T0374423

VOICES from THE WORD

Bill Dunphy

WESTBOW
PRESS®
A DIVISION OF THOMAS NELSON
& ZONDERVAN

Scripture quotations in this publications are from The Message. Copyright © by Eugene H. Peterson 1993, 1994, 1995, 1996, 2000, 2001, 2002. Used by permission of NavPress Publishing Group.

Two Scripture passages: Epigraph on page vii and Aaron's Blessing on page 28 are from the King James Version of the Bible. No copyright nor permission needed.

WestBow Press books may be ordered through booksellers or by contacting:

WestBow Press
A Division of Thomas Nelson & Zondervan
1663 Liberty Drive
Bloomington, IN 47403
www.westbowpress.com
1 (866) 928-1240

ISBN: 978-1-5127-7284-5 (sc)
ISBN: 978-1-5127-7286-9 (hc)
ISBN: 978-1-5127-7285-2 (e)

Library of Congress Control Number: 2017900916

Print information available on the last page.

WestBow Press rev. date: 05/17/2017

To the glory of God.
and
to Caroline,
my understanding and loving wife,
an artist and the mother of our two creative adult children

And I heard as it were the voice of a great multitude,
and as the voice of many waters,
and as the voice of mighty thunderings, saying,
Alleluia: for the Lord God omnipotent reigneth.
(Revelation 19:6 KJV)

Contents

Dialogues and More

Preface

This is a different kind of Bible story book. The stories will ring a bell with many of you, but the details of the stories may not be known to you ... yet! Their "voices" should sound familiar to you as you read their stories. You will meet kings, soldiers, mothers, fathers, teenagers, babies, shepherds, visionaries, fishermen, good people, and a few bad ones, among them desperados, and many others. They may be strangers to you, but as you get to know them, you may recognize their voices as not being that much different from your own, or from people you know.

Some of these stories may be familiar to you, but many of the people in them are hidden away as minor characters in the primary stories of the main message of the Bible. That message is of God's entrance into the world He created. His invasion of the world was accomplished by His Son, Jesus Christ, whose birth, life, teaching ministry, death, and resurrection is the paramount message of the Father's action in the world. After the ascension of the Christ, the third person of the Holy Trinity, the Holy Spirit, became the presence of the Godhead in the world.

Without tampering with the essential message of the scriptures, the author of these stories constructed the probable actions and possible speech of the people you will meet. Of course, the actions and words you will read are fictional but are based on research into the life and times in which the biblical characters lived.

Attitudes and reactions to events and other people are assumed to be much like ours when in similar circumstances. To some extent, the author has given a contemporary slant to the words people used in speaking to each other. One source that assisted in this "slant" was the translation of the Bible, *The Message: The Bible in Contemporary Language*, done by Eugene H. Peterson and printed by NavPress, in alliance with Tyndale House Publishers.

Note: You will find suggestions for how to use these stories at the end of this book.

The superscript numbers you find throughout the book will direct you to specific notes page 293.

Acknowledgments

A handful of people contributed to this book in a variety of significant ways:

- My daughter, Maureen Dunphy, the recently published author of *Great Island Escapes: Ferries and Bridges to Adventure*, not only encouraged me to write, but also was the primary editor of this book. She worked tirelessly with me, helping and teaching me what she uses in her work as a teacher and coach of published authors.

- My wife, Caroline Dunphy (the artist C. Dunphy), designed the cover of the book you are holding in your hands and patiently assisted in the editing process in various roles through long hours of reading them with me.

- Rev. Roy McBeth, deceased pastor of Strathmoor-Judson Baptist Church, Detroit, Michigan, started me on my journey of faith as a Christian camp director and as a pastor.

- Four past, interim, and current pastors of Rosedale Gardens Presbyterian Church in Livonia, Michigan:

- o Rev. Kellie Whitlock, Senior Pastor, a relentless encourager and promoter.

- o Rev. Richard Peters, Pastor Emeritus, whose sermons and illustrations were always memorable.

- o Rev. Stephen Clark, our former pastor, whose preaching of the Word gave me the idea for this book.

- o Rev. Anne Schaefer, Interim Pastor, whose sermon on Jonah opened my eyes to him and his motivations.

- Eugene H. Peterson, translator of THE MESSAGE: The Bible in Contemporary Language. With two exceptions, this translation is used exclusively for the Bible passages included in this text. The clarity of his translation is one of the sparks that gives light to the stories in this book.

- The members of Rosedale Gardens Presbyterian Church, who listened to some of these stories in worship services, at work camps, and in formal services, as well, and insisted on having them put into a book.

The Mother of Nations

The Voice of Sarah, Abraham's Wife

Wouldn't you know—just when a girl gets settled into a life with her friends and things to do, when she knows all the shops and markets and thinks life is finally settling down, her husband comes up with a story about moving to the other side of the world. On the one hand, I don't know of any other women who have had this experience, and on the other hand, I'm sure my women friends would tell me I'm crazy to even think about it—much less go through with it.

What I didn't know was that my husband, Abram, had been talking to his God, who told him to move to the other side of the world. God didn't even tell my husband where that side of the world was located. It was something like a "just start out, and I'll tell you when to stop" kind of thing.

Abram walked into our tent and abruptly announced, "Sarai, we are going on a trip, but I don't know where we are going."

"Abram," I said, "Give me a break. A trip? Do you think we'll be gone for a long time? What shall I plan on taking? How's the weather there? What servants shall I ask to go? Oh, when will we be leaving? Oh, by the way, what about your father, Terah, and your nephew, Lot? Are they going too? I need to know if I have to

1

plan for them too. Shall I pack lunches, or do you think we'll find a place along the way to eat? I had better start making my lists.

"What do you mean you don't know the answers to my questions? Really? Sometimes I just don't understand you, Abram. Why didn't you ask your God some of these questions? You always leave the planning, the questions, and the details to me.

"I'm sorry, Abram, if I ask so many questions—but you really threw me for a loop. I'm not as young as I was when we first married, you know, so you can't expect me to jump for joy at this news. After all, I am now all of twenty-five years of age. However, there is one good thing about all of this—I won't have to hang my head in shame anymore because we don't have children. Our neighbors and my friends are beginning to talk about why the gods are cursing me. All my friends are having their first babies, and they laughed and laughed as they told me that I'd probably be the last one to have a child. Humph! Little did they know how right they'd be."

Eventually we left for somewhere—with a caravan of people and herds of sheep, cattle, goats, and other assorted animals. We were hauling all our belongings from Ur, which is down near the Persian Gulf. We headed westward up toward the two great rivers, the Tigris and the Euphrates.

After more than two months of traveling, Abram and Terah, his father, decided to stop at Haran, a busy city at the major crossroad on the trade route from Asia to the Great Sea coast. Terah had become ill on the long trip, so Haran seemed like a good place to stay for a while. I assumed that once we were settled, I'd get pregnant and have my first child. Well, *that* didn't happen.

We ended up staying there many years until Terah died at the ripe old age of 205. Lot, Abram's nephew, stayed with us until we buried Terah, and then he helped us prepare for our trip down to Canaan, the original destination promised to us by Abram's God.

Being older, we couldn't hurry as fast as we had when we left Ur. We still had a lot of stuff to move in addition to all we had picked up in Haran. But there was one thing missing—we still didn't have a child. I think I had given up on that ever being a possibility in spite of what Abram said his God had promised—a son to him.

Before we left, I bought a young, attractive slave girl to be my personal handmaid. I realized that I was joining the elite group of women who had their own handmaidens. That made me a little bit satisfied. Nevertheless, I would rather have had a son.

I had no idea about the time all this traveling would take. The trip to Canaan was a four-month journey by caravan down to Shechem on the far north side of another great sea, which looked as though it were *dead*. Abram built an altar there and listened again to his God's voice, saying that he was promising to give this land to his children. *Promises again!* I had heard about enough of these promises. I just wanted to settle down, but I had the feeling that this wasn't our last stop on the way to wherever Abram's God wanted us to be.

I was right. That wasn't our last stop. (We were the "movingest" family I have ever heard of!) The next place we pitched our tents was in Bethel, but we were only there temporarily until we went farther south to the Negev. Unfortunately, there was a horrible famine in the entire region, so we went even farther down—into Egypt. (One thing for sure, I was getting to see a lot of the world!) Egypt had some problems for us though—and at least one that involved me.

Abram can be so sweet and dear! He thinks I am still a beautiful woman, and he worried about losing me to a man who had more to offer than he had. The upshot of this was that Abram, in order to save his own life, said I should say that I was his sister if the pharaoh, a very powerful man, insisted that I live with him. Oh, no! That's exactly what happened. (I think I'd better take another look at myself in the mirror.) In time, Pharaoh came down with some serious diseases, as did his entire household. In the end, it all worked out. The pharaoh discovered our ruse and kicked us out of the palace, saying to Abram, "Take her and go!"

I don't know how he did it, but during the time we were in Egypt, Abram acquired more animals in addition to some silver and gold. The good news of this was that we could keep all that Abram had acquired while we were in Egypt. (They must have been extremely happy to see us leave.) So back toward Canaan we went, and Lot, Abram's nephew, was still with us. A son he wasn't, but at least he was some company for my husband even though he meant more work for me and our servants.

To me, it seemed as though we drifted around the desert, packing up and unpacking, first to Bethel, then over to Ai, and that's where there was some trouble between our herdsmen and those of Lot. Abram and Lot decided to split up and each go his own way. Lot looked over the landscape and realized that the Jordan River was more fertile and well-watered, so he took the prime real estate for himself, his family, and all his possessions and moved to one of the cities, Sodom.[1] That's a story for another time.

Lot ended up in trouble with some kings who wanted his land, his home, and his flocks. It never ends—trouble, I mean. The kings absconded with Lot and all he had, and they took off for the north country. Of course, it was up to Abram to rescue him and bring him back to the Jordan Valley. I didn't go on that long journey—been there, done that. I had had all the traveling I needed in my life.

Abram had another spat with a king who wanted me to live with him. This story was similar to the story involving the pharaoh, and again we were told to go home and never come back. (By the way, I looked in my mirror and was flattered that my husband thinks I am still beautiful.) I must cook him a special meal—one of his favorites! How about lamb shank and rice?

However, still no heir to our fortune! I finally took matters into my own hands and figured out a way to make this happen. I thought I'd help Abram's God—just a little. Since it is an accepted custom in our part of the world, I offered Abram a way out of our predicament by giving my maidservant, Hagar, to him so he could have a child. It worked out as I had planned, and Ishmael was born. That was just the result of my practical intuition hard at work, and I'll admit, the result of more than a little impatience and annoyance with Abram's God!

Did I say it all worked out? It did, but not well at all! Hagar, my servant, started to get quite uppity with me because she had a child and I didn't. I couldn't stand having her in the same place with or even near me. It became so unbearable having her around that I suppose I let my feelings get the best of me and took out my anger and disappointment on her. One morning, she wasn't there when I awoke. The other servants told us she had run away. Good riddance!

The worst part in this whole scheme was that since Ishmael was Abram's son, it appeared that the promise that Abram's son would be the beginning of a great nation would be fulfilled through Ishmael. God had never said anything about *me* having a son. Oh well, Hagar was gone—or so I thought. However, back she came saying that God had told her to return to me. I now have a beef—or a camel—with Abram's God. How could he do this to me?

About the time I was getting mentally adjusted to this new arrangement, I became pregnant, had a son, Isaac, and was as happy as a person could be. Of course, I was about ninety years old by now, but this made me feel much younger. I finally came to accept that Abram's God could also be my God. He came through when I was sure it was just Abram's pipe dream to get me to move and put up with all the troubles I had endured over the many years of travel, moving all over the world, and even being forced to live with a king or two. Forgive me if I sound like a drama queen.

When we had the weaning party for Isaac, Ishmael, who was now fourteen and becoming quite a man, stood on the sidelines and began to mock and laugh at the three of us. I watched him, finally went to my husband, and demanded that Hagar and her son be sent packing. I did not want my son to be associated with that teenager ever again. Later Abram told me this had put him in one of the most distressing moments and hours of his life. He loved Ishmael. He had taught him all about farming, husbandry, and the care of our animals. The two had grown close to each other over the years—had fished together, played games together, and together had discussed and solved problems of the land that together they held. Both assumed that all they could see would someday belong to Ishmael. Now I had asked Abram to forget all that and disown his own son. I think he and I started to grow apart during this entire ordeal—he grew tired of my complaining about not having a child, then about Hagar, and then I added Ishmael to my complaint mix.

Abram told me to send Hagar and her son away, so I did. We later heard that she and her son almost died in the wilderness without food and water. Abram had packed a lunch for them and a skin of water. However, that was quickly gone. After all, Ishmael was a teenager, and I found out from Isaac when he became one how fast an adolescent boy can demolish a basket of lunch. We heard later from a traveler that they survived in the Desert of Paran and that Ishmael had become an archer, and Hagar had gone down into Egypt to find him a wife. That was one chapter of my life about which I have strong mixed feelings, thoughts, and some guilt.

Finally, just when Isaac was approaching adolescence, and I thought the world and we were settling down, Abram surprised me with another announcement. He and Isaac were heading north to Mt. Moriah[2] for a special event, which would only last for a few days. He said God wanted him to make a sacrifice on that mountain, which actually wasn't much of a mountain, but a strange, skull-shaped hill.

I didn't know what was to have been sacrificed until they returned from the trip. *Isaac* was to have been the sacrifice. If I had known that before they left, I would have gone berserk, and would have stayed crazy for the entire week they were gone. I was so prepared to let my husband, Abram have a piece of my mind, but then he told me that God had put a ram in the bushes by the altar and told my husband to sacrifice the ram instead of Isaac. That sounded silly to me until I heard the rest of the story. God was pleased with my husband's commitment and obedience to Him and repeated the promise that Isaac would be the father of a new nation that would bless the entire world and whose inhabitants would be as numerous as the stars in the sky. God also told him that my name was changed to Sarah, which means, "to rule." At the same time, Abram's name was changed to Abraham.

I never had any grandchildren to hug, hold on my lap, or tell my life's story to, but I rested easier knowing that our God would be taking care of Isaac and all his children and all the generations that would follow. I only hope that those inhabitants, those generations to come, as numerous as the sands of the seashore, will be the blessing to the world as God promised, and that the nation will be as faithful to God as Abraham was. We made some mistakes—most of them were my mistakes—but we learned that God is faithful in forgiving us our errors as we learned to put our trust and our futures in his hands.

We also learned that when we felt that God intended for us to do something or go somewhere, He expected us *to do* and *to go*.

Biblical background: This story is based on the biblical account found in Genesis 11–23. The account of Sarai (Sarah) is one of the earliest accounts in the Bible. Abraham and Sarah are the parents of the Jewish nation going back to the latter years of the Middle Bronze Age, 2200–1550 BC. Read more about these two early lovers in the book of Genesis.

Scripture: Genesis 11:26–25:18
Reading: Genesis 12:1–6
Discussion possibilities:

1. Describe how Sarai must have felt about her life and its demands and moves.
2. Identify some issues *we* might face that would put us in similar situations as that in which Sarah found herself.
3. How did Sarah deal with all the many changes in her life?

The Wrong Mother for a Promised Son

Voice of Hagar

What happened to us? Why did he do this to us? What can I do now to save us? Where is his God now when we need him? How can I get him to listen to me, or will he ever listen to me? These questions lie in my head like the dried-up, dead bushes all around me in this God-forsaken desert. There's my teenage son lying whimpering under that bush that gives him almost no shade from this hideous sun, and there isn't any water to heal our parched tongues or to cool our dry bodies. We rationed the water that Abraham sent with us, but it's gone. The desert is just too big—all we can see is sand and a few scrub bushes that are as thirsty as we are.

It's a rather long, sad story, and to be honest, I guess I was a contributor to what happened and to this predicament we are in. I learned the background from my mistress, Sarai, soon after she bought me before the trip she and Abram took from Haran down to Canaan.

They both promised me that they would be good to me. The master seemed like a good man, who prayed to his God often. His wife, Sarai, told me that her husband, Abram, had a message from his God to leave their home in Ur of the Chaldees and strike out for the west. I guess something like, "Go west, young man, go west!" Abram seemed like a good guy, and his wife … well, I'm still not so sure about her. Sometimes she was good to me, but lately, not so good!

Abram's father, Terah, was in Ur and went with them to Haran, along with Abram's nephew, Lot. Lot was something else—young, impetuous, and ready to go for broke at the drop of a headpiece. I never knew Terah, but if I had, part of my duties would have been to nurse him back to health when they arrived in Haran. He had taken ill on their long trip between the great rivers, Tigris and Euphrates, from Ur over to Haran. He didn't recover but died, and the family buried him a little north of Haran. After Terah's death, Abram's God told him to head south to the land of the desert, the Negev, to the land that he would show him, and make it his and his descendants after him.

His descendants? He doesn't have any—at least, none that I have seen. I should have suspected something was up when I heard the two of them talking and talking about having a son. It seemed to me that whenever they had more than a few minutes together, that's all they talked about. But what? A son? They had to have been kidding. They're *old*! I know enough about such things to know that a woman of her age can't have children. Are they nuts, crazy, or just dreaming?

Sarai devised a plan, dubiously a manipulative plan that I doubted would work, but she convinced me that I would be happy with her plan if it worked out as she figured it would. I went along with her plan. A plan? A scheme? Whatever it was, it wasn't good except in Sarai's head. I wasn't sure about the "whatever it was," but Sarai convinced me that she knew best.

You see, it was customary in our land for a servant girl to have a child with the master, if his wife couldn't bear a child. I had no choice in the matter. Sarai talked Abram into the scheme, and as usual, he went along with her. Apparently, Abram's God had promised them a son, and this was the only way that Sarai figured it was going to happen. It was a plan, and I think Sarai was the schemer. What I couldn't understand was, if Abram's God was so great, where was He in all this planning?

Then you can probably guess what began to occur. I am ashamed, but I started playing one-up-womanship with Sarai now that she and I both knew I was having her husband's child. Our relationship quickly went from good to bad to worst. Sarai, of course, blamed Abram for the entire problem and told him to take care of the whole thing. He wiggled out of it by telling his wife that I was her slave and this was her problem, and to do whatever she wanted to do. Her response? To make life miserable for me. I couldn't take it anymore, so I ran away from them. Well, not exactly ran. Remember, I was pregnant!

We kept Abram's God busy—one of his angels found me in the desert and told me to return to Sarai. The angel promised me too that my child would be a son and would be like a bucking bronco of a man, doing a lot of fighting and being a trouble maker. He would be hostile to almost everyone, and everyone would be hostile to him. I'm not sure how comforting that was, but it did give me my own son. My child (and Abram's son) was born, and I was happy. However, I was back in Sarai's home again and still keeping my tongue quiet whenever her jealousy had the upper hand in our relationship. I hadn't known that a child could bring so much joy into a life. He was a wild little guy (God had told me, didn't he, that my son would be like a "wild donkey?"), mischievous and playful. Abram named him, Ishmael and took to him as any father would. I think you can figure out what this did to Sarai and her relationship with me.

Ishmael was the apple of my eye, but not only of my eye but also of Abram's eye. Abram was a good dad even though he was eighty-six when Ishmael was born. Our son was also a bond between Abram and me. We were a family, and I was thrilled to have an almost ... real family, although Sarai was always somewhere in the picture, too.

Oh, yes—Sarai! Always somewhere in the picture, but never *out* of the picture. I was still her maidservant. Talk about a tough role and relationship—for both of us! To make matters worse, when Abram was ninety-nine, his God appeared to him saying, "I am God Almighty, and I'm here to confirm my covenant between the two of us. I will greatly increase your numbers" (Genesis 18:17–19). God told him that he was going to be the father of many nations, have a son, that all of Canaan would be an everlasting possession for him and his descendants, and that his name would be changed to Abraham. (That's when circumcision became a law for all of his male descendants.) Oh, and Sarai's name was changed to Sarah, and she would become a mother! She was already eighty-nine. That must be some kind of a record to be posted in a book sometime.

You'd think, wouldn't you, that Sarah's attitude would be better? It was for a while. She even laughed when they had some visitors (angels?) who announced the news again to them, and when she told others about their good news, they laughed with her. Isaac was born, and she was a changed woman. However, that all changed when Abraham and Sarah had the weaning party for Isaac. Ishmael stood over to one side, and Sarah said she caught him mocking them. You can believe she quickly got over to Abraham and told him, "Get rid of that slave woman and her son, for that slave woman's son will *never* share in the inheritance with my son, Isaac." Jealousy does stir up deep resentment and anger, doesn't it? Notice that Isaac is now her son? Ishmael's father, with tears in his eyes, told me the bad news. We had to go!

Oh sure, we were given some lunch and a skin of water, but the snack disappeared in a day or two. My fourteen-year-old son ate the sandwiches in one gulp, or so it seemed. However, what else could a good mother do? I kept thinking, now we were both starving to death, far from home, and no one would care if we lived or died, if anyone *even* heard of our deaths. How did I ever get us into this predicament? Now how do we get out of it? Oh, I know, *I know* how we got into this mess, but I couldn't figure out a way to get us out of it. How can people who plan something get so angry when it works out their way?

There we were in Beersheba, down near Egypt, on the edge of the desert. The angel showed up again. Busy angel! I was hoping he would tell me to go back to Sarah and Abraham. However, he didn't say those words I was waiting to hear. Instead, he told me to take Ishmael's hand, get him back on his feet, and stop worrying. *Stop worrying?* Just how does a mother do that? We were dying of hunger and thirst! I opened my eyes, took Ishmael up, and nearby there was a well of water. What a great God we have!

Ishmael grew up and became an archer, and while he began to make himself a life in the desert, I found him a wife down in Egypt. I'm not sure how we managed. Obviously, we didn't go back to our old home with Abraham and Sarah, but Abraham loved Ishmael, his son, so he had arranged for us to have a life together as mother and son.

I heard that Sarah lived to be 127 years old. Abraham had bought a family burial plot near Hebron, and that's where they buried Sarah. Abraham was also buried there when he died at the age of 175 years. Both of his sons, Ishmael and Isaac, conducted his burial.

What a life! I wouldn't wish it on anyone. Some lessons I learned were difficult to learn, but I struggled with the education, and lived to be happy, even without a husband—I had my beloved son, who fathered twelve children, each one of whom formed a tribe. I often share with him and his family the stories of our lives as we remembered some of the hardships but also the blessings of God to us. These were some of the lessons we had learned together:

1. Watch out for schemes that put me in the middle of a family, other than my own.
2. Don't become a confidant to a boss-lady or boss-man.
3. Be thankful for all those who help and assist me.
4. Realize that God is the Almighty One who watches out for me all the time.
5. Jealousy has an evil power that destroys relationships.

These were tough lessons that we learned together, but as I told Ishmael, they were invaluable in helping me keep my sanity. "You'll do well to teach them to my grandchildren so they don't have to learn them the hard way we did."

Biblical background: This story is based on the biblical account found in Genesis 11:26—25:18. The author of this story of Hagar, Abraham, Sarah, Ismael, and Isaac has filled in the blanks of the lives of the biblical characters using information about the life and times of that period of history, the Middle Bronze Age.
Scripture: Genesis 21:14–21
Discussion Possibilities:

1. How do you think Hagar evolved into a woman of courage and strength in the face of her difficulties?
2. Discuss Sarah's role in this family's issues.
3. What does this account tell us about getting involved in other people's problems?

I Always Thought I Was Special

Voice of Ishmael

I have wondered for many years why my dad seemed so much older than other dads I know. Come to think of it, I don't get to see many other people except the servants. I can't ask my dad about his age because it might embarrass him that I think he is so much older than our servants. Most of the dads of the boys I play with are strong men who work hard in the fields and with the hundreds of animals we have.

The question still bugs me, though, why is my dad so much older than the other dads around here? Sarah (I never knew what to call her) is also older than the other mothers. My own mom, Hagar, says there is something strange about Abram and Sarah's life. She said that when I'm older she'll tell me what it is. But I want to know now. I like to know the secrets that other people hide away from their families and friends. You never know when those secrets can be helpful to someone who likes to plan and scheme as I do.

Even though my dad is much older than dads of my friends, I really enjoy the work that my dad and I do together in the fields and with the animals. For fun times, he and I go fishing whenever there is enough rain to fill the brooks. He told me that someday we might go way up north to a great fishing place on the way to

15

Haran, near where my grandfather, Terah, is buried. There is a big lake there called Galilee, and it has lots of good fishing. We've also done some hiking, but the desert isn't exactly a great place to hike, especially in the hot weather, although the trails around the Dead Sea are interesting and sometimes can be challenging.

I think that my dad enjoys being with me as much as I enjoy being with him. When we work or play together, it gets us away from the two women in the family who always seem to be at each other in ways that I don't understand. They know how to get each other upset with just a word or a look. Sometimes I can't get to sleep at night trying to figure out what's going on with them. Someday I'll solve this mystery, or I'll get Dad to tell me the story that I've heard bits and pieces of about Sarah wanting a child. Why? They have me. Besides, Sarah is too old, or so my mother tells me. I'll never understand how a woman's mind works except that maybe it works overtime!

You can understand my surprise when I learned that Sarah gave birth to a baby son. She seemed to be satisfied—*finally*! Abram named the little kid Isaac. I'm not sure what I'll call him—maybe I can call him the kid! Sarah having her own child should take care of most of the problems between Sarah and my mom. Well … we'll see if it does, but for sure I'm not going to take any bets on that happening!

I'm glad I didn't take any bets, because just about the time things had started to settle down, and I thought that the world was not going to fall apart, everything changed. One day, unexpectedly, Sarah said she couldn't stand to have Mom and me around here anymore, and that we had to leave. Leave? Why? I had to know why. This must have been a part of the big mystery that they all had among themselves without telling me.

I had just celebrated my fourteenth birthday when my dad had given me my own horse—what a day that was. He taught me how to ride it to help corral the cattle and the other animals. I was in my glory. However, the excitement didn't last very long. When I walked in on the weaning party, when they celebrated the birth of the new kid, Isaac, I couldn't stop laughing at them. They seemed so old, and Isaac was so small. I couldn't get it out of my mind how strange it all seemed. Then the thought hit me ... was this new little kid going to cheat me out of my father? I wouldn't be surprised if Sarai would try something, anything to make Isaac my replacement in Dad's mind and life. Would he—could he let that happen? I laughed at the whole idea. Dad and I were too close for all of that to happen. He'd never let it happen, would he?

During the party, Sarah, unfortunately, caught me over in the corner laughing, and I suppose she assumed I was mocking them or something like that. I saw her stop in the middle of a conversation with another woman, march over to my dad looking as angry as I had ever seen her, and almost yelled at Dad. (And I had seen her angry many times, but never like this.)

Dad looked upset, and I think I saw tears in his eyes. I wanted to run over and give him a squeeze to let him know I was there with him, and that I felt so sorry he was distraught. I didn't see him for a day or two, and when we got together, he told me all about it. He told me it was one of the worst decisions in his life, and the hardest he had ever had to make. Sarah, he said, couldn't let me take away Isaac's birthright, and she demanded that Dad tell my mom and me to leave and go far away from our home. I tried to hold my tears back, but I couldn't, and threw myself into Dad's arms, where he held me as though he wouldn't ever let me go.

That's when he told me the whole story of their lives from their beginning in Ur down by the Persian Gulf right up to that day when he told me I had to leave him. He told me about his God's message about leaving their home and going to a place his God would show him. That was the time when his God had promised him a son who would be the beginning of a great nation. Dad thought that I was the son that he had been promised, but Sarah wasn't convinced that I was the promised son and had that idea reinforced by some heavenly visitors just before she became pregnant. She had been upset about this for the last thirteen or fourteen years, and finally, I guess, she had just had enough. I was a threat to her happiness, and she couldn't stand the thought of that. So, we had to go!

Dad packed us some food in a basket and a skin of water, said a tearful good-bye to both of us, and turned as he left us looking at our future—which at that moment looked worse than bleak. We hadn't had much to eat that morning, so I was as hungry as any fourteen-year-old boy can get. The sandwiches, or whatever they were, didn't last long, but we rationed the water between us. I don't remember where we slept that first night, but toward the end of the second day, I was exhausted, so I found a bush that still had a few leaves on it for shade and crawled under it and fell asleep sobbing. Before I slept, however, these head-pounding and heart-shaking questions wouldn't leave me alone.

- Why had my dad caved in to Sarah's demand, letting her get away with something I was sure he didn't buy into? I knew I was special to him, so how could he just let me go? Where was his strength?

- Why did Sarah hate us so much that she could be so inhumane and ugly about us? My mom had never stolen anything from her, and from what Mom told me, she was always quick to do everything she wanted. She felt she needed to keep on Sarah's good side for both of our sakes.

- How could I ever forget all I had with my dad—the work we did together, the play times we had, the fishing we both loved, and the long discussions we had about Dad's God and what his God had promised to Dad?

- Had we been left to die of hunger and thirst in this God-forsaken desert?

I fell sleep with all these questions going around and around in my head. Then suddenly Mom woke me up and told me that she had been talking with Dad's God and that God had assured her that we would be all right. As soon as we were standing and looking around, we saw a well that I swear had not been there when I fell asleep. I don't know when I have ever had a drink of such good ... sweet ... water. We were alive, refreshed, and able to face the sandy desert.

In the following years I learned that the desert had a lot going for it—I loved it! Hunting was good, so I learned to use a bow and arrows that I had bought from some nomads who were wandering around the desert. Mom convinced me that I needed a wife, so she went over to Egypt to find me one. I think she was afraid to let me do that for myself because I might find one that was like Sarah, and neither of us could live with someone like Sarah. I have a feeling that my mom will be living with us for a long time. I hope that she and my wife will get along better than she and her mistress did!

Biblical background: This adaptation is based on the biblical account found in Genesis 11:26—25:18. The author of this story of Hagar, Abraham, Sarah, Ishmael, and Isaac has filled in the blanks in the story of the biblical characters using information about the life and times of that period of history, the Middle

Bronze Age. There is more to read about the problems of this mixed family in the chapters noted above.

Scripture: Genesis 16:7–17, 21:8–21

Reading: Genesis 21:14–21

Discussion possibilities:

1. Discuss Abraham's decisions and their results.
2. Talk about God's watchfulness of our lives: your experiences and outcomes.
3. Describe the personal lessons you learned from this emotionally charged story.

Dad Always Liked You Best!

Voice of Reuben

I knew it, I *knew* it, I *always* knew it would come back to bite us! It was a comment one of my brothers made years ago that would haunt us and probably mess up our lives for longer than we cared to think. You see, Joseph, one of our younger brothers, was our least-favorite person. In fact, several of us hated him. My brothers and I spent considerable time figuring ways to eliminate him temporarily or even permanently from the family. We watched for any behavior that would validate our hatred. It was obvious to all of us that he was our dad's favorite, but we probably exaggerated some of what we observed to rationalize our hatred for him. I guess that's natural for people to do in such circumstances.

There are twelve of us boys—well really, men now. The four you will meet in this story are Joseph, Simeon, Benjamin, and I am Reuben. Our dad is Jacob, but we have different mothers. You see, back in our day there was a need for many children to work on our farms and care for our herds, so multiple wives were common. As close as we could figure, Dad had at least two wives and was the father of four of us by our mothers' servants. Our dad cashed in on that: twelve of us to tend to the cattle, and the rest of the huge land holdings we had. Our family hadn't been in the area all that long, and we had a lot of land. Our neighbors said they considered us very good farmers.

Great-Grandfather Abraham was born a long way from here, beyond the big rivers, Tigris and Euphrates. Our Grandpa Isaac was born after Great-Grandpa's journey to Canaan with Sarah, his wife and our great-grandmother. Then our dad, Jacob, settled in these parts many years ago after some difficulties with his father-in-law, Laban, who was also Dad's uncle. Figure all that out for yourself! You can check the genealogical charts for what happened to Uncle Esau, dad's brother.

Grandpa Isaac tried to help Dad do the right thing, but as you well know, dads don't always listen too well to their own fathers. I guess they listen about as well as any father listens to his sons. Those difficulties gave us boys some delicious laughs as we compared stories of Dad's escapades and the jokes we created about those problems he had with his old-country father-in-law, Laban. There were some shenanigans that Dad pulled on his father-in-law, and he had the cooperation of his two wives, Laban's daughters, in those clever schemes. They left Laban and headed back here to Canaan—home. But it was not without some problems with Uncle Esau. When the book is written about all of this, you can read and learn more about Dad's problems with women. That account will probably be in the first book of our scriptures. Good grief—why can't families get along? Enough of the problems of our parents! We had a few larger problems of our own.

One of our problems was the kind that sometimes tears a family apart. Our problem was our brother, Joseph, the one that Dad loved best! He was annoying to say the least: always bragging, or so it seemed to us, about himself and his future. Can you believe this? He would tell us his dreams about how someday he would rule over us, and we would bow down to him. It didn't take us long to catch the drift of these wild, crazy, ego-satisfying dreams. (Yes, we knew all about egos and how big they could get!) One dream was about the sun, moon, and stars with the stars all bowing down to him. Another dream: he and we, his brothers, were in the field binding up the grain sheaves when his sheaf stood up and the other eleven bowed low before it! Wouldn't that frost you? Then we heard that he was tattling to Dad about some of the stunts we were pulling while we were away from home. That further fueled the fire of hatred that was burning us up.

On top of all that, Dad made him a special gift—a brightly colored coat. Dad said it was because Joseph had been born when Dad was an old man. *Ha*! Man oh man, we learned to hate Joseph enough to want to kill him. His dreams were bad enough, but the problem was piled up even higher with his cocky attitude. Of course, he was the son of Dad's first love, Rachel, but I was Dad's very *first son*. That should have given me some priority in the nature of things, don't you think? After all, this boy, just a twerp, was actually, only about seventeen years old—a smart-alecky teenager if there ever was one.

This all came together when Dad asked Joseph to go up to Shechem, just a little north from home, to check up on us and the herds, and then he was to get back to Dad about his findings. However, we had moved the herds a little to the west over to Dothan, but he found us there. There didn't seem to be any way to get away from him, the big mouth. We looked to the east and saw that he was coming closer to us. One of my brothers said that we should kill him and tell Dad that a vicious animal ate him. Now *I* was scared. This had gone too far. I didn't want him dead, so I said, "We can't do that. Let's just throw him in the cistern here, but let's not kill him. He'll just die a natural death." (I fully intended to come back later and get Joe out of the dried-up old well.) So, that's what we did, but not before we took that hated coat from him. Then we relaxed and ate well, considering we had just practically consigned our brother to death. At least, my brothers could rest easily knowing that they had taken care of our big problem!

While we having a good supper, we noticed in the distance a string of camels coming toward us. Traders are always going on this regular trade route from the east hugging the coast of the great sea down to Egypt with spices, perfumes, and other exotic items. Judah, my brother, had a brainstorm, "Hey, let's make some shekels on him and sell him to the traders. We don't have to kill him; after all, he is our brother, even if we can't stand him." So, that's what they did! I had slipped away from the group earlier, but when I came back to get Joe out of the well, they told me what they had done. I was so angry and frustrated that I ripped off my clothes and tried to figure out what we were now going to do.

Simeon suggested, "Let's kill one of our goats, drip the blood on his ugly coat, and take it home to Dad, and let him assume what he wants to." So that's what we did! Dad assumed the worst. That's when we found out how much Dad loved our stuck-up brother. We thought he would never stop crying.

Meanwhile, back in Egypt, Joseph was in deep doo-doo. From what we learned later, the traders sold him to a member of Pharaoh's personal staff. Things went well, and apparently Joe's career really took off until he became the chief administrator of Potiphar's estate. Joseph was extraordinarily handsome, so handsome that Potiphar's wife decided that she wanted him just for herself. That did not go well for Joseph or for Potiphar's wife, and Joe paid the price with a term in prison that would be long enough that he would probably be left to rot in his cell. However, Joe was Joe, always able to turn a problem into an opportunity, and soon he was the chief administrator of the prison. However, the dream scene went on, only this time it was the dreams of a couple of the other prisoners. One had been the chief baker and the other prisoner was the official wine taster for Pharaoh. He interpreted their dreams, they were released, and he asked them to mention him to Pharaoh. The dreams came true, but Joe was immediately forgotten. So much for honor among thieves.

Two years later Pharaoh had two dreams that he could not interpret, and that's when the wine taster's memory kicked in, and he remembered his promise to mention Joe to Pharaoh. A pleased Pharaoh had Joseph brought back from prison. Now Joe was always careful of his appearance, so he shaved first and changed out of his prison garb, and then went to see Pharaoh. I wouldn't have been surprised if he even had had a haircut to enhance his good looks. The dreams were good news/bad news for Egypt: seven years of prosperity with bumper crops, followed by seven years of famine. Pharaoh was so impressed by Joe's interpretation of the dreams that he appointed Joseph to be the chief-in-charge of all Egypt. His plan was to store the grain and then to use it during the famine years to dole it to the people, even to the people of other countries that surrounded Egypt. When we heard about the plan, we dubbed it the "International Joseph Plan."

Now back to the rest of us. The famine hit us too, but, unlike Joe in Egypt, we were not prepared for it even though famines were not unusual in our area. It was usually feast or famine. Both Great-Grandfather Abraham and Grandfather Isaac had been through similar famines. Dad somehow heard that Egypt had grain for sale and told us to "get with it" and get down there to buy some before "we all starve to death." The situation was as desperate as it sounded! One stipulation: Benjamin could not go with us. Benji was now Dad's youngest son and Joe's only full brother. Dad didn't want anything to happen to his youngest son as had happened to his favorite one. We started wondering if

Dad had any idea about Joe's disappearance, but we were quite sure he didn't.

Joe made it tough for us, demanding that we go home and get Benjamin or he would have us thrown into jail. He relented and let nine of us go, kept Simeon in jail, and gave us grain to take home with us. It took quite a negotiating session to reach that agreement.

On the way back home to Canaan, we stopped overnight, opened one of the bags of grain to feed the donkeys and found our money in the bag on top of the grain. I knew it, I *knew* it! I remembered what had happened fifteen or so years before when we sold Joe into slavery. I reminded the others that I had warned them, and now we were all going to die because of what they did all those many years ago. It was a tough way to learn that actions do have consequences! Sometimes it takes a long time for the other sandal to drop, but it does drop ... eventually.

That scared the wits out of us, and when we told Dad, it also frightened him. Then we told Dad the plan: we had to take Benjamin with us the next time to prove that we were not spies. Dad was strongly against this and thought he could veto our plan. I stepped up to the plate. "Dad, you can kill my two sons if I don't bring Benji back to you. I'll be responsible for him." Dad said as adamantly as he could "No way!" He would not relent. "No," he said. Eventually, Dad finally did give us permission to take Benji back with us: our cupboard was bare—the situation had become unbearably desperate. You see, while we did the farm work, Dad kept the books, as well as a tight rein on our inventories. There were herds to feed, servants who were in need, and there was a shortage of food for us. He knew how deeply in trouble we were.

The drama was just beginning! The details are complex, but Joseph insisted after our second trip to Egypt for more grain, that we leave Benji with him while we returned to Canaan. Judah stepped up to the bar and pled with Joseph to keep him and let Benji return to us for our father's sake. Now the plot gets even thicker. Joseph dismissed everyone in the room except us, and told us who he was—our brother, Joseph. I am telling you, it was the time for tears and fears. Tears from Joseph, but fears from us because we were terrified. We figured it was now payback time for us: the empty well, our sale of him to the traders, and our hatred of him. We couldn't look at Joseph and only glanced at each other.

He allayed our fears and declared that it had worked out for good. God had sent him to Egypt so he could eventually meet our needs. He said, "I am Joseph, your brother whom you sold into Egypt. But don't feel badly, and don't blame yourselves for selling me. God was behind it. God sent me here ahead of you to save lives." (Genesis 45:1–15)

Now hurry back to your father and to my father and bring him back with you. Hurry, don't delay. We'll set you up in Goshen while the famine runs its course—there are five more years of famine.

It all worked out as you probably figured it would. The scene when Joseph welcomed us back was worthy of a play set to music. I think something like "Joseph and the Amazing Coat of Many Colors" would be a good title. The next time we went back to Egypt, Dad went with us, and that was even a more extravagant event, with tears, hugs, kisses, and food, every kind of food except Reuben sandwiches, whatever *they* are. Joe and his boss, the pharaoh, gave us some prime real estate in Goshen and had us go back and bring our flocks and herds with us to settle there.

Dad died in peace after giving each of us his blessings and assurances that someday our families and heirs would go back to Canaan and become a great nation. I often wonder when that will be—if ever.

If I had never believed in the goodness and faithfulness of

Jehovah God, I did after all of these experiences. I just hope and pray that everyone who hears my story will know and love this Jehovah God with all their hearts, souls, and minds. As someone in our family is sure to write this, I think I'll beat them to the punch:

> The Lord bless thee and keep thee,
> the Lord make his face to shine upon thee,
> and be gracious unto thee, and
> give thee peace. Amen.
> (Numbers 6:24–26 KJV)

Biblical background: The story is an adaptation of the Joseph story found in Genesis 28–50. Not all the details are included in this story, but all the essentials are here. Some of the words come from Eugene Peterson's translation of the Bible, *The Message*, published by NavPress. Read more about this large family and its problems in the book of Genesis.

Scripture: Genesis 28–50
Reading: Genesis 41:28–43
Discussion possibilities:

1. How does God work in the lives of our families to bring good out of our poor decisions?
2. What are God's messages to us as parents in this account? As adult children?
3. Describe the consequences of anger, hatred, and favoritism.

Riches to Rags to Riches

Voices of Ruth and Naomi

Been there and done that! I was rich, I became poor, and then I became rich again. To tell the truth, I'd much rather be rich! But I never would have made it through the ups and downs of my young life if it hadn't been for my mother-in-law. Yes, you heard me, that's right, my mother-in-law!

It all started with my mother-in-law, Naomi, and her husband, Elimelech, moving from Bethlehem of Judah across the Jordan River to Moab just thirty miles away. You see, there was a famine in Israel, their native country, and they decided to take their sons, Mahlon and Chilion, to a place where there was adequate food. They were very comfortable in their ability to pay their way wherever they went; some people even considered them rich. Elimelech was not a young man, and before long, he died, leaving Naomi and their two sons in the foreign land of Moab. However, the family was able to manage on the estate that Elimelech had left behind. The boys were typical guys who had their eyes on the young girls in their village, and it wasn't long before Orpah and I, Ruth, became a part of the family as the wives of those two handsome brothers.

Life was not easy without Elimelech, but we managed. We all worked together, and both Mahlon and Chilion were hard workers. Tragedy struck again, and struck hard. Mahlon and Chilion both died, leaving Orpah and me with Naomi, their mother. Soon word came across the Jordan River that the famine had ended in Bethlehem and that God had provided food for his chosen people. Being more than just a little homesick, Naomi, now that her husband and two sons were dead, wanted to return to her family home in Bethlehem. Orpah and I, now in our early twenties, decided that we had no place else to go, so we began to pack up to move with Naomi.

If we had decided not to go with Naomi, we would not be able to show our faces in our Moab village. Our lives were inextricably linked to Naomi and her deceased sons. In our culture a widow could have no expectations, other than poverty and more gossip than any young person would probably want to live with.

While we were alone together doing our packing, Orpah took a deep breath, paused, and admitted, "I really don't want to go over to Bethlehem and leave Moab. All our friends and our gods are here, and we don't know anyone over there. Our husbands told us about the laws and customs of life over there, and it doesn't sound like the kind of place that would accept us or a place where we would fit in. Does it to you? We could stay here, probably find new husbands, and try to get our lives back. I know I'd miss my family, especially my mother, more than I could bear."

"I don't know about that, Orpah," I responded, thinking out loud. "If we stay here, I know I would worry about Naomi all alone over in Bethlehem. She has been like a mother to us and wanted so much to be a grandmother to our children. We failed her on that count, and I would feel much worse if anything happened to her on the trip. We'd never know, but you know me—I'd worry about her for the rest of my life. You've seen the difference in her since Elimelech and our husbands died. It's as if she has become an old woman with nothing to live for. I feel that

I have to go with her, but you do what you need to do. If things don't work out, I can always come back here."

Under ancient laws, as widows, we were considered undesirable for marriage and were now almost destitute. However, there were relatives back in Bethlehem who might be of some assistance to us. Naomi, distraught from her recent tragedies, must have realized at the beginning of the trip that the two of us would not fit into life in Israel. We were Moabite women and as such were forbidden from having any claims on anyone or anything in Israel. In fact, we were probably not welcome in Israel and might even be on Israel's hit list as foreigners, and the Mosaic law forbade Israelites from marrying us. It looked to us that we were just out of luck—poverty was staring us in the face without any escape.

Neither Orpah nor I wanted Naomi to leave us. In spite of Orpah's hesitation, we decided to go with Naomi, since she had been caring and helpful to us as young widows. However, no sooner had we packed what few possessions we had, then Naomi surprised us by seeming to be commanding us to return to the households of our mothers. Naomi said to us, "The Lord, I am sure, will treat both of you well because of the way you treated your husbands and me. He will provide security for you in the households of new husbands."

We begged Naomi to let us go with her, although I didn't hear the depth of conviction in Orpah's voice that I felt in *my* heart. However, I still said, "I don't want to contradict you, but I'm going with you to your people." After she kissed us, Naomi became practical. She said, "Now look, girls, be reasonable, I'm too old to have more sons, and if I did, would you stick around until my newborn sons would be old enough to marry you? I don't think so. You'd be much older than they would be. This is more bitter for me than it is for you, since the Lord has treated me harshly."

We cried together some more, but Orpah realized that she just could not go with us. After more hugging and crying, she left us to return to her own mother. When Naomi suggested that I take the same action, I said, "Don't urge me to abandon you. I can't turn back from following you. I'm going wherever you go and am planning to stay with you too. I'm going to accept your God and your people. Wherever you die, that's where I'll be buried. I don't want to leave you and be separated from you." That ended that conversation! She didn't say another word about me turning back to Moab. Instead, she told me about Bethlehem, some of the people there, and what I could expect life to be like in a different place, and especially, in a strange religion with its own, but different, God.

The women of Bethlehem welcomed Naomi back, "Can this really be Naomi?" They remembered her as the peaceful, pleasant woman she was when she left them. She responded and told them, "Don't call me Naomi, but call me Mara, because the Lord has made me very bitter I left here full, but I'm returning empty. I don't think that the Lord has treated me very well." Now Naomi was back home but had no place to live and nothing to eat.

Naomi told me about a law in Israel—a levirate arrangement when a husband dies. Sounded confusing to me, but it worked out well for both Naomi and me. A husband's widow becomes the responsibility, and I suppose even a liability, of the husband's nearest relative. That relative is the "redeemer" of the widow and of any property her deceased husband leaves behind. Any outstanding debts are to be paid by the "redeemer," who is also responsible for having a child with her, a child who would be considered the heir to the deceased. This was an ancient eastern social security program when children, especially boys, and property were essential for both a woman and the nation. This seemed strange to me, but they called it a levirate marriage.

Naomi remembered this custom, which was actually more than just a custom; it was a law ... Mosaic law. She also remembered that her husband, Elimelech, had such a relative who now became responsible for her and her late husband's property. As she told Ruth, "Even though he is responsible for us, he may decide that he does not want to take on that much responsibility. There is a second man, Boaz, related to Elimelech who, I think, will be more than happy to assume that responsibility. Aren't we fortunate that Boaz is also a wealthy man, and that it's barley harvest time?"

"So, listen up, Ruth, here's what we're going to do. It is the law in Israel that during harvest, the reapers who tie the grain stalks into sheaves must leave behind on the ground the heads of grain that fall off the stalks when they are cut. This is another part of our social security system. The poor and needy are welcome to come into the harvest field and pick up all they can carry. Now all you have to do is get your pretty self out to Boaz's field and start picking up the leftover heads of grain. A personal word to you: I know you tend to be shy, Ruth. Don't be shy if Boaz likes what he sees when he looks at you."

I found out later that Boaz had noticed me in the field and had instructed his workers to protect me while I gleaned in the fields. He also told them to strip some of the grain heads from some other barley stalks so there would be more grain for me to glean. He also seemed to know all about Naomi, me, and our relationship. I thought it rather interesting that he would have an interest in our affairs and know so much about us. It must have been just because I was the youngest gleaner in the group.

At mealtime, he asked me to come to his table and have some of his bread and gravy. That also seemed strange to me, since none of the other gleaners were invited. I was starting to see a side of this well-to-do planter that I didn't realize could be or would be possible to someone of his status in the community. I spent much of the rest of day trying to figure how this would play out for all of us. However, this was only the beginning.

Now the plan and plot thickens. I don't know how Naomi knew this, but she told me the next step to the plan. I have to believe that she was using her network in the village to her own advantage as well as to mine. I quickly realized that this mother-in-law of mine was no slouch when it came to strategic thinking. She was more than just casually interested in her future and mine since she left very little, if anything, to chance or fate. She knew Boaz would be winnowing the barley sheaves and then sleeping on the threshing floor that night. "Ruth, wash, perfume your hair, and get all gussied up and go down to the threshing floor, but don't let him see you until he has finished eating and drinking. As soon as he falls asleep, uncover his feet and lie down and wait for him to talk." She was not only a master of strategy but also a learned mistress of tactical reasoning as well. I didn't realize this at first, but I went along with her plan because she was adamantly convinced it was the only way to operate to achieve her goal.

After working a full day and then eating and drinking to his fill, Boaz quickly fell asleep. In the middle of the night, something startled him; he turned and discovered a woman lying at his feet. "Who are you?" he asked. "I am your servant, Ruth. I am a little cold. Please spread the corner of your garment over me, since you are a kinsman-redeemer."

He was quick to respond: "It's okay. Stay here for the night, and in the morning I will check with a relative who is a closer kin than I am. If he is not willing to redeem you, as surely as the Lord lives, I will redeem both you and your mother-in-law, Naomi."

It was a surprise to me, but not to Naomi, that when I came home the next morning, she learned that it had all gone as planned.

I told Naomi that he knew all about the troubles we have had and about our return to Bethlehem.

He went to the city gate to talk with our kinsman and arrange for our redemption. He also gave me these six measures of barley. I told Naomi that he didn't want me to return to her empty-handed. He even suggested that I stay with his workers until they finish harvesting all his grain, so it looked like I'd be in his fields for a while since the wheat harvest was next.

At the city gate where all business is done, Boaz talked with the closer relative. "You've probably heard by now that our relative, Naomi, is back home from Moab and had put up a 'for sale' sign on Elimilech's property. Why don't you buy it as the redeemer-kinsman? It's rightfully yours, and the witnesses are here. But if you don't, I'm next in line and I will buy it. I realize that you know the law, but I'll remind you that when you buy the property, it's a package deal. You also assume a marriage with our dead man's widow. It's important, as you know, that children be reared in Elimilech's name." Then the man, who shall remain nameless, said, "I cannot redeem it because I might endanger my estate and it could cause a problem with my own heirs. You redeem it. I cannot." Then as is our custom, he took off a shoe and handed it to Boaz to seal the bargain (Ruth 4:7–8).

When Boaz told Naomi and Ruth what had happened at the city gate, I'm sure I heard Naomi whisper, "I could not have planned it any better myself." As Boaz told us his story, I am sure I heard him chuckling to himself, as he whispered, "Amen."

Boaz redeemed both Naomi and me and Elimelech's property. Boaz and I were married and had a son, Obed. Boaz asked the men at the gate to witness all these transactions, with shoes flying all over the gateway.

Biblical background: This short story is based on the biblical account found in the Old Testament book of Ruth, probably written in the time of the Judges who ruled over some of the tribes of the Hebrew people. Read the short book of Ruth to get the full story of this unusual family's problems and solutions.

Scripture: Ruth 1:6–22

Discussion possibilities:

1. Consider the differences between Ruth and Orpah on the ideas of responsibility for and alignment between older and younger people.
2. What do you see as the major theme(s) of this short biblical account? Why is it included in the Bible?
3. What are the major conflicts among the people and the cultures in this account?
4. How do we accommodate people of other cultures and traditions in our neighborhoods and churches?

Tall Saul

Voice of King Saul

I've felt guilty ever since I was declared a king! I know why I took the job—I was hungry for recognition and fame. I'd spent too many days and years as a virtual nobody. Now it was my turn to shine and make a difference for myself and for my small nation. However, I have had more than just a little trouble keeping my head straight between those two differences, which was the more important one—myself or my nation!

My dad, Kish, of the tribe of Benjamin, sent me on what seemed like a wild goose chase to find some lost donkeys—no, not a wild donkey chase to find some lost geese, although that's what we started calling it after three days of looking in a few places and not finding them. We came to Zuph and were ready to turn around, to go home, and to admit to Dad that they were gone—they were only donkeys after all, just donkeys! One of my servants told us about a holy man who lived nearby. On our way up the hill to the town, we met some girls climbing up to a well. They told us that a holy man was on his way to a shrine close to the city and we would find him there. They were correct—there he was, Samuel! Never heard of him, but I guess many people recognized him.

Samuel seemed to know who we were—how'd he do that?

Samuel told us how that happened. Apparently, he had been talking with his God, who told him that he would be having a visitor whom he was to anoint as a prince over "his people Israel. Israel's future is in your hands." That must have been where I came into the picture. I knew I was tall and handsome, but a prince? Wow! Handsome wins out every time, I guess.

"But, but … but … I'm *only* a Benjaminite, from the smallest of Israel's tribes, and from the least significant clan in the tribe at that. Why are you talking to me like this?"

Samuel told me to send my servant home and meet him the next day at his home. He had something important to tell me—a message from God. Then he did something weird—he took a flask of oil and poured it over my head. It was slimy and gooey, and I didn't like it and couldn't imagine why he did that. However, he quickly told me that this was God anointing me to be the prince over God's inheritance. He added that I'd meet a couple of guys on my way back home, and they would tell me where to find Dad's donkeys. I did as I was told, and it all happened as Samuel said. All the rituals that took place confused me, but I guess it must have been okay, because nothing bad happened. Samuel's final words were something like these: "After all of this you'll know that you're ready. Whatever job you're given to do, do it. God is with you" (1 Samuel 10:7).

I felt like a new person, and I think I was.

I came to a group of prophets on their way home playing instruments, so I joined them and did a little prophesying myself. That seemed strange because I just wasn't that *kind* of guy, playing music, and saying things I would never say among friends … but I said them! I was soon home and my uncle asked me about the trip, the donkeys, and Samuel. I told him where we had looked and that we had eventually found the donkeys. I didn't tell him what Samuel had said about the king business. You know, the more I thought about it, the more nervous I became. I was not a king, didn't *feel* like one, and was not even sure what a king did. We'd never had such a person in Israel.

When Samuel called the tribes and clans together, lined them all up, and pointed at our tribe, Benjamin then looked right at our clan, Matri, and asked, "Where is Saul, the son of Kish?" Oh, no! I looked around, realizing that I had not bargained for this, so I hid in someone's luggage. God knew where I was and was quick to tell Samuel where I was hiding. I decided that I was not ready for this! However, Dad had told me that the whole nation had decided that we needed a king. They weren't satisfied to be ruled by the judges like Samson, Gideon, and Samuel, who had appeared when we needed to be rescued from one enemy or another. The elders let Samuel know that we needed a king to keep up with the neighbors. A king would be responsible for all the tribes and not just for whichever tribe was in trouble with a marauding enemy, and God knows we had plenty of enemies.

My first venture into army life was unique. King Nahash of the Ammonites was brutalizing our forces, and we were about ready to surrender to become the servants of Nahash. One of his conditions in accepting the Israelite warriors into his army was that each soldier had to gouge out his right eye and give it to the king. (What a great guy for a king and a leader!) He promised to humiliate every person in Israel before he was finished with them.

However, our army sent messages to all our villages to round up more fighting guys. Some of them came to our village of Gibeah just as I was coming back from the field with my oxen. The enemy's message infuriated me, so I sent messages to all of Israel saying that any man who refused to join up with Samuel and me in fighting the Ammonites would be punished. (Ask Samuel about that punishment!)[3] So help me—thirty-three thousand men showed up ready to fight. We were successful in the battle, and we celebrated Israel's victory at Gilgal, where Samuel reconsecrated me as their first king. However, he warned Israel that God was not pleased by being replaced as their king by one of us even though I was young, tall, and handsome.

Then it was battle and more battles—war after war after war. After one of the wars, I was carried away with my victory (notice I said *my* victory). In my enthusiasm, I took it upon myself to make sacrifices without a priest officiating. That's a big—*very* big—no-no in Israel. We had our God-given law from Mt. Sinai, but I broke it. Oh, no! Samuel showed up and let me "have it" big time. He informed me that God was sending him to find a replacement for me. However, I have a son, a good son, Jonathan, who is more than capable of being my heir and king when I join my ancestors in death. I guess that wasn't good enough for God or for Samuel either. God said that he would pick my successor—not the elders of Israel.

I knew of David because of his and our victory over Goliath of the Philistines. I heard that David was a musician, so I had a servant seek him out and bring him to court to play his lyre to quiet my nerves. One of my favorite songs, and his as well, was one that spoke of the Lord as his Shepherd, who took him through green pastures and beside still waters. The song went on to say that when he was in the care of the Shepherd, he would not fear evil because the Shepherd would be with him. It ended with the Shepherd providing a place in the house of the Lord for him forever.[4]

Usually, that song quieted me and restored my entire being so I could finally rest. I wished many times that I could have somehow been able to copy David's music and songs because I was in a much better mood when I heard them.

As I now look back on my life, I could feel myself gradually slipping away—in my head. I couldn't keep myself together as I could earlier in my life. I blamed this slippage on the bad news about my kingship, but that would have been too easy a reason. I seemed to fly into a rage, unable to control myself, and I would let my rage fly at the closest person near me. I once let my spear fly at David, who was my court musician, and who could sing the most soothing music while playing his lyre. That usually quieted my anxiety and assuaged my guilty fears.

But not always. I let my spear fly at others, too. I would feel embarrassed when I came to my senses again. However, it seemed as though I just couldn't help myself. The court doctors couldn't figure it out, or if they knew what it was, they weren't about to tell me, their king. I guess they didn't want to be skewered on the end of my spear and become a "doctor en brochette." I had a good son, Jonathan. He was my second-in-command in the army and was an excellent strategist and a brave soldier. He was responsible for some of our victories—but that didn't bother me. However, what did burn me and maybe was responsible for my head problems was the people's adulation of David. If I heard it once, I heard it many times—but that may have been just in my head:

> Saul kills by the thousands,
> But, David by the ten thousands!
> (1 Samuel 18:6–9)

I was the *king!* Not a poor, illiterate shepherd boy who played his lyre all day to mindless sheep, and occasionally had to fight off a bear or a lion when all they wanted was just a good meal. I was the king, and I couldn't stand the thought that someday he … *he* would take my place as king. Not Jonathan, but David, of all people!

Oh, talking about my son, Jonathan, there is another issue that constantly bugged me. I figured out there was some kind of conspiracy between my son and my possible successor, David.

They were as unlikely a pair as you could imagine—a prince and a lowly shepherd-court musician. I knew they were plotting something, but I couldn't figure it out, until I had one of my spies track them down. I had put out an order to have David killed. One time I had him sent into a battle feeling confident that someone would kill him, but instead he claimed another victory. Then I heard the people singing it again about David's ten thousand being killed. Another time I sent men to stake out his house and kill him when he appeared. However, David's wife, my daughter, heard about the plot, and hustled him out a back window, letting him escape. I wouldn't be surprised if somewhere in all that confusion, Jonathan was involved.

I knew they were all liars—including my own children—Michal and Jonathan. One day, my son walked with me out into a field near where he knew David was hiding from me so David could hear our conversation about my plans to kill him. About that time, I had learned about their close friendship and challenged Jonathan with the loss of the kingdom unless he turned David in. I'm sure you know what happened. He didn't turn him in, but that was end of their conspiracy against me. Chalk one up for me! David escaped from me many times. At one time, I challenged a priest of God when I thought that he, Ahimelech, had helped David escape after another of my many trips around Israel to find him.

The priest, stood up to me, confronting me with his plea for David's life. My response to his challenge was, "Death to you and your family," as I ordered my men to immediately kill the priest and his family. My men refused, but I found Doeg and ordered him to kill them all. He did, and then turned on all those who wore the sacred priestly robes. Only one priest escaped, Abiathar, who sought out David and joined him.

I spent most of the rest of my life hunting down David, but

he always got away from me. Samuel told me that he was writing down the stories of my life, Jonathan's, and David's too—I guess it is nice to be remembered for something—all the victories. The one thing I regret is that I never was able to get the better of David. I'll go to my grave with that regret. Jonathan told me that David's God was protecting him from all his enemies, including me. I really didn't believe that—my son was just a good friend defending his own good friend. But I never quit trying. I should have known better than to try to kill a man that God had chosen to be king. Too late in life I learned that fighting against God is useless, *totally* useless.

The end was more than a little gruesome. The Philistines were again at war with us, and we were not doing well. I was losing my troops while the Philistines were knocking us around badly. They killed my three sons, Jonathan, Abinadab, and Malki-Shua, who had all been fighting alongside me, and I realized that I was next on the hit list. I told my weapon-bearer to take his sword and put me of out my misery. We didn't need to give these pagan pigs a game out of killing me. He seemed to be terrified and refused. I drew my own sword and intended to fall on it. However, a young man from my camp showed up as I was leaning on my sword. I asked him to come over to me and put me out of my misery. I'm nearly dead already, but my life hangs on." The last thing I heard was, "I'll do it."

Biblical background: This story is an adaptation of the biblical account of King Saul found in the Bible in 1 Samuel 8–31. The prophet Samuel is the recorder and narrator of the accounts of Saul, David, and Jonathan. The biblical portions are from *The Message,* the Bible translated by Eugene Peterson. Saul's life story is fascinating. You can read much more of it in the book of 1 Samuel.

Scripture: 1 Samuel 15:22–23
Discussion possibilities:

1. Think of contemporary situations in which people make decisions to accommodate elements of other people's thinking similar to Israel's demand for a king.
2. Think what it must have been for Saul to end his life still angry enough to kill David.
3. Describe Saul's downward spiral in his relationship with Jonathan and David.
4. Have you ever been involved with someone like Saul? How did it feel?

Mighty Prince, Warrior, Loyal Friend

Voice of Jonathon

Those Philistines, those no-good Philistines were the next worse things to traitors as far as I was concerned. They hunted us down, and if they were not hunting us, they were haunting us by making us wonder when and where they might next choose to challenge us. They seemed to think that we were born for one purpose only: to serve them, and to be targets for their army. Our army was frightened of them, but also angry that they could get away with their evil and continuous baiting.

Our entire nation made a big deal of a couple of my battles, as though I was the champion of the world boxing or wrestling games, or even of the Olympic Games in Greece. Set your mind at ease—I am not! I'm just an ordinary guy who found out early in life that I had some skills I could use to my country's advantage. My father, King Saul, was very proud of me and often let me know just how proud he was of me. Like any other boy, I was always more than glad to hear my dad tell me how proud he was of me.

I inherited some of my skills, and others I learned to develop on my own. My father was tall, handsome, and quite athletic—I thank him for passing those traits down to me. As I grew older, I realized that I was also fortunate that I didn't inherit some of his problems. As it turned out, at times, he became darkly despondent, and he seemed to be ruled by some other spirit than the one I had learned to love as a little boy—carefree, wise, and loving.

We were of the tribe of Ephraim, so along with all my friends, I learned as a child how to use the bow and arrow that my father had given to me when I was still young. I worked hard at being the best in my age group and can still hear Dad say, "Great shot, Jonathon!" or "Well done, Son!" A boy can never hear stuff like that or experience the thrill of hearing it too often.

My father trusted me enough to help him fight our small country's enemies as soon as I could yell out commands and exercise my judgment in planning our battle strategy and tactics. Dad and I both learned a lot from Samuel, God's prophet to us. He was also my mentor and guide. Samuel would also remind us of the ways in which God had led our people out of Egypt many years ago, and how he would continue to lead us if we obeyed him and his will for us. That required us to listen for His voice, and to check with Him before we decided on strategic moves in our lives and in those of our military force.

Our greatest enemy was the despised Philistine army, which far outnumbered our army. They were constantly in our face—threatening us, demanding our money and our manpower. They were more than just a nuisance—they were killers, murderers, thieves, and rapists. Father asked Samuel, who then asked God, what to do about them. Samuel told us that God told him to tell us to go for it—battle them and that he would bless us in the battle. That was all my dad needed to hear. We were ready—I was to lead one small army while Dad took the rest of the army with him. Talk ... about ... excitement! This was going to be so much better than playing army with my friends, or setting up sticks in the sand pretending they were soldiers. I was beside myself! Dad trusted me. I was in charge of real soldiers, and I knew I wouldn't fail because God had said, "Okay, go for it!" We went for it in a big, huge way.

I'll tell you just one example of how Dad and I worked together, and how God gave us a victory in battles with our enemy. It turned out well for Israel and for me, but not so well for my dad, the king. I was learning the art of war, and the Philistines were across a big divide from us, the Israelite army, if you could call us an army. I decided to try to go around a deep ravine and get to the top of a large hill where the Philistines were camped. We knew we had to see what they were all about. My armor bearer, Josh, agreed to the plan and seemed excited to attempt to take out the disgusting excuses for people. It all worked out as he and I had planned it. Josh and I took out an entire crew of guards—about twenty of them. Before we were through, they were actually slicing at each other with their swords and pikes.[5] We had them on the run, and did they ever run! What a night that was. I figured that Josh and I would get some high-fives when we arrived back at camp. Well, we were given a hand, but not exactly the kind we thought we should get.

Dad and his units were nearby, saw the Philistines in flight, and started to run after them with much success—so much so that the enemy was totally dispersed. Some of our soldiers who had been hiding out in the backwoods of Ephraim came out of the woods to fight with the king and me, or that's what they said. Who knows? That's when our army grew to be about ten thousand soldiers. They literally came out of the wood ... work!

Dad saw that his fortunes had turned, but he did something very foolish on that great day. While Josh and I were not with them, my dad had given an executive order: no one was to eat anything until the Philistines had been thoroughly routed, dispersed, killed, and he had had his vengeance on his enemies. Samuel had not been consulted, and no one else was asked if that order was a good idea, let alone if it was such a good idea or sensible for fighting men to go without food. There was no prayer to God asking about the wisdom of this ban—nothing but Dad's overly excitable enthusiasm. I learned a lot from that incident. A leader *doesn't* know it all! My dad won't be the only leader who doesn't consult with others who could be essential to an outcome. I hope I never make such an executive decision based only on my own most recent emotional experiences.

Meanwhile, Josh and I were working our way back to the rest of the army and being hungry, I stuck the tip of my staff into one of the many honeycombs in the field—um, so sweet and refreshing! One of the soldiers who had heard Dad's dictum mentioned that he had heard Dad put a curse on anyone who ate anything that day. Whoops! *That would be me!* Of course, I didn't implicate Josh in any of this foolishness, but I couldn't believe what Dad had done. He had imperiled the lives of our soldiers and had reduced the number of enemies we could have dispatched from this life to their next, wherever that may be.

When Josh and I returned, we discovered that the army had not obeyed Dad's crazy ban but had plundered and slaughtered sheep and cattle, killed what they wanted, and ended up eating what they had killed—raw and still bloody. Now, doing that was against our Mosaic law. Dad told the troops, "Let's go after them even farther."

The soldiers gladly shouted, "Let's do it!" They not only had broken our own law by eating meat without cooking it, but also were bloodthirsty enough to want even more.

"Whoa," the priest said. Remembering his failure the last time around, he said, "Not so fast. I know you are the king, but don't you think maybe we ought to ask God for his thinking about this plan?"

My dad quickly responded, "Oh, yeah."

Admittedly late, my dad asked God if he should pursue the Philistines farther. Oh, oh! God didn't answer. I'm sure Dad wondered, *now* what do I do? He must have decided that someone in the camp had not obeyed his ban on eating.

"We are going to find out who disobeyed my order. Step forward, all you officers. You stand on one side, and Jonathon and I will stand over here. For all we know, it may be Jonathan who must die. God will give us a sign and show us who is guilty of disobedience."

The sign pointed to me, his son. He asked me, and I told him about the finger-licking bit of honey. "And for that you going to have me killed?"

My dad said it was out of his hands and in God's hands. He said that he couldn't go against God, could he?

The army was incensed and rose up against him. "Jonathon—die? Never! He has just won a great victory for our nation. No one will touch even a hair of his head. God and he have been working together all day." I think I heard a threat in their response to Dad, but I'm not sure if I did or not.

However, Samuel must have had Dad's number, and I guess he was ready to call it in. He ordered Dad to go after Amalek to pay him back for the ambush he had laid on Israel when they came out of Egypt many years before this current dust-up. Dad again put a ban on taking any plunder from the Amalekites, except for King Agag, and choice cattle and sheep. It was Dad's ban but not God's.

Samuel told me later that he confronted Dad about the exceptions to God's order that Dad had granted. God had apparently told Samuel that Dad lost his kingship because on more than one occasion, Dad had refused to accept God's word. Samuel was distraught and angry all night and then tried to find Dad the next morning to settle the issue. However, Dad had gone to Mt. Carmel to set up a monument to himself for his victory. While there, he had built an altar and had sacrificed a burnt offering to God using the cattle and sheep the army had plundered in the battle with the Amalekites. My stomach started to roil as I listened to Samuel. I knew what was coming. I had known before this and was reminded again that Dad had not, nor had anyone else asked God for his blessing. I learned that we can't get away with saying no to God. Maybe once … but not as many times as Dad had. My guess is that there will be many more dads who will be guilty of saying no to God. Dad plaintively assured Samuel that he had done everything God had asked him to do. Samuel made a classic response I'll never forget: "So what is this I'm hearing—this bleating of sheep, this mooing of cattle?" (1 Samuel 15:14).

Dad tried to make apologies and asked forgiveness for making a sacrifice when he knew he was not permitted to do that. Samuel's response:

> "Do you think that all God wants are
> sacrifices—empty rituals just for show? He
> wants you to listen to him! Plain listening
> is the thing, not staging a lavish religious
> production. Not doing what God tells you
> is far worse than fooling around with the
> occult. Getting self-important around God is
> far worse than making deals with your dead
> ancestors. Because you said, 'No' to God's
> command He says 'No' to your kingship."
> (1 Samuel 15:22–23)

This is where the story gets more exciting, at least for me, changing my life's focus and energy. I needed what God gave me—a purpose for living a worthwhile life. First, I thank God, then Goliath, then Samuel for this excellent gift—they all played a role in giving it to me. Strange partners, I'd say, but I realized that God has many ways to influence our lives and actions.

You probably know the story of how David ended the scare

our nation endured when Goliath showed up on the shore of the river down in Oak Valley. That was a shock none of us were ready for—a big … ten … foot shock! Our army was petrified: some decided to run, others hid when the brute showed up daily to yell at them, but more of them stuck it out as the good soldiers they were. Then the golden-haired boy showed up! He was a little guy. I'd guess probably much less than six feet, yeah, closer to five feet tall. Some of the soldiers, including one of his older brothers, laughed at him and told him that the sheep, his "lambies," needed him back on the hills of Bethlehem. "Feel free to leave now that you delivered the food. We don't need you here since you are too young and too little to fight with us experienced big guys."

One of the soldiers took David to see my dad, the king, who gently remonstrated with him about the war experiences of Goliath compared to David's total lack of such experience. The smaller guy wouldn't hear of it—nope, he would take care of this oversized threat to Israel and feed his carcass to the crows and coyotes. Sounded like a bit of bragging to me, but he insisted that he had dispatched to their graves lions and bears who had attacked his sheep. Dad at length gave in to the young boy's insistence. But I had to laugh when I saw that Dad had put his own armor—six feet of it, sword and spear, too—on this fair-haired little shepherd boy. David looked more like a little boy in his own dad's suit. Of course, he shrugged it off, and instead, from the riverside, he picked five stones as his only weapons. I could only pray to God that he would protect this handsome, little boy from harm as he went to face this gargantuan giant.

David … did … it! The most feared person on the battlefield was dead, and to all of us, David was the hero of the day. My dad called him in to reward him for his heroism. This gave me the opportunity to meet him and personally thank him for dispatching the brute, the menace to our nation. Without realizing what was happening to me, I became entranced by this courageous young lad, who was probably not more than ten years my junior. What neither of us recognized at the time was how intertwined our lives would become and how dependent we would become on each other.

This was not David's first meeting with my dad. He had been called to the court earlier to play his harp to quiet my dad's nerves and improve his moods. Dad had a strange problem in his head that threw him off his stride and made him angry beyond that which would be considered appropriate for the cause of the anger. No one could explain it to any of us, but he would suddenly go into a tirade and strike out at a person we were sure he did not dislike. For instance, once while David was soothing him with his harp and voice, Dad grabbed his spear and flung it at David, apparently intending to pin him to the wall. David was quick and ducked, but he became wary of Dad's moods after that. However, Dad's threat to David took on additional meaning after Samuel discovered Dad was involved in a couple of cover-up schemes involving attempts to circumvent God's commands related to the land God had promised to Israel. Dad's conceit led him to build a monument to himself on Mt. Carmel. I couldn't believe it—a monument to himself!

As far as my dad was concerned, it was now war with David. He did everything he could to kill my buddy, even enlisting my sister, Michal. She had become David's wife as a prize from the king for David's outstanding war record against the Philistines. Dad told Michal to encourage David to go to the battlefield and destroy our enemies. "I'll be waiting to hear of your victory, and celebrating with you when you get home." David, as would anyone, was excited to be thought of so highly by his king. Little did he know that my dad had also charged all of his servants to make sure that David did not live through the encounter with the enemy. Not only Michal, David's wife, but I was also to take part in David's murder. What do I do now? David and I were now blood brothers. I could not have any part of Dad's malicious scheme. During a sleepless night, I came up with a plan that I needed to share with my "brother."

I found David and told him about the plan, and together we firmed up an arrangement to avert this tragedy. I hid David in a field before walking with Dad into the field where David would be able to hear my conversation with Dad. In the morning, my talk with Dad brought up David's war record, all the good things David had done for Dad, even putting his own life on the line for Dad's sake. "You were *there*, you *saw* what happened, and you *applauded* him along with everyone else. So why would you even want to think about sinning against such an innocent person for no good reason at all, let alone sinning against our God?"

For that time, it worked. Dad and David were back in working order. However, the intrigue continued. David had more victories, was praised by the people, and the expected result was, you guessed it—Dad's anger against David became even more deadly. However, I was having heart trouble—this was getting to be too much. I was torn in two directions—torn in half, between my dad and my best friend, David. This time, Michal, David's wife, rescued him, sending him out a back window when the king sent his men to their home to murder him. Michal told a fib to get out from under her father's disapproval for her action. Disapproval? That's too kind a word for what Dad called her.

Strange stuff happened when Dad followed up on David's escape, but I don't have time to go into all of that now. Ask Samuel about it—and weep or laugh! I did both, and people are still talking about those strange happenings.[6]

After Dad's embarrassing event, he really became obsessed with David's death. That's all he could think about, scheme about, and compulsively anticipate. However, he was on to us—David and me. He finally figured out our relationship, and he did not approve. David and I planned another escape for the hero. We chose a similar method: David hiding in a field, but this time a servant was secretly brought into the picture. The servant was to pick up an arrow that I would shoot into the field near David's hiding place. This would give David a message to run or stay. I also told my dad a fib, saying that I approved David's going to his home in Bethlehem for the New Moon celebration.

My father exploded. He called me some of the worst names I had ever been called and threatened to disown me—my future as the next king of Israel was dead in the water. I was on the other end of one of his spear throws, which I also ducked, just as David and others had done before me. David got the message and knew the scheme had failed. After the servant went back to his home, and knowing that David must leave us for his own safety, I went out to the field to say good-bye to David. Of all things, David fell on the ground three times, prostrating himself before me. We kissed, said our good-byes, and wept friend over friend. David had an especially difficult time. I told him, "Go in peace! We have vowed friendship in God's name. God will be the bond between you and me and between my children and your children forever! If you are able, please care for my little boy, Mephibosheth, if something should happen to me."

I saw David after our tearful parting in the field. He was fearless, but he was still afraid. I don't quite know how to describe what I saw in him, but I encouraged him: "Don't give up. My father wouldn't dare lay a hand on you for fear of the army and of God. Some day you will be king, and I'll be with you to help in every way I can. My dad knows this but can't bring himself to say it." David and I renewed our covenant and then went our separate ways. We didn't know that it was the last time we'd ever see each other, hold each other, or repeat our vows of friendship and unity.

As I lay dying with my dad in the battlefield after another tragic war with the Philistines, I thought of David and knew that when he heard of my death, he'd weep and have a few quotable words to say about us. I closed my eyes in death, thinking back not on the battles I had fought and won, but on the life-giving encouragement and the strength of a powerful friendship that made a prince and warrior like me into a friend and a servant to a shepherd boy.

Biblical background: This story is an adaptation of several chapters in the Old Testament of the Bible in the books of Samuel. This author maintained the original story line. Some of the accounts have been abridged and words added to make the story flow in contemporary language. You can read the entire account in 1 Samuel 13–31. David's lament at the burial is in 2 Samuel 1. Too get the full impact of Jonathon's life, read the chapters in 1 Samuel. This story follows the account in the Bible, Eugene Peterson's translation, *The Message*.
Scripture: 2 Samuel 1:22–27 (David's lament at the death of Jonathon and Saul; read *after* the story has been told.)
Discussion possibilities:

1. Talk about the steadfastness of David's faithfulness to both Saul and Jonathon. What bound them all together?
2. Describe what it must have been for Jonathon to give up his inheritance of the throne to David, a shepherd boy.
3. What does it mean to be a "blood brother" to persons such as David and Jonathon?
4. Have you ever experienced with another person such a relationship as Jonathon and David had?

They Changed My Name

Voice of Mephibosheth

Why would anyone in his right mind ever give that name to a sweet, little newborn baby boy? Mephibosheth? Really? *Mephibosheth*? Took me years to learn to pronounce it and more than a few more years to learn how to spell it!

That wasn't my parents' first choice or even their second choice! I was originally called Mirab Baal, which means "Opponent of Baal." Baal is the name of one of the many gods of the pagans that live around us. As I tell you my story, you'll learn why it was changed from Mirab Baal to Mephibosheth. But that name isn't much better, is it?

My grandfather was King Saul, the first great king of Israel and Judah and the greatest king in the world at that time. My father was Prince Jonathan, who was one of the most handsome men in the kingdom. So that makes me royalty! How about that!

Suddenly, in just one day my whole world turned upside down. Until that day, everything seemed to come my way—gifts, friends, and fun—because I was royalty. However, that day my name was changed to Mephibosheth. (I almost have trouble saying it myself.)

The change happened this way. I was five years old playing with some other boys when a man—sweaty and exhausted—burst through the palace gates yelling, "King Saul and all his sons are dead!"

He said it again: "King Saul and all his sons are dead!"

Even though I didn't understand much about it, I could tell it was terrible news. Immediately, the world became crazy when just moments before it had been calm and peaceful. One minute I was playing with my friends and having fun and now this! I looked for nurse, but I couldn't see her. All I could hear and see were people shouting and running in all directions while others stood frozen in place, apparently unable to decide what to do or where to go. I don't know what happened to my friends, where they went, or even who took care of them—they just suddenly disappeared. Everyone was in a panic mode—some were crying, and the servants seemed petrified. When I started to run to where I thought nurse might be, she came running to me with just a few things in her hand as she screamed while running: "Run, Mirab Baal, run for your life! *Run now!*"

I realized quickly that we weren't playing a little boy's game, but I didn't know what we *were* playing, although I figured it wasn't a game. Was it some kind of a drill? So I ran as fast as I could, but being only five years old, my short little legs just couldn't go fast enough, I guess, because my nurse turned me around, picked me up, and ran with me in her arms. This slowed her down even more but didn't stop her. She ran and ran, but didn't notice something in the road ahead of her. She tripped and fell.

She told me later that I flew out of her hands and landed with a hard thud on my back. Nurse was so scared that she didn't check to see if anything was wrong with me. She told me that I was screaming—from pain she thought—she picked me up and tried to run on her sore ankle. She told me later that she knew she had to get me to a place where we both would be safe.

Nurse tried to get me to walk, but I couldn't. Every time I tried, I fell to the ground. My back was broken, so my legs and feet were useless. I didn't understand what all that meant until much later. That day, nurse took me far away from the palace. I don't remember how we traveled or how far. I finally fell asleep even with the horrible pain. Eventually, we ended up at the house of Makir, in LoDebar up near the Sea of Galilee. That's when I became Mephibosheth.

No one would be interested in a boy named "Son of Shame" (that's what my new name meant.) My legs were useless but I still had them. They just trailed behind me as I crawled around. For a couple of years, I blamed nurse for my problem, but finally I realized that she had done all she could do to save my life. For her I was and am grateful.

I had to learn how to get around by crawling, but the worst part was learning to live without my handsome dad and my grandpa. That was the most difficult thing to learn. Only five years old and no dad or grandpa! Later, I learned that many children in our region had similar family situations. I am sure I wasn't the first and I wouldn't be the last little kid to be crippled or orphaned or both. My foster parents were patient with me crawling around, under their feet, and needing special care. Eventually, I did learn to appreciate their kindness and tried to be as good a boy as I could be, but I'm sure I must have often been a nuisance to them.

When I was old enough to understand, I heard that my grandpa had done something he should not have done. I had trouble believing this, but people told me that Grandpa had done something bad, I mean, *really bad*. He had tried many times to kill David whom God had chosen to be our next king. Someone told me that God couldn't have Saul as king, ruling over God's own people, the Hebrews. He was a would-be murderer!

Apparently, God holds rulers and leaders to a higher standard than the rest of us. He must expect leaders to be merciful to their subjects—kind, truthful, transparent, and considerate. When Grandpa was killed, my dad was also killed, and all of my uncles that the king's men could find. Uncle David, I guess, was not on their list, because they didn't look for him. Even though Uncle David was not in my family, he was one of my favorites. He and my dad were very close friends—much like brothers.

So now for years I was left to look out for myself. I had a servant who was fairly faithful, but he had a streak of selfishness in him. His name was Ziba. I never felt that I could fully trust him. You can read in one of our books how right I was to suspect him of treachery.[7]

Anyway, I remained hidden from the palace people for many years in the house of Makir the son of Ammiel. It was there that for the second time in my life my world was again turned upside down. It was unbelievable. That was the day that Ziba rushed into the house shouting, "King David wants to see Mephibosheth *now!*"

My heart stopped beating. This was it! I *knew* it. You see, in our part of the world it was customary that when one king succeeded another one, the new king sought out all the family members of the deposed king and disposed of all of them. A new king could not be safe unless there were no rivals in the old king's family who would challenge the new king to the throne. Wars had been fought in our region because the new king hadn't killed everyone in the former king's family. No one was safe. The new king's soldiers were relentless in tracking us down.

However, the question remained, how did King David even know where I was, or that I was even alive? Only one answer: Ziba! Ziba was in charge of what property I had, and I knew he had always had his eye on my property. So what better way for him to get his hands on my property than to turn me in so that the new king could eliminate me and then all the property would belong to Ziba? I had heard that King David had sent out a call for people to let him know if there was anyone of Saul's family still living. Ziba had been quick to answer, for it would mean a lot for his future and his fortune. I think I already told you that Ziba was not to be trusted. He did some more bad stuff later. But that story is for another time. This time I couldn't run, and I was now too big for nurse (wherever she might be) to help me. I figured that the only thing for me to do was to face the end of my life with honor and dignity, go to see King David, and take what I had coming to me. By this time, I was tired of the secrecy and the hiding. I knew I couldn't keep living this way—hiding and running for the rest of my life. What I didn't know until later was that King David had asked for information about my grandfather's family so he could show kindness for my father, Jonathan's, sake. King David's love for my father was greater than all the "rules" of life for a king.

I felt as though I was cursed just because my grandfather had sinned in God's eyes. Sometimes I wished I had not been born a prince, but of course, I couldn't change that. And now Ziba was at the door.

"King David wants to see Mephibosheth—*now*!"

Almost immediately, soldiers of the king were there to pick me up and race all the way south to Jerusalem and up to the king's palace. No one would tell me what this was all about or explain why King David wanted to see me. They carried me to the palace, through the gates, through door after door. I could remember some of those rooms from the times when I had played in them with my friends. Finally, we came to the king's chambers where the throne was. I was scared and knew I was going to die. I wanted to pray to Jehovah, but I was so frightened, I wasn't able to even think of words to say to him. All I could do was shake—and I *shook!* Did I ever!

As was our custom in pleading for mercy, I lay on the floor

with my face on the floor and stretched out my hands, waiting and hoping that it would all be over quickly. I could almost feel the sword over my neck just waiting for the word of the king sentencing me to death. I prayed that it would be quick, but then I heard a voice softly say: "Mephibosheth ... Mephibosheth."

But Uncle David's voice didn't sound angry. "Oh, Mephibosheth."

His voice was very emotional. Perhaps he was on the verge of crying, and if anyone knew about crying, I did. I knew all about tears!

Without even looking up, I said, "Your servant ..."

"Don't be afraid," King David said, "for I will surely show you kindness for the sake of your father Jonathan. I will restore to you all the land that belonged to your grandfather, Saul, and you will always eat at my table."

All I could say was, "Why are you being so considerate of me? I don't understand. Given what the king thinks of me, I might as well be a dead dog to him."

I don't think I'll ever know how or why Uncle David's love for my handsome Father was passed down to me, his son.

Eat at his table? I was deformed, and no one in my condition should ever have been permitted to be before the king, let alone eat at his table. This was beyond kindness; it was pure grace, the king's grace of a mighty king piled upon more of the king's grace. It's no wonder my father, Jonathan, loved Uncle David so much. At that moment, I loved him as much as I loved my father. I knew then that King David had God's love in his heart. He showed me that same love enough to make me a prince again and be a part of his royal family.

It was as though I was a part of God's family and eating at God's table at every meal. I was not only rescued; I was made a child of the king. After all those years, my king had redeemed me, and it was a forever redemption.

A friend told me that Uncle David had composed a song for my dad at his funeral. The last lines were especially about his love for my dad.

> O my dear brother Jonathan,
>   I'm crushed by your death.
> Your friendship was a miracle-wonder,
>   love far exceeding anything I've known—
>   or ever hope to know.
> The mighty warriors—fallen, fallen.
>   And the arms of war broken to bits.
> (2 Samuel 1:26–27)

There was nothing I could do to show my appreciation to my king uncle except to love him and serve him in every way I could, even though I would never be able to outdo his love to me. I know he had accepted me for my dad's sake and transferred his love for my dad to me. I'm beginning to realize that Jehovah's love for me works that way, too. Alleluia!

Biblical background: This story is based on the account in the Old Testament in the books of 1 and 2 Samuel about Mephibosheth, the son of Prince Jonathan. King David researched and found from Ziba the boy's inheritance and returned it to Mephibosheth The story of Jonathon's son is only a small part of the whole family story. Read the rest of the story in 2 Samuel.

Scripture: 2 Samuel: 9:9–13

Discussion possibilities:

1. Do you know the feeling of being afraid for your life? How did that feel?

2. What relevance does this story of David and Mephibosheth have for us today?
3. Whom do you know that has had the love of God shown to them as clearly as Mephibosheth had it shown to him?
4. When in your life has someone shown you similar care and love?

I Hate Them All!

Voice of Jonah

I guess I was brought up in rabidly biased family where discussions were easily spouted about our supposedly national enemies. We were rarely corrected by our parent or even our religious teachers when we repeated what we had heard from them. Hey, if our parents were leading by example, you could say that the neighboring countries were filled with all kinds of bad people, and it seemed only right that we kids could take up the same language and lingo. Of course, we were dependent on the accounts of only a few prophets and travelers for our information about all the horrible things that those people did. In a way, it was exciting to think and imagine what all those unmentionable things were. We kids would often get together in the street after dinner or after Sabbath services to compare notes on what we had most recently heard. As a result of these influences, I must have learned the emotion of hate. It wasn't difficult to learn how to hate, probably as easy to learn hate as it would have been to learn how to love. Maybe even easier.

My family lived in a rinky-dink village over near Nazareth, just a little north of Lake Tiberias sometimes called the Sea of Galilee. There wasn't much for a boy to do there, so during breaks in our school day, lunch, or recess, we had time to talk about how sinful the Assyrians and Chaldeans were. Bad people! But when we even just talked about them, they took on a life of their own and became tantalizing to us teenage guys. I think we knew we shouldn't talk about them, but there was always something exciting and forbidden about them that made us keep our ears and then our mouths open to the tales we heard and retold.

We were certain we were the only nation that Jehovah loved, and that all of creation was made just for us. We alone of all the nations around us were the people Jehovah had firmly planted and were allowed to bloom. We believed that the Assyrians, Chaldeans, and all the rest had sinned so much that God had grown tired of them and was waiting to punish them and possibly destroy them. We were the "chosen people." We knew that and were proud of it. The older I became, the stronger became my sense of my special place in Jehovah's world and in His plan for His people, the Israelites.

Then out of the blue, Jehovah blew me away by telling me that He wanted me, Jonah—me of all people—to go to the city of Nineveh, the worst of the worst, and tell them how angry He was with them for all the stuff they never stopped doing. He told me that I was to tell them they had only six weeks to live, and if they didn't repent of all their sin, they and their beautiful city would be totally destroyed. By the way, their city *was* beautiful beyond words and was the largest known city in the world.

I was beside myself! They were dogs, and I was supposed to go and warn them—warn them of all people—that they were destined for destruction. I'd be the laughingstock not only of them, but of everyone who would listen to their wild stories of "this crazy guy" who was yelling in their streets that their beautiful, tree-lined streets with the huge mansions and exotic gardens would soon by destroyed. I, an Israelite of scrupulous taste and decorum, would be humiliated in front of not only the citizens of Nineveh, but by anyone to whom they told this ridiculous story. The story would inevitably get back not only to my own people in Nazareth but also to all of Galilee. I wouldn't be able to show my face ever again if I even ended up with a face. I decided one sleepless night that there was no way I was ever going to put myself in that kind of a situation. But I knew better than to confront Jehovah, "No, this job is not for me!" So, I had to think of a different way to say no without being obnoxious and rude.

All I could think of was to run away from God's sight. "Out of sight, out of mind" was my plan. I headed west to Tarshish at the edge of the world where the sun sets every day, on the seacoast possibly of the last place on earth, Iberia, where the Great Sea[8] enters into the unknown waters. I secured passage on a ship in Joppa, on the west coast of Israel. I was the only Israelite on the heavily laden ship, so they put me in steerage in the hold of the ship next to the animals.

While I was sleeping down in the hold, a terrific storm came up as they can do on the Great Sea. The storm alarmed every waking person while I slept on with no more worries or thoughts about Nineveh or about my God. Suddenly, a couple of sailors woke me by screaming at me, "How can you sleep while *we* are going to the bottom of the sea?" They told me that they had already thrown much of their cargo in the sea to lighten the load, including some of my animal roommates who ended up in the drink. Slowly I began to realize that the storm and the present danger to the ship was Jehovah's way of getting my attention. Obviously, he certainly doesn't mince words or actions when he needs to get the attention of his people. The sailors asked me about my God and if I could get him to stop the storm, and if that didn't work, they were going to start abandoning their ship as self-sacrifices to their many gods. Jehovah must have finally gotten through my thick skull, because I told them, "I am the cause of this tragedy. Throw me overboard and save the ship and yourselves." They seemed positively delighted to get rid of me, so, wasting no time, they threw me into the raging waters. And the raging waters quieted. *Voila!*

I knew I was a goner. (Even my self-nobility didn't save me or the day.) Jehovah was through with me! I had pushed Him too far, and He had had it with me. Just before I drowned, a huge fish opened his gigantic mouth, and down I slipped into his mammoth belly. Pray? I poured out my heart and soul to the one who rules the sea and its waves. "Forgive me, Lord, I have sinned. I'm ready to do Your will even if it means going to the wicked city of Nineveh. I don't want to go there. I can't change that, but I will go if You send me." I figured I was quite safe. Here I was inside a huge fish and Nineveh was far, far away. As someone said, big fish don't enjoy eating people so, whoops, the next thing I knew, I was out on a lonely shore and the fish was on his way—I hope back to his home with a story none of his fish friends would ever believe.

After another long trip looking ragged and disheveled, I made it back to surroundings that seemed more familiar—to Nineveh. I looked as though I had just been rescued from some outlandish adventure as I walked up and down their streets and lanes shouting, "You have forty days to repent. If you don't, you will all die and your city will be smashed."

What I didn't know was that in the space of time when I was fighting for my life in a raging sea and in the belly of an unbelievably big fish, Nineveh was being looked at and not so amorously. Their enemies were licking their lips for a fight for the treasures that Nineveh's rulers had stolen from all the nations they had conquered. Their enemy's conquered magnificent temples and mansions had been decimated through all the wars they had lost over the many years of battles and the looting that followed. Now, Nineveh's enemies were ready to pounce and take their "pound of flesh" from the hated rulers of Nineveh. The prized possessions of the conquered countries were now in Nineveh's palaces and mansions, and in the throne rooms of their king. Given these circumstances, Nineveh was more than ready to hear me. In fact, they repented on the first day of my preaching. I hadn't realized until then that my preaching could be so effective. Or did I just scare them into believing?

Someone told me that their king had heard of my rantings and had ordered all the people to repent, put on sackcloth, sit in ashes, and refuse to eat or drink until God decided to let them live. Even the animals were to follow the king's edicts by being dressed in sackcloth, sitting in ashes, and not eating for a few days or drinking any water. The people were hoping that God would hear their repentance and relent, but I am sure the animals had no idea why this was happening to them. (Poor things!) Jehovah did relent! That's right, He *relented*! Can you believe it? After all *I* had gone through! And just after one day of my preaching. Wow!

Can you imagine how I felt about this unimaginable change of events? You are *so* right! I was angry—*very* angry! I didn't waste a minute to give Jehovah an earful. "What is it with you? I did everything you told me to do. Reluctantly, I admit, but I did it. How could you do this to me? I should have known this would happen. This is exactly what I thought you would do—give them a reprieve and make me the laughingstock of the entire city and all those they tell about this tragedy. I know you are a merciful God, slow to anger, but quick to respond to repentance and then you go and cancel your plans for destroying these wicked people. No gold stars on my forehead, and not even a thank you note! Now, just kill me … please! I'd rather be dead than alive since what I told them would happen unless they repented, but never did happen. Did you do this to humiliate me? If that was your purpose, well, it worked. I'll *never* be able to face people again—they'll just laugh at me."

I went up on a hill outside that city of criminals and people guilty of all the sins a person could imagine. I sulked, yes, I *sulked* and built a shelter from the sun out of a quickly growing tree so I could watch what God might do. Jehovah sent a strange worm that ate through the tree root overnight, killed the tree, and the sun burned me so badly that I almost fainted. Angry at the *tree*, at *God* and at the entire *world*, I said, "Death is better than this! Much better!"

Jehovah asked me, "What right do you have to be angry about a tree just because it died?" I spoke right back to Him, "Plenty of right. It's made me angry enough to want to die!" (Jonah 4:9). It didn't take Him long to respond to my plaintive sob story. "Jonah," He said, "how is it that you can change your feelings overnight from pleasure to anger about a mere shade tree that you did nothing to get? You didn't plant it, and you certainly never watered it. You are just feeling sorry for yourself. However, being God, I can change from what *I* feel about Nineveh from anger to pleasure for a great city as Nineveh with its 120,000 people, who are in utterly spiritual darkness to say nothing of all those poor, innocent animals ... *Jonah ... get ... a ... grip!*"

I left Nineveh and wandered around before returning to my home in Galilee. I was desolate. I felt spiritually destroyed because I was sure that Jehovah had let me down. He showed patience with a sinful city and its outrageously criminal bureaucracy and made me a liar, or so I figured. I didn't even know if their repentance was real, but if I were a betting man, I would bet it wasn't real, or that it would be short-lived.

My questions to Jehovah were simple ones:

- How can you be so forgiving to the worst of people?"

- "What is it about you that makes you *want* to forgive people?"
- "Is it because you originally made us just so you would have someone to love, and who would love you in return?"
- "I wonder about you and what kind of God you really are."

Biblical background: This story is an adaptation of the biblical account in the book of Jonah, one of the prophets, whose book is near the end of the Old Testament. The author of this adaptation has added words and also surmised the attitudes of the people involved to make it more relevant to readers of this century. Many of the quotes are from *The Message*. The writer of this story is convinced that chapter 4 is the key to the book of Jonah. Use the few minutes it will take to read the four chapters of the book to understand how pernicious "hate" is with its terrible results.

Scripture: Jonah 4

Discussion possibilities:

1. Consider the questions at the end of the story that Jonah asked God.
2. What was working in Jonah's mind that must have raised these questions?
3. Discuss the result of egotism in doing God's work.
4. Discuss the evolution of hatred in a person's life and in society.

Between BC and AD

Voices of Zacharias, Elizabeth, and Mary

"Praise Jehovah, Zacharias, you're finally home!" Elizabeth, my wife, said as soon as I walked in the door. But she was acting strangely with her head bobbing, her curls flying around, and her feet moving as though she was doing one of our sacred dances that are a part of our festive occasions.

For a couple of seconds, I thought maybe my wife had completely flipped her curly gray hair or had been hitting the Manischewitz while I had been gone. I'd only been gone a few weeks this time. Certainly not enough time to get her this excited about my return.

When I am gone, I am fulfilling my role as a priest in our temple in Jerusalem. I belong to a group of priests who do various tasks in the temple. These tasks may be as simple as keeping the incense lamps burning and keeping the temple clean and in good order or as important as sacrificing the lambs and goats for the sacrifices our people bring to atone for their sins or to offer for other purposes. Since I'm relatively close to Jerusalem, my trips are not as big of a deal as they are for many priests who live in Galilee, many miles much farther north.

Elizabeth has had plenty of time to get used to my travel schedule—it hasn't varied much in all our years together. We had married our first sweethearts more years ago than either of us will admit. We only have one problem in our marriage, but it is a very serious problem. We don't have a child, and my wife has never been able to reconcile herself to being childless, especially when she sees other mothers playing with their children in the village streets. It also hurts, she says, when she sees families heading off to religious services, and she must walk alone when I'm away or when it is just the two of us when I'm home.

You may have trouble believing this, but while I was away this time, standing by the temple's table of incense, an angel talked to me about the very issue of us having no child. Angel Gabriel told me that we were going to have a child and that his name was to be John. I felt the same way you'd probably feel if an angel told you such good news! I was speechless! I just couldn't believe him. After all, I'm an old man, and my wife is an old woman. I fought the idea and fearlessly remonstrated with the Angel Gabriel. In response to my arguments, he made my speechlessness, at least for now, permanent. Because I had refused to believe him, he told me, I wouldn't be able to speak for about nine months. Nine months! Should you ever meet an angel, try to summon up enough faith to believe him. No matter how you initially feel about his message, believe whatever the angel tells you.

After Gabriel's visit, and while still at the temple, I worked hard at gesturing, but still had difficulty communicating with the other priests. I knew I'd even have more trouble when my temple shift was finished and I returned home to my loving wife.

And here I was now at home, and I thought that Elizabeth was going to burst. It seemed as though she had something very important to tell me and couldn't wait for me to listen to her. As the good husband I try to be, I finally let her know that I was listening by putting my hands behind my ears and waggling my mouth while pointing to her mouth. And as soon as she realized that I was truly listening, she shouted: "We're going to have a baby!"

How did she know? Who told her? Now the hard work began for me. How to let her know that I already knew this? I understand enough about female psychology to know that for such important news, it was strategic that she thought this was also news to me.

I tried to answer Elizabeth's exuberance, but remember, I couldn't speak. I had to mouth my words, "What!" And then I pulled out the slate I'd carried with me on my trip home so I could communicate if I needed to let someone know something—anything. "How do you know this?" was all I could write, wondering what she could possibly say.

Her response was no surprise. "This you won't believe. I didn't believe it at first either. I had a visit from an angel of the Lord," she replied as though she was talking about the next-door neighbor dropping off some matzo balls for Sabbath.

"A real angel?" I wrote.

"Yes, of course, a real angel," she said.

"But you have never seen a real angel, or any other kind of angel, have you?" I wrote.

"No, but that's how the person identified himself, as Gabriel," she responded.

(Talk about one family keeping one angel busy!)

I grabbed my scroll again and wrote: "Are you okay with this? At our age? I hope we are up for this, and that Jehovah knows what He is doing! Raising a child is no picnic. We have noticed from watching other parents, even when the parents are young, but at our age? And a boy, too?"

My wife spoke for many childless women in Israel. "Oh, yes, I don't have to hang my head in shame any longer. Now we know that Jehovah has shown us His favor and has taken away my disgrace among the people."

I figured that now I needed to come clean and make myself clear. "I guess I better tell you about my experience with Gabriel." I wrote and gestured. "I was in the temple at the table where we burn the incense. Suddenly, Gabriel appeared, leaned against one of the ancient pillars, and told me what was about to happen. When I arrived home and couldn't speak, did you think that I had gotten a cold on my way back from Jerusalem? I didn't get sick, but it was because I didn't believe Gabriel's words, and he told me that I wouldn't speak until our child was born. So, now it is really going to happen—we'll have a baby of our own!"

We looked at each other with love in our eyes, thankful that God had heard our prayers and was ready to make our lives complete with a family to cherish. Spoken words would have been irrelevant at that moment: we were beside ourselves with joyful anticipation.

Bringing us back to the present, Elizabeth said, "The angel also told me that Mary of Nazareth, a relative of mine, was going to have a baby soon, too."

Now, this was news to me. I hadn't been told about that!

Mary arrived from Nazareth soon after this. It's a few days' trip from Mary's home in Galilee to our home in the Judean highlands. I suppose she made the trip with a caravan since she had to go through some dangerous places on her trip, and I'm sure that neither her parents nor Joseph would allow a young teenage girl to travel alone on our roads even on a fast donkey doing about two miles per hour up and down the hills.

When Mary came into the house, she was enthralled with Elizabeth's greeting, which went something similar to this:

> You're so blessed among women, and the babe
> in your womb, also blessed! And why am I so
> blessed that the mother of my Lord visits me? The

moment the sound of your greeting entered my
ears, the babe in my womb skipped like a lamb
for sheer joy. Blessed woman, who believed what
God said, believed every word would come true!
(Luke 1:42-45)

Almost immediately, Mary broke into song with words that I
venture will live for a long time:

> I'm bursting with Good news;
> > I'm dancing the song of my Savior God.
> God took one good look at me, and look what
> happened—
> > I'm the most fortunate woman on earth!
> What God had done for me will never be forgotten,
> > the God whose very name is holy, set apart
> from all others. ...
> He ...
> > scattered the bluffing braggarts.
> He knocked tyrants off their high horses,
> > pulled victims out of the mud.
> The starving poor sat down to a banquet;
> > the callous rich were left out in the cold.
> He embraced his chosen child, Israel;
> > he remembered and piled on the mercies,
> > piled them high.
> It's exactly what he promised,
> > beginning with Abraham and right up to
> > now. (Luke 1:46–55)

I hope that someday a composer will sit down at his harp and
work out a melody to fit these beautiful words.
Mary stayed a little more than three months until our baby

was born and then went to Nazareth and to her family so they could be near her when she gave birth to her baby. We packed her up and made sure she would be safe on her return journey. I image that someday someone will think of a way to make such a trip easier and faster.

Our story only gets better. After our baby was born, we started to prepare for the eighth-day ceremony and party. Friends and relatives from all over the place descended on our home, along with the rabbi. This was the time to give our baby his name.

I guess the guests assumed that he would be my namesake, Zacharias Jr. But his mother said, "No. He must be named John." I can tell you that this didn't set very well with the guests who wanted to argue with her. "There is no one in your entire family by that name." So, they turned to me, gesturing to me their arguments. They found that difficult, but I found it rather amusing. Of course, I couldn't talk, so I motioned my slate and wrote, "His name is John."

As I wrote that name, I also spoke it! This surprised all of them, but it shocked me. I had my voice back just as Gabriel said I would. See—you can believe an angel of the Lord when he tells you he will do something—he will! I don't think I said a single word for several minutes. I was so shocked that it silenced me as much as the angel's action had silenced me at the temple.

We could not believe how quickly the news of John's birth went from house to house in our village and eventually even to other highland towns. As one old-timer told me. "We couldn't help but wonder what John will become and what God has in store for him."

I didn't tell them everything that Gabriel had told me in the temple. I'm sure they would have trouble accepting it, and I didn't want to sound proud and arrogant. I know that if this had happened to one of my neighbors, who shall remain nameless, he'd be spreading it on so thick, you could walk on it or may be in it! Gabriel had given me some directions:

> You are to name him John. You're going to leap like a gazelle for joy, and not only you—many will delight in his birth. He'll achieve great stature with God.

> He'll drink neither wine nor beer. He'll be filled with the Holy Spirit from the moment he leaves his mother's womb. He will turn many sons and daughters of Israel back to their God. He will herald God's arrival in the style and strength of Elijah, soften the hearts of parents to children, and kindle devout understanding among hardened skeptics—he'll get the people ready for God. (Luke 1:13–17)

Do you now understand why I couldn't or wouldn't share this information with other people? If there is enough interest in it, someday I'll probably tell someone this story from start to finish. I suppose it could even be included in a best-seller.

Now, to wrap up the events of that great ceremonial day, I felt a strong need to express some of my own thoughts and hope for my new son. Gabriel had said much of this, but I put it into simple, plain Hebrew so that if you had been there, you would have understood it, too. As soon as I started speaking, I knew that I was not the one speaking, but that the Holy Spirit was speaking through me, as he did through our prophets of old. I said a couple things about God's mercy to us as Israelites, and then spoke about John's role in God's plan.

And you, my child, 'Prophet of the Highest,'
    will go ahead of the Master to prepare his ways,
Present the offer of salvation to his people,
    the forgiveness of their sins.
Through the heartfelt mercies of our God,
    God's Sunrise will break in upon us,
Shining on those in darkness,
    Those sitting in the shadow of death.
Then showing us the way, one foot at a time,
    down the path of peace. (Luke 1:76–79)

We watched John grow into a fine young boy. It was obvious to us that God was with him, and that he loved God. If someone ever writes this down, you'll probably enjoy reading about our son and what happened to him as a grown man. As strange as his life began, we can't imagine how it will continue and end.

Biblical background: This story is an adaptation of the biblical account of the birth of John the Baptist found in Luke. The author had added phrases and has surmised the actions and feelings of the four major participants: Gabriel, Zacharias, Elizabeth, and Mary plus their families and friends who attended the party.
Scripture: Luke 1:5–17 (Entire story: Luke 1:5–80)
Discussion possibilities

1. Why do you think this story is in the Bible?
2. What does the story say about hope?
3. How do we see this as a connecting link between the Old Testament and the New Testament?
4. Discuss the place of faith in a person's life.

We Followed Our Star

Voice of Kasper, the Wise Man

You may think that travel is fun, educational, stimulating, and even exciting. Let me tell you that when you are sitting on the back of a camel, travel is not fun. It may be educational, but that's about it—even for short trips—to say nothing of the long trip we had just finished.

Since as astrologers, we believe that the stars reveal vital information, we search the heavens every night to see what the stars can tell us. One special night we saw a bright new star. This was the first new star that we had ever discovered in the heavens. We didn't know what it meant, but we knew that whatever it meant, given its brilliance, it was extraordinarily significant.

We read everything we had collected, but we could not find out anything about it. No one was saying a word about it at the marketplace or out on the street. Apparently, no one else had observed it or else anyone who had observed it was as dumbfounded as we were. It is not uncommon that some people who discover something new are often slow to announce it to the world. We were fearful that other people could try to trump us by claiming they knew about the star before we did. We were also afraid of the ridicule of others if it turned out that we were wrong. Therefore, we usually keep such information close to the robe, really close to the robe, as we say.

To us, a new star can only mean one thing: somewhere on earth a new king had been born. From our research, the three of us believe that the brilliance of the star is directly related to the stature of the newborn king and to the significance of his reign.

Not having much else to do, we decided to follow the star and head to the western nations. We were sure that such a trip would be a long one. However, the three of us knew that our lives would be miserable if we didn't at least look for the new king. Life gets quite dull when there is no goal challenging us forward, so now we had a goal. We might find the new king, or the entire trip could end up just being a wild king chase. We had hope, lots of it, and we had big expectations of finding the new king and being a part of spreading the news of our discovery.

My fellow travelers call me Kasper. I am the oldest of the magi who made the trip from the East to Judah. The others were Melchior and Balthazar. People who heard about our journey wondered why some wealthy men from Persia would want to go looking for a new king. Now that's a good question! Being the old man of the group, I, myself, asked that question more than once while we were traveling. The answer from my colleagues was always the same—our star. At least, that's what we had started to call it—our star.

It wasn't easy getting a staff and all our traveling equipment together to make the long trip, especially since we had no idea where we were going, how long it would take us, or if we would even find what we were looking for. However, what else do a few rich astrologers have to do? We loaded up the camel train with enough provisions to last several months, including food, tents, carpets, and of course, gifts for the new king. Considering the probability of the king's significance, only the finest gifts would be appropriate.

Since we suspected that the new star was an omen of good things to come, we packed up and followed it. Camels are far from the ideal mode of transportation, but our options were very limited: oxen, horses, camels, or walking. I hope for the sake of future generations that someone comes up with better modes of moving around our world. If only camels could fly!

The trip was excruciatingly long. In fact, it was too long to be on the back of a camel or on anything else that bounces along through the desert. It seemed as though it would take forever to reach our destination. Melchior kept asking, "Are we there yet?" He alternated that question with, "How much farther is it?" Balthasar and I threatened several times to make him go to the end of the camel train if he didn't stop asking so many questions. Of course, we would always break at dusk, set up the tents, cook our meals, and sleep as best we could. There were many times when windstorms would whip up the sand, almost blinding us, and of course, there was not much rain, since most of our trip was through desert in the dry time of the year. Several times, we stayed in the homes of residents in the cities. I'll never forget little, crippled Amahl, who insisted on making the journey with us to see the new king, hoping that he would be healed of his crippling sickness. However, his mother was not at all happy about that possibility. We had to convince her that we were not three old rich men who wanted to abscond with her son. We finally did convince her, promising that he was safe with us. He livened up our trip considerably with his youthful chatter and antics.

Eventually, we arrived in Jerusalem. We knew nothing about this city or its residents. We soon learned, however, that the residents were called Jews, had a king named Herod, and were under the domination of Rome, and the area was a small part of the Roman Empire. We asked everyone we met where we could find the new king who had been born. King Herod heard about us and quickly was at full attention. He asked us to come to his palace—what a place! The gardens, oh my! The palace had the newest and best of everything we had ever seen. Herod told us that after we had found the newborn child, he wanted us to return and tell him where we had found him so he could also go and worship him. Herod called in some of the Jewish priests and asked them where the child might be. The priests replied that their holy scrolls predicted that a special child would be born in Bethlehem. They told us that Bethlehem was not very far from Jerusalem. We reminded Melchior that, yes, we were almost there—less than a day's journey away.

We spent the night in Jerusalem and left for Bethlehem the next morning. As we journeyed south the few short miles to our final destination, the three of us discussed the details of our visit with Herod, his interest in the new king, and especially the reaction of the Jewish priests and scribes to the news of the birth of a king that had been prophesied in their holy scrolls. The three of us were surprised—no, we were shocked—by the priests' and scribes' reactions. Melchior was surprised that their holy scrolls would have predicted such an event. Balthazar couldn't believe their apparent lack of interest in something that had been prophesied or predicted so long ago.

I wondered why they wouldn't have been at least as excited as we were about such a significant event. After all, we had traveled hundreds and hundreds of miles to see the new king, but they didn't seem at all interested in finding out for themselves about him, and it appeared that he was only a few miles away from them. After all, the news couldn't have been too surprising to them since they seemed to already know the information Herod wanted.

We realized then that the chief priests and scribes were similar to many of our fellow astrologers. They read their books, studied the stars, knew so much information, but then did nothing about what they knew, nor took any action on that knowledge. All that information didn't move the priests enough to get them off their backsides and do something. We figured that at the very least, they would have been interested in what we learned in Bethlehem, but we never heard from them again.

We stopped at an inn in that small Judean village, Bethlehem, where the host and his wife warmly greeted us and told us that the small family for which we were looking had moved from their inn to a home in the village. The host was kind enough to guide us to the home, and as we looked up to the heavens, there was our star right above the house! Melchior was happy! We had completed our journey! We met the little boy, apparently the new king, knelt down in worship, and presented our gifts of gold, frankincense, and myrrh. The little fellow didn't know what to make of the gifts, but his parents had no trouble figuring it all out. We thought that we might be embarrassed to worship such a young boy, but when we were down on our knees, I felt as though that was exactly the place where we belonged—on our knees.

Now what were we to do? Herod had asked us to let him know where the boy was so he could also come and worship him. You know, after some thought, we didn't care for the sound of his request. Something seemed very fishy to us. Could it be a setup?

Balthazar had a dream that confirmed our suspicions. The dream warned us that Herod was planning to do dastardly violence to Jesus, so we returned to our homeland by way of a different route. Melchior didn't say much on the way home except to comment on the scenery or sometimes, the lack of it.

While Balthazar was having his dream, Joseph had a similar one about Herod's evil intentions toward Jesus. Joseph told

Balthazar about it when we went to say good-bye to the family we had come to love. Joseph, with Mary and their baby, Jesus, had planned to flee to Egypt to escape Herod's evil intentions. We wished them God's blessing on their trip and their futures.

On the way back to Persia, a traveling storyteller told us an unsettling story about Herod. If his story were true, Herod was a despicable man. After we had left Bethlehem, he ordered his soldiers to go to Bethlehem and kill all baby boys aged two and under. This King Herod had serious problems! Apparently, his position as the king was the result of bloodshed, conspiracy, and uncertain allies. For example, two of his political friends were Mark Antony and Cleopatra who themselves were in serious trouble. We also learned that King Herod had murdered his first wife and even some of his children. He had married again and again and again, probably about ten times. Strange, we were saying, how powerful people seem to want only one thing: more and more power. It appears that such people will do almost anything to hold onto their power, whatever the consequences may be. We decided that power must be so seductive that politicians cannot resist it. Power must be an aphrodisiac that dulls their minds and causes them to make very strange decisions, and to act in very strange ways. Maybe that explains Herod's paranoid, conniving, and disgusting behavior as well as his fear of a little boy. Fear of a little boy? A baby? *Give ... me ... a ... break!*

All the way back to Persia, we couldn't stop talking about the object of our journey. The little boy was probably about two years old, handsome, quick, and we predicted that he would be a fast learner. But there was something more. Balthazar reminded me about those few moments when Jesus climbed up on Amahl's lap, looked into his eyes, and smiled as though he knew who Amahl was. I took the little guy on my lap, too, and had the same feeling. There I was, an old man, a stranger in strange clothing, but I felt an overpowering love for him, and not, surprisingly, I felt that love returned. At that moment, I realized that there was probably nothing that could ever keep Jesus from loving anyone. I predicted, being the wise man that I am, that nothing could ever separate anyone in any place from the love of this new king. For certain, he was not an ordinary person. Oh, no! There was something so intriguing about him that Balthazar insisted that we spend time on our journey home discussing this among ourselves. After many long discussions, we concluded that Jesus had all the makings of a king, but not similar to any king we had ever heard of.

However, we tried to imagine where his kingdom would be. He could be a powerful successor to Herod, although we sensed a greatness in him that would easily surpass the needs of the small kingdom of Judah. Nor would he fit in well as a Caesar in the Roman Empire, which by this time included not only most of the barbarian nations but also all of Asia, because most of the world was Roman. No, he wouldn't be a suitable monarch for Rome. We could sense the kindness and tenderness in him that would endear him to the citizens, but not to administrators or to the vast bureaucracy of Rome and its military.

On the other hand, Balthazar said, "I can foresee a firmness and decisiveness in his nature that would ensure fairness and balance in his dealings with others." This we were sure of: he would never be an ordinary person or king. But we also sensed a hint of mystery in his future.

Melchior finally stopped admiring the scenery and said something not related to the scenery. "I am sure that some tragedy will end his life." We all suspected that at his end there would be tragedy, but that is as far we could see. We felt positive, though, that great wonders would result from the tragedy, and that there would be victory and majesty in his future. Our question: was tragedy his ultimate end, or victory, or in some strange way, both?

My final contribution to this discussion was, "I also have a strong intuition that Melchior is right, and that the sometime in the future, Mary's heart will be broken because of him."

The more we analyzed the situation, the more distressed we became. We spent hours and days discussing it, while we rode those beasts of the desert, as we ate our meals, even as we prepared to sleep at night. The more we talked about it, the more genuinely frustrated we became. For the life of us, we could not discern more about his future. This usually does not happen to us. After all, we were the wise men, the magi, the forecasters of the future who had our reputations to protect. Even if we don't know the future, we must at least pretend that we do!

We spent the rest of the trip surmising what his life would be. Would his life affect others in the region, Judea, and maybe the world? Unfortunately, our powers of forecasting didn't help us this time. We couldn't see his future, but we felt sure within our hearts that his presence in the world was going to be earth shaking. We figured that only future generations would fully know his contributions to the world.

The new, small boy's impact on our lives during those days was far beyond anything we could ever have imagined. We're now going back to our homes as different men with a desire in our lives to worship him, and to share our experiences of those few months with others who are seeking knowledge of a living and loving king.

Our star had not disappointed us. It had led us to the one whom we know will always be the King of all Kings! Will you follow your star? If we can help, seek out a wise person who could help you find your star.

Biblical reference: This story assumes the authenticity of the account in Matthew and builds the story around the Magi, the wise men, who journeyed from the East, probably Persia, to Bethlehem. The journey was long and probably treacherous, but they pursued their goal, their star, until they arrived to worship the newborn King.

Scripture: Matthew 2:1–12

Discussion possibilities:

1. Why does this account appear only in the gospel of Matthew? (Matthew wrote for a Jewish audience for whom the account would help authenticate the kingship of Jesus.)

2. Why do you suppose the chief priests and scribes did not go to Bethlehem, or even lead the Magi to the new king?

3. Discuss the reluctance of many Christians today to follow their goal to find God's will for their lives.

4. What motivation do goals provide to a person in search of a career, task, or project?

Who Is This Kid?

Voice of the Bethlehem Innkeeper

"How was I to know who they were? The crowds were huge. Everyone was so demanding and exhausted. I did my best to accommodate as many of them as I could. There are only so many things one small town innkeeper can do. Right?"

"Amos, who were the last people you had to turn away?" my wife Deborah had asked when I walked back to the kitchen to see if there was anything I could do to help with dinner. I told her it was just a young couple from up north in Galilee. They had pleaded with me for a room, saying that the wife was pregnant with her first child. I had to tell them the inn was full, and there just wasn't room for any more guests.

"You did what?" my wife said. "Amos, how could you? You actually turned away a woman who is expecting a baby. I don't believe you! How could you be so cold-hearted?" She added, "Oh, why didn't I go to the front desk? I would never have turned them away. Did you give them a recommendation for another inn, or what did you do? Well, don't just stand there, *what ... did ... you ... do?*"

I didn't know what to say. If you have ever faced your wife or girlfriend when she is throwing questions at you like a child throwing stones at a brick wall, then you know how I felt. Good grief, what had I gotten myself into? I swear, it doesn't much matter what I do; I am always in the wrong. Oh, I know that she is worn out with meals to prepare, rooms to clean, and questions to answer. But I'm tired, too. And then Caesar Augustus lays another tax on us along with the census, making more work for all of us. People having to travel to their place of family origin to be counted, causing traffic jams, jangled nerves, and situations similar to the one I had just handled. Wouldn't you think someone in the government could have figured out a way to automate this whole process? Well, maybe someday. And while they're at it, figure out a way to handle reservations, too. This first-come, first-served process is for the birds.

"Deborah, that is not what I did!" I responded, probably a little too loudly. "I told them the stable was available and they could use it." Now what did I do? No sooner did I say it I knew I was in trouble again! When will I learn to think before I speak, especially when she is so upset about everything? It seems as though I can *never* be right. Now I prepared to hear it all again. I could almost guess what she was going to say next! And I was right!

Deborah practically yelled at me, *"You did what?* You sent them to the stable? With the animals, the smells, the noise? Please tell me you didn't do that. *Please,* Amos, tell me you are kidding, right?"

I knew I was stuck and the longer I waited to respond, the worse the situation would become. I told her, "That was the only way to resolve the problem. At least it's warm out there; it's better than spending the cold night sleeping outdoors, isn't it? What was I to do, give them *our* bed for the night?" As soon as I said that, I knew I had said the wrong thing again. There went my comfortable bed for the night.

Before she could deliver a comeback, strange things began to happen. Suddenly, the sky seemed to light up, and the most beautiful sounds I've ever heard rang across the heavens. Some shepherds from the hills told us more about this later. They said they were "watching their flocks by night, all seated on the ground, when, they said, the angel of the Lord came down, and glory shone all around." They continued with their story. "The sounds we heard," they said, "were angels singing about someone who had just been born here in our little village." The angels told them to get up, leave their flocks, and get themselves over here to Bethlehem.

Oh, Lord, I hope they don't expect to stay here tonight. They are dirty, smell like sheep, and look hungry too. I really don't want to tell my wife about them, and I hope she doesn't show up while they are at the door. All I could tell them was, "Not more than an hour ago, I sent a pregnant woman and her husband to the stable, and maybe she was giving birth. She certainly looked as though she was ready for this big event in their lives."

"Which way to the stable?" was all they could say.

"Right that way," I said as I pointed to the cave behind the inn.

They rushed off, almost stumbling over each other in their hurry to verify what the angels had said, and to see this thing that had come to pass. I can tell you, I was glad to have them and their smell away from the inn and from me. Phew, what a stench a bunch of dirty shepherds can leave behind. Things were happening so fast that I couldn't figure out what was going on. What did it all mean? So many unusual events:

- Angels singing to *shepherds!*
- Angels telling *shepherds* about a baby being born!
- Shepherds leaving their sheep to see a *baby?*
- Shepherds don't *do* this—to see a *baby*! I don't *think* so!
- Who *is* this kid?

I shook myself from my wonderings and decided that I couldn't keep this news from my wife, so together we left the inn to check this out for ourselves. My wife seemed to be overcome with grief for what I had done to this young couple. She apologized to them for what I had done and poked me in the ribs to make me add my apologies to hers. The young couple were so nice about it, making us feel even worse. It would have been easier if they had been *upset* with us. They even thanked us for the use of the stable. Ouch, that made it worse.

I have learned that one of the important questions to ask new parents is, "What's the baby's name?" Joseph responded to my inquiry. That surprised me because the baby's mother is often the one to answer that question. He simply said, "Jesus." Then he told all of us standing around that an angel told him that name in a dream and also the reason for that name. Now the name is not unusual among our people. It simply means "Savior," and goes as far back as Israel's leader, Joshua, the man who became our leader when Moses couldn't take Israel into the Promised Land. The angel had told Joseph that the newborn child "would save his people from their sins." Just how does a baby save people from their sins?

As we walked back to the inn, I asked Deborah, "Did you notice anything unusual about the baby Jesus? To me, he seemed different in some way. I can't put my finger now on what that difference is. I guess I need to think about it after I collapse tonight."

The next day, Joseph, the new dad, went to enroll at the town hall and pay their tax, leaving Mary, the new mother, alone with some of the townspeople who had heard the commotion in the heavens and had followed the shepherds. Of course, the shepherds by this time had returned to their flocks in the hills. I suspect they might have been having second thoughts about leaving all those sheep out there with no protection from the bears, lions, and rustlers. On their way back to the pastures, they told everyone who would listen what the angels had told them and who they had seen in the manger.

My wife got her way about the living arrangements, as I knew she would. By the way, our rabbi had told me after we were married that marriages seem to be less stressful when the husband lets the wife make most of the decisions—at least those decisions about the household and the family. Her decision as related to the family in the stable was that they were to move into the inn, take our room, and stay until Mary and the baby could safely travel. Grudgingly, I went along with the plan. I think it was either this or find *myself* out in the stable.

You had better believe that as soon as the crowds left town, I started looking for a small house the new family could use until they traveled back to Nazareth. I found one, and Joseph and I arranged to have them move within the next week. People brought them meals, some changes of clothing, and even a couple of toys for the baby. The house had some furniture in it, so there was no need to supply additional tables or chairs. My wife told me that Joseph and Mary were quite content to stay in Bethlehem and live here for a long time. If anyone would know, my Deborah would!

Now I could breathe again with that problem solved. My wife was happy, and when Mama is happy, everyone is happy, right? Of much less importance, I was back in my own bed. However, this quiet time was just the calm before another storm. This kid's birth was creating more problems than you can imagine. I hope his life doesn't continue to create problems for people, but I have an uncanny feeling that it will. My mind keeps asking the same question: Who *is* this kid?

I guess Joseph and Mary were comfortable here. Joseph took on some construction work, and everything seemed to be going along just fine. My wife and Mary became friends, and they were frequently running back and forth between the two houses, I suppose keeping each other up on the news and the gossip. From what my wife told me, Mary shared some of the details of her prenatal experiences: her visit with her cousin, Elizabeth, and the unusual events of that three-month visit, her dream about the birth of her child, and Joseph's dream, too. These stories seem so strange now, and I wouldn't be surprised if someday someone writes a book of them.

Then the next storm hit. Rumors had drifted south to Bethlehem from Jerusalem about some strange visitors who had been asking King Herod questions about where a new king was born. Knowing just the little I'd heard about Herod, that must have been the same as being hit in the head with a brick. He had the reputation of being a conniving, evil, and treacherous man. The strangers arrived here soon, saying that a star had led them to this place, or rather, to the house where Mary, Joseph, and Jesus lived. Come to think of it, when I went out to the stable last night to check on the animals, I did see a bright star that seemed to have stopped right over our village. After what we had been through, I conveniently forgot to mention it to my wife. I didn't see any point in adding any more fuel to the fire, the fire I had started a few months ago. I'm not sure she has come to terms with what she now calls my ineptness with handling guests. I just don't want them coming to our inn for rooms. They are too elegant for our small-town inn.

From what some of the neighbors are telling me, the visitors are richly dressed and have gifts for Jesus, gifts that could keep Joseph well fixed for income for a long time: gold, frankincense, and myrrh. They didn't stay long, just long enough to throw themselves down before the little boy to worship him. To some of the people at the synagogue that seemed to be a very strange thing for anyone to do, especially such important men like the Magi. What is going on here? Just who is this kid that even foreigners travel for months to see him and worship him ... worship him?

Again, as I watched the Magi worship Jesus, I thought about my earlier wonderings about the difference I had first noticed about Jesus. I felt in a way that maybe I, too, should be worshiping him along with the Wise Men. But I didn't want to seem weird to those who were watching. Who knows what the rabbi would say about that?

However, I suspected there was some kind of evil behind all of this. One of the Magi told me, when I just happened to be down at Joseph's place borrowing a tool, that Herod had asked them to return to Jerusalem and let him know where the new king was living, so he could come and worship him, too. Now that is all we need in our village, to have one of the worst kings in our history visit us. I doubt that we have the necessary social class that would encourage him to stay with us or at our inn. For once, my wife can be happy we hadn't upgraded our facility. Wisely, the visitors went home another way without going back through Jerusalem. That took one worry from me—no visit from Herod!

However, that wasn't the end the story. Joseph told me that he was warned in a dream that harm was about to come to Jesus. He packed up their few animals and fled with Mary and Jesus to Egypt. He needed to get out of Herod's way. It was a good thing he did because Herod sent his soldiers to Bethlehem to kill every baby boy who was two years old and younger. If someone was looking for a reason to hate King Herod, this was it! Parents were beside themselves seeking hiding places for their young sons. The rabbi told us that Jeremiah, one of our prophets,[9] had predicted something similar to this would happen. I have the feeling that Herod's actions will be remembered not only here in Bethlehem, but in many places as "the slaughter of the innocents." The mourning for those precious boys lasted for months just because one man felt his position and power threatened by a baby boy!

Why was Herod so afraid of a young peasant boy not even

two years old? What did Herod know about him? The same question keeps haunting me: Who *is* this kid?

Joseph sent back word to us through a traveler from Egypt that an angel had visited Joseph. This time the message was: "Herod is dead, and it is safe to return to your homeland." We assumed they would return to Bethlehem. Then we remembered that Herod's son was the new king. Could Joseph be sure it would be safe to return to our village? We hoped Joseph would realize this and avoid coming back through Bethlehem. We assume he realized what the changes could mean. We didn't see them again.

All this drama had started to get to me: There must be something very significant about this new baby. There are just too many unusual events around this child's birth. My original question about "Who *is* this kid?" is starting to resolve itself in my mind! Here are the clues:

- Mary and Joseph having dreams about the new baby's birth
- the shepherds hearing angels and music
- Magi coming from the east following a star to bring them to Bethlehem
- ... and worshiping the boy;
- then King Herod's strange interest in Jesus
- ... and ordering the slaughter of the young boy babies
- The Magi's dreams about avoiding Herod
- Joseph fleeing with Mary and Jesus to Egypt.

I finally realized that Jesus was very different from any other boy I had ever seen. I didn't even dare to say aloud what I was starting to believe: he was the promised Messiah, the Christ of God, the Prince of Peace, the Emmanuel or the God with us Person.

I think I have figured out what it all means! The prophets were right. It is happening right here and right now. This is the child who is the one to save us and all other people from our sins, point us to a better kingdom, and establish a new creation.

I've never been a praying man, but my heart has been strangely moved by all of these events, so I am praying that what I have suspected all along is happening, really is happening. If Jesus ever comes back to Bethlehem, he will be more than welcome to stay in our inn. I hope that I, too, will have the opportunity someday to kneel and worship him.

Our little village will never be the same. I know Deborah and I will never be the same. Who is this kid? He is the Son of God! We have seen the face of God in this little boy. We often wonder what will happen to Joseph, Mary, and Jesus in the future. I hope that life holds a more peaceful and quiet future for all of them, but somehow, I doubt it will. I feel sure this is just the beginning of sorrows for that family.

Biblical reference: This story is an adaptation of the accounts in the gospel records of the events that surrounded the birth of Jesus, the Christ. Read again the accounts in the scriptures keeping in mind that the author of this book's intent in writing this story was only to dramatize the significance of Christ's birth.

Scripture: Luke 2:1–20 or Matthew 2:1–23 (For prophecies, see: Micah 5:2, Jeremiah 31:15.)

Discussion possibilities:

1. What do you think the innkeeper will do with all the information he has about Jesus?
2. The prophets had predicted what would happen to the Messiah. Why do you think the innkeeper didn't know about these prophesies?
3. What was going on in Jerusalem with the priests and elders?

Terrified by an Angel

Voice of a Christmas Shepherd

I'd never admit this to anyone except to my best bud, but I have been scared by many things in my short life, but before now, never by an angel. My brief life has never had any contact with an angel. At least, I am not aware of meeting one or having one pass me on the road with a "Hi there, Dude, 's up?"

In my job as a shepherd, I have had some wild and crazy things happen that have frightened me or caused me at least to stop and think, *Now, why did that happen?* or *What am I supposed to do with that?* Or *Who should I talk to with that information?* I am an inquisitive guy, and at night when we can't sleep, I am sometimes kidded by my buds about being the "wordy herder." They tell me I ask too many questions and probably wish I would just shut up once in a while.

There have been a few times, though, when I have been really scared. In fact, more than just a few times. Out on the Judean hills, which are six miles south of the big city, Jerusalem, where we watch our father's sheep, the cowardly wolves sneak up on us at night and try to catch a lamb or two before we can even see the thieving beasts crawling on their yellow bellies up to the flock. There are usually wild dogs hanging around waiting for the wolves (natural enemies I guess), and the circus begins. The circus gives us, the shepherds, about the only entertainment we get. I know we aren't supposed to place bets, but we enjoy making wagers about who will be the winners for the night: the wolves or the wild dogs. In all the excitement, it isn't unusual for human thieves to use the distractions to attempt to get a lamb or two for themselves and their families.

On this particular night on the hills, it was just like every other starlit night. We had a contest to see who could name the most star constellations. I didn't win that night, because I had a very uneasy feeling that something out of the ordinary was about to happen. You know how you get that feeling of anticipation that something unusual is in the offing? I can't describe that feeling, but it's similar to the feeling I get just before a large storm breaks over the eastern hills. There must be something in the air or in the wind that foretells that something unusual is on its way. The other guys think I must be a little crazy, too, in addition to talking too much. But I'm sure they are just kidding, or at least I hope they are.

The wild dogs had just chased the wolves away when it began to happen. All of a sudden, a light—I mean, a bright, bright light—lit up the entire countryside. We can only describe our reaction: we were terrified, and I do mean terrified! The only possible conclusion we came to was it had to be an angel and he was right in the center of the light. A voice from the skies boomed out, "Don't be terrified." Thinking about it now, it's a wonder I didn't open my big, sassy mouth and respond with something like, "That's easy enough for you to say. When was the last time *you* were surprised by someone talking to you from another world?"

Instead, he responded with some travel directions after giving us an announcement that we found difficult to believe, especially since it was from the skies and delivered by an angel. I mean, how would you respond if, out of the blue, someone spoke to you this way? The angel further said that the news was for all people, apparently not just for us.

The angel told us to go into the town of David (we called it Bethlehem) and that a newborn baby we would find there was the Savior, Christ the Lord. This certainly was successful in getting our attention—a Savior for all people! Personally, I had given up on that possibility a long time ago. I heard the rabbis telling us this many times. However, since it hadn't happened and instead we had the hated Romans around—who, by the way, are the greatest soldiers in the world—where does a Savior fit into that story? However, there was more! This Savior was a baby wrapped in loose-fitting clothes in a manger as his bed. One of the other shepherds looked at me, saying, "Give me a break—a baby? You gotta be kidding!" A baby, a savior?

There's more, hang on! While we were still shaking in our sandals, the sky was filled with beautiful music—music I'm sure that was not of this earth. Suddenly, a huge crowd of angels joined the first one, singing at the top of their lungs (if angels have lungs), "Glory to God in the heavenly heights, Peace to all men and women on earth who please him." We went to check out the story the angels had told us, even though we didn't expect to see much. The oldest shepherd on our watch, Jesse, said, "I'll stay here and watch the flocks. You young guys go and see what you can find out about this strange story. You can tell me the details when you get back."

It didn't take us very long to get down to Bethlehem, but while walking there, we started to think. Why were *we* the ones to hear this message from heaven? Why us? Why not the rabbis and the priests up in Jerusalem? Or even the governor from Rome? But guys like us, just shepherds? It didn't take us long to get to the place after we met the innkeeper who had loaned the stable and manger to the parents of the new baby. By the way, for some reason, he didn't seem happy to see us. I suspect not many shepherds stop at his inn.

By the time we arrived at the stable, we were less terrified, but still more than just a little nervous and overwhelmed. We were shocked that such an event took place in a stable rather than in a palace. We were just as surprised that the parents seemed as though they were ordinary people who probably had not much more than just a few shekels to rub together in their saddlebags.

I just have to tell you that on the way back to our flocks, we were different guys. We couldn't stop talking about who and what we had seen. There were some people out and about even at that time of the night. We had to tell them all about what we had seen even though it meant that we didn't get back to our flocks as soon as we thought we would—or should. Some people were excited about our news, but others doubted just as we had doubted when we first heard the news.

When we told Jesse, who had stayed with the flocks, what had happened, he also had trouble believing us. He was skeptical as were many we had already met on way back to the hills. "Sure you did," he said, "let's just wait and see what happens over the next few years to this Savior for all humankind. I am sure that Rome will not be as excited as you are, nor will the hotshots in Jerusalem's temple be as enthusiastic as you seem to be about your news. You do know that our people have had many messiahs who promised all kinds of goodies only to be killed when they didn't deliver the goods. Let's see what he does to deliver us from our troubles: the Romans. I'm going to keep an open mind on this, so let me know when you get further word from your sources."

None of us got much sleep that night even though we had our sleeping shifts planned. We couldn't stop talking about what had happened—from the angel's words, to the heavenly singers, to the quiet peacefulness of the birth scene, and the awe we felt as we saw the baby in the manger.

Sometime later, we heard that men from far away came to visit the baby boy and his parents. They said that a star led them to Bethlehem after a brief stop at the king's palace in Jerusalem. The neighbors told us that these men brought fabulous gifts for the boy because, as they said, someday he would be a king. That made sense to us because about that same time, Herod, the king, sent soldiers to Bethlehem to slaughter all young male children. We found it unbelievably strange that a king would feel threatened by a newborn child. A king threatened by a child? By a *child*?

That night we realized that we had a new focus in life and a new purpose for our lives. We still kept questioning each other and ourselves about the probability of God choosing *us* to be among the first witnesses of this miracle. You can be sure we craved every piece of information we could get about this baby's life. A couple of us were still in the sheep business when we heard about his crucifixion and his resurrection three days after his death. It all made sense to us—one of his followers explained it to us. The baby grew and was the Lamb of God that Isaiah had talked and written about in our scriptures This Lamb of God was slain for our redemption. Our questions were answered—we are the children of God. We can't keep quiet about it—we tell just about everyone we meet the good news that God has come to us so we can come home to God.

Biblical background: This story is based on the account found in Luke 2:2–20.
Scripture: Luke 2:2–20
Discussion possibilities:

1. What do you think God was thinking when He gave the news first to lowly shepherds?
2. If you were one of the shepherds, what would be the effects on rest of your life?

Suggested hymn: "While Shepherds Watched Their Flocks by Night"

Could I Have Said No?

Voice of Mother Mary

I was beside myself with fear as I tried to keep from screaming, "Where is he? Have you seen him? I thought he was with Deborah's family, but I just checked with her, and they haven't seen him either. He has never done anything like this before, and now he's gone!"

I could feel the tears beginning to well up in my eyes. "We started home this morning, and here it is dinnertime, Joseph, and he still isn't here. Where can he be?" Joseph and I checked with all our friends, but we still couldn't find him. "Now what?" I knew that Joseph was just as worried as I was about Jesus, but he doesn't show panic in the same way that I do.

He tried to calm me down by quietly saying, "Mary, let's just focus on getting back to Jerusalem, where I'm sure we'll find him. I know we will. Take this cloth, wipe your eyes, blow your nose, and let's get turned around and start heading back to Jerusalem. But keep your eyes open and look for him on the way. He may have strayed off the road."

Since Jesus was now twelve years old, we had taken him with us so he could be a part of the Passover celebrations. He met some of his cousins who had come up from Bethlehem for the feast. I think we had assumed that he was having such a good time with them that he didn't hear our calls when it was time to go back to Nazareth. Our friends were also concerned about this turn of events, but we assured them that we would soon find him and catch up with them later that night.

We finally found him after three days of looking all over the city. Of course, the last place we looked was in the temple, and there he was, having discussions with the teachers and asking them questions. We were dumbfounded! And so were the teachers—they were amazed at his understanding of our Torah and his answers to their questions.

Well, we had a few questions, too! "Son, we've been worried about you. We've been back in the city for three days looking for you. Why didn't you stay with us?"

His response shook us up more than just a little bit. "Why were you looking for me? Didn't you know that I'd be right here in my Father's house?"

We didn't understand what he was talking about—*his* father's house? We were going back to *our* house, our house was in Nazareth, so what house was he talking about?

He had been a miracle child in many ways, and that I was his mother was something that I had trouble believing from the very first. I realize that every birth is a miracle, but of course, his birth was my first and so it was my miracle, too. Similar to most girls in Nazareth, my life had been quite ordinary. I did all the normal stuff that girls did with families, friends, and neighbors. Life with its customs hadn't changed much from the way they had been for my grandmothers or for their grandmothers either. While our brothers were in school, each girl had her tasks to do—gardening, sewing and mending, cleaning the small house, sweeping the paths in the yard, feeding the chickens and ducks, and sometimes milking the few animals that were kept out in the shed. Life was good! It never crossed my mind that all of this could change—*dramatically change*—for all of us.

Entering into womanhood was exciting and full of promise—at least as promising as it could be to a young Jewish girl in a small Galilean village. I helped my mother take care of my younger brothers and sisters in preparation for the eventual arrival of my own children. My mother and aunts were patient with me as they taught me the practical lessons of family life while my brothers were off at the synagogue school learning their lessons from our scriptures and laws, events in our national history, and whatever else they had to learn. One thing that was a little different for me than for most of my girlfriends was that my mother also taught me to read and write.

Even with all of this, I still had time for the typical daydreams of how life would be when Joseph and I would be married and have our own home and family. I still remember the first time I had noticed Joseph, a good-looking, husky carpenter who must have been about twenty-five years old and who walked by our home almost daily. When I walked by a house he was working on, I'd often slow my pace and steal a look at him. I'd even go out of my way sometimes in order to do this. I didn't know if he had any special feelings for me since we didn't talk about such things. In fact, we didn't talk to each other except to say, "Good morning," or "Good afternoon." Anything more than that would have been in extremely poor taste and would have caused all kinds of gossip among the neighbors.

I dreamed and realized that I had to be satisfied with only the dreams until I would be older. On the other hand, I had a growing sense that he was having similar feelings about me. There was something in his glances when we happened to cross paths that made me think he might be thinking about more than just saying hello. On the advice of a cousin, I had checked out the other guys in the village to see if any of them came up to my standards. However, I just knew Joseph had everything I was sure that I'd ever want in a husband. But then I probably had another year before my dreams could become my reality. Of course, Joseph was the one who would decide if I met *his* standards. I kept forgetting that little fact. I just assumed that I did! Of course, my father and his father would have the final word.

In our village, life centered on the Sabbath. We anticipated that day and kept it holy by attending synagogue services and by refraining from doing anything that even looked like work. One sure way to start the tongues wagging in Nazareth would have been to be seen doing anything that our laws prohibited. By the way, we have so many laws and regulations that it was often difficult to remember what was written in our scriptures—the Torah and the Prophets—much less to make sure that we were doing what was right, and not doing what we were forbidden to do. One thing I dared not do was to make it obvious that I had my eye on Joseph. The best I could do was to pray and hope that he had his eye on me. I loved Jehovah, my God, and everything I did had to be according to His will for my life.

It was at one Sabbath dinner that I learned some exciting news. My father and Joseph's father had agreed to a marriage between Joseph and me. We were betrothed, espoused, or engaged. I didn't care what word was used—my dreams were coming true. "Thank You, Jehovah, for making this happen!"

I was promised to Joseph, and suddenly all my dreams changed. Now I could dream about my *own* home with Joseph and a family that we would start. Of course, we'd follow tradition: the engagement, which was the important ceremony, would last about a year, and then we would be married. But I'm still having difficulty believing what happened just *before we were* married.

I almost fell off my kitchen stool when I had a visit from a messenger of God, an angel no less. Moreover, it wasn't a dream. He suddenly just appeared beside me when I was preparing soup and salad for our noontime meal. He was real, with a message that was exciting but also disturbing and even frightening. Here I was, doing what I should be doing, saying my prayers, obeying my parents, being good to my neighbors, and helping them when I could. Surprise! An angel was standing by me with a message, bursting in on me like a desert dust storm that obliterated all my teenage hopes and dreams. I felt at that moment that the desert dust was choking off my breath, or that I was drowning in the storm-driven waves of the nearby Sea of Galilee. How can a girl even breathe when an angel is standing beside her and speaking to her as though you were just a couple of neighbors chatting about their gardens?

Oh, you ask, what was that life-changing announcement? I'm sorry, but it still astounds me so deeply that I just assumed you already knew. The messenger from God, Gabriel, told me that I was to have a baby, a male child. The Holy Spirit was going to make it happen, and the child would be holy and was, in fact, God's Son.

Fast and furiously, I threw these questions at Gabriel: "How can this be? I don't have a husband. I will be thrown out of the synagogue, out of our village. What will I do alone on my own with a baby?"

Other questions popped into my mind: "May I have a day or two to think about this before I give you an answer? Do I have a choice: Could I say no? Isn't there someone more suitable for this honor? Why me, here in Nazareth, one of the least among all the cities of Judah, and known by all in Israel as a place from which no good can come? I am also engaged to Joseph. When he finds this out, what will he say? He could divorce me, or even worse, have me stoned to death."

Gabriel's response was quite simple. "Cool it, daughter. Rejoice, Favored One. Don't be afraid, and stop worrying. Remember, we are talking here about Jehovah God, the Creator, and about His plan for the world and for you. He'll handle Joseph. In fact, Joseph's on my list to visit when I leave here. In the meantime, go visit your relative, Elizabeth, down in the hill country. I was down there a few months ago, so I know that she could use your help for a little while since she is also pregnant and her husband, Zacharias, will soon be in Jerusalem on priestly business."

I couldn't believe that all of this was happening to me—a simple girl of Nazareth, a nobody in the larger scheme of things. Why did God choose me out of all women, many of whom would kill to have this chance to be the mother of the Messiah, the Son of God? Well, I didn't really mean kill. After all, we do have a prohibition against murder. But we're talking big here, the successor to King David and the one who will rule over the house of Jacob forever, whose kingdom would have no end. Can you understand my shock?

As you have probably guessed by now, I capitulated to God's will and said words something similar to, "Yes, I see it now. I am the Lord's maid. I accept what you have said, and I am ready to serve." That's all it took! As soon as I told Gabriel those words, he was gone. He had already told me that his next stop was to see Joseph. I'd wait until I get back from Elizabeth's to hear about that visit.

So off I went—south then up into the hill county to visit Elizabeth. Wow, what a reception I had there! Prophecy and singing like you've never heard. Liz and I had a great time together talking about our futures and our babies' futures. Zacharias came back from Jerusalem while I was there, and what a surprise that was, too. He couldn't talk, but had to write notes to us. But that's another story. I stayed with them until their baby was born and

Liz was able to function on her own. They were both so happy, and the eighth day party was a huge success. That party was the big event when the baby was named. In spite of the family's and friends' opposition to the name, they named him John, the name that Gabriel had told Zacharias to give him.

Soon after the party, I returned to Nazareth, about a week's journey, to see my family again and Joseph. Joseph had his visit from Gabriel soon after the angel had visited me. I had been worried that Joseph wouldn't believe all that Gabriel had told him, but he did. He told me that for the past couple of years, he had had his eye on me, too. That, at least, took care of one of my worries. I know, I know, Gabriel had told me not to worry, but how can a girl not worry when such a momentous message is delivered by no one less than Jehovah's angel?

I won't bore you with the details of the next few years. In another account, I'll try to get the details straight for you. The story about the birth of our child is amazing, but then you've heard from other mothers their amazing stories about the births of their children. The birth of a child is always a mind-blowing event. The birth of our child, Jesus, amazed not only Joseph and me, but most of the people who were around at the time, even shepherds and Magi.

Just before the birth of our son, of all things to happen, the emperor (whatever his name) called for a census of everyone in Israel. Even worse, we had to go to the city of our family's origin, which for us was Bethlehem. That meant a long trip and with only about a month to go before our baby was to be born. Talk about timing! Could it have been any worse? I didn't know what we were to do—should we go or should we stay.

Joseph was convinced that we had to go. So what did we do? We went! Now that I think about it, I must have been crazy to even consider such a trip. Joseph said it wouldn't be so bad. Just south to Bethlehem—only a week's trip on the back of a donkey. No problem! I was to deliver my first baby sometime in the next month. Crazy, huh? I had never realized how bony a beast's backbone could be until I sat on one day after day after day. I begged Joseph to let me walk with him or at least, to trade places with me occasionally. Let him feel those sharp bones for a while. After this was all over, I realized he was just being kind to me. At least, that's what he said. I'm learning quickly that a husband doesn't always think about things the same way that we girls think about them. However, we had to pay our taxes and register, so we were off to David's royal city.

We finally arrived in Bethlehem, the family homestead where our forebears settled centuries ago, and where King David had been a shepherd before he became the king. Even before King David, it was the village where Ruth and Boaz had settled down as wealthy farmers.

I don't know why we hadn't thought that finding a place to hang our hats and give birth to a new baby might be difficult, but we hadn't. It never occurred to us that so many of our relatives would also be arriving. We had family all over the place, so they had to be registered, too. However, we never gave them a thought. The competition for places to stay was much tighter than we had dreamed it would be. After a day of looking, we realized that there was no place for the two of us. After a day of looking all over town and asking everyone we met if anyone knew of an opening, I heard Joseph mutter, "Where is Gabriel when we really need him?" At the last place we stopped, they also had no room in their inn, but they offered a stable-cave where they sheltered their animals. Joseph was ready to turn it down, when I said, "Joseph, I'm pretty sure we don't have any more time to look around. This baby is about to be born whether we have a nice place or not."

That's all it took to get Joseph excited, nervous, and all

thumbs. As I thought back on the experience, I remembered I had wondered if he would get that way with every child we had and every major event in our lives. I know now that it was not just that one time, but every time. The daughter of the innkeepers, a young girl who was just a little younger than I was, helped us get settled in and helped me with the delivery. She said she had served as a junior midwife a couple of times. I'd give her a reference any day.

We were hardly over with the delivery when a group of dirty, smelly shepherds poked their heads in the cave opening, asking, "Is this where the Savior of the world has just been born?" They told us that angels (angels again!) sang to them from heaven and told them to "get down here and see the newborn child, so here we are!"

We didn't get much rest that night! We were exhausted! If my mother could have seen me—I knew I'd never hear the last of it. "What were you thinking? Why didn't you send those smelly shepherds on their way? Don't tell me you believed their stories? What were you thinking—in a cave you gave birth to your first baby, my grandchild? If I live to be a hundred, I will never understand it!" Of course, eventually she did, although I'm not sure if she ever completely forgave Joseph for carting me on a donkey all the way down to Bethlehem.

This was just the beginning of an unbelievable series of events for our new son, me, our village, our synagogue, and Israel, and possibly for the world. But we can't say we hadn't been warned. I shudder to think that I could have said no, but I didn't. I said yes to Jehovah. For that, I thank Him every day. I'm sure there are many in Israel who would shout a loud "Hosanna!" for his life. He fed the poor, healed the sick, and even raised at least a couple of people from the dead: I think Jairus and his wife would be praising Jehovah every day for the life of their little girl brought back to life by our son. Mary and Martha also would be thankful to Jesus for the resurrection of their brother, Lazarus.

My memories of those miracles far exceeded all the difficulties that Joseph and I encountered because of his coming into the world that one blessed night.

Biblical background: This story is based on St. Luke's account in Luke 1 of the events leading up to the birth of Jesus. The human sides of these two major persons, Mary and Joseph, are consistent with those of most people then and now
Scripture: Luke 1:26–38
Discussion possibilities:

1. Put yourself into Mary's sandals and think about what you would have said and done.
2. Identify some of Mary's major concerns about this entire situation.
3. Put yourself in Joseph's shoes and think about all of the concerns he probably had.
4. How do you think Joseph and Mary dealt with the issues that neighbors and relatives possibly raised to them about the unusual circumstances of the birth of Jesus?

Baskets of Bread, Buckets of Fish

Voice of a Teenage Boy

"Mother, I need my lunch," I yelled from just outside the door of our little house.

"Zach, it is right here on the table," she called back. "Come and get it now or you'll be late for school."

What she didn't know was that I had no intention of going to school that day. Actually, she was responsible for my decision to skip school. She had been bugging me to go and hear the new rabbi, but I do know that she didn't mean for me to miss school just to hear him. As far as my parents were concerned, school was the most important part of my life. However, thinking back now after ten years, my life was changed forever by skipping school that day. The events of that day are still so real to me that I really want to relive them as they happened, and as though they had happened just in the past couple of days. I never tire of going back in time to those few days that had such an impact on my life.

That morning I walked as far as the dusty lane that runs past our house when I realized I would not be alone on my walk. There were small groups of people hurrying along, so I joined the first group I saw. I checked back to see if my mother had seen me, but she hadn't. I was in the clear. People were talking and wondering about the man we were going to see. I didn't care who he was. I had a chance to skip school, so I took the chance. The only concern I had was keeping my parents from knowing that I had skipped school. I knew for sure that there would be trouble to pay if they found out.

When I asked if anyone knew the man's name, I learned that his name was Jesus. I knew that name—it was the same as Joshua and had the same meaning that Joshua's name had—savior—that famous man who had brought our people into this Promised Land centuries ago.

A man about my dad's age told me that this Jesus had been healing people in some of the cities and towns in our area of Galilee. A woman in the walking crowd called out that he was also doing other miracles: making cripples walk, restoring hearing to others, and even healing people with leprosy. Now that is something I would call a miracle!

As I tried to work my way to the front of the crowd, an argument was going on in another group I joined. Some people were saying that Jesus was the prophet Elijah back from the dead. Now that's a scary thought! Back from the dead? Others said, "No, he isn't Elijah; he's one of our other prophets. That concerned me since we've had many prophets in Israel—some good ones, but I'd say more bad ones than good ones. I didn't much care about who they thought he was. I'd make up my own mind. I just wanted to get close enough to see for myself who he was and what he could do. You know, I'm starting to get excited! I hoped that I'd get to see a miracle or two. That would certainly be better than sitting in school all day—much more educational, I think, than spending another day in school.

I'd have a lot to tell Andy, my best bud, when I saw him that afternoon. I was sure he would wish he had come with me instead of practicing his running for the big race the following week. Andy was a great runner, and even though our rabbi didn't think that sports were very important, Andy always wanted to win. I enjoyed running, too, and often ran with him to keep him company and challenge him to do his best. Winning was important to me, but I wasn't a winning runner. Instead, I tried to be the best student in our school. Dad thought both sports and intellect were important. He said that it was important to educate both the body and the mind. I appreciated my dad's ideas on that.

Some of the people I walked with that day were not familiar with Bethsaida. When anyone asked me about our village, the one thing I always said was that it was a great place to fish. In fact, our name meant, "fishing village." Andy and I often went to the lake to catch fish for our families' dinners.

But on that morning I was not going fishing. I was on a hot, dusty road climbing up the side of a large hill getting lots of exercise, just to see what was going to happen with this new rabbi, Jesus. Andy often said, "Anything to get out of another boring day at school." That reminds me—Mother or Dad will be sure to ask me at dinner tonight: "How did school go today?" I'll say what I always say, "Same old, same old!"

The new rabbi told us to sit down, and he started talking to us about the kingdom of God. Our task, he said, was to do the *work* of God. The kingdom he was talking about was far different from the Roman kingdom, that's for sure. In the kingdom Jesus was talking about, the rulers gained allegiance to it by loving and caring about the citizens. A law of love would rule in the new kingdom. I can't even imagine a world run on love, can you?

By midafternoon, all around me I could hear stomachs rumbling and people grumbling about being hungry. I got my lunch out and was ready to eat, but I felt a little strange because I was the only one around me who had brought food. What were all these other people going to eat? My mother taught me always to be concerned about other people's needs first, and never to eat unless other people also had food. I didn't know what to do. Our school teacher would say that I was in "a moral dilemma."

If I hadn't felt so uncomfortable, I probably wouldn't have responded so quickly when one of the rabbi's followers asked, "Who brought some food?" Right away, I raised my hand and responded, "Here, I have some that my mother made for me. Who wants to know?"

"Jesus has need of it," Andrew said. I learned later that Andrew was one of the disciples of Jesus. Even though Andrew was a few years older than I am, we became friends, especially after we found out that we didn't live very far from each other in Bethsaida.

So, here we all were on a hillside about two thousand feet above Lake Galilee, hot, tired, hungry. Wouldn't you think that some smart adult would have brought some food along to sell? With four or five thousand hungry people, someone could have made a haul. Philip, another disciple, said that it would take eight month's wages to buy enough to feed this crowd. That's when Andrew figured I had something to contribute to the lunch menu.

Andrew, the disciple, took me to meet Jesus. He was nothing like any rabbi I had ever known. He was a down-to-earth, ordinary man, similar to my dad but younger. He didn't resemble some of the strange men we see going around preaching "the end of the age" messages, scaring people out of their wits. I decided right then and there that if I could, I was going to stick around for a while to see if this was all just a show or if this Jesus was for real. I was hoping that he was in the "good" category of prophets. I've read about both kinds of them in the Torah, our scriptures.

Jesus seemed glad to see me. He asked my name, who my parents were, and where I went to school. For a minute, I worried that maybe he was going to let someone know I had skipped school. Then Andrew showed Jesus the small lunch I had brought of five barley loaves and two fishes. I had figured that Jesus needed them for himself. However, when Andrew said that such a small lunch wouldn't go very far with such a large crowd, I had the feeling that something *big* was about to happen. Jesus took the loaves, thanked Jehovah for them, and gave them to his disciples in big baskets to distribute.

He did the same with the fishes. Now this is the miraculous part that still blows my mind every time I remember it. People took some bread and some fish, but the baskets were never emptied. There was always more, so everyone had as much as he or she could eat. Can you believe it? There was enough for everyone to have as much as they needed. By this time, I was feeling such a part of the action that I even volunteered to help clean up the mess that was left. That was not me! What a mess it was! There were more than enough leftovers to feed another four or five thousand people.

I ran all the way home to tell my mother about the miracles, and how many people ate from that little lunch she had made for me!

"Five thousand!" she screamed. "You must be kidding."

"And that's not all," I said. "There were a lot of leftovers, too."

"How do you know so much, Smarty Pants?" was her next question. "Did you count them yourself?"

"No, Mother, but I did help count them. I became friends with a couple of the disciples of Jesus, and helped them the clean up the mess. Do you know Philip and Andrew, two of our neighbors here in Bethsaida? I helped them with the clean-up."

(Oh, no! I realized that I had just made my big mistake of the day. I had ratted on myself about skipping school.)

"Anyway, Philip and Andrew asked me to come back tomorrow morning and help them again when Jesus talks with the people over in Capernaum. Can I go, Mother? *Please*? I really want to see Jesus again." (If Mother had said no, I'd just ask my dad. He'd probably say, okay.)

"No, you can't! Tomorrow is an important school day and you already figured out a way to skip today, but no more. *Is ... that ... clear?* If you should figure out a way to miss another day of school, neither your dad nor I will stick up for you with your teacher. Besides, your new friends sound as though they are very busy people who don't have time for a lot of questions from a young boy. I know how you are when you get curious. They have more to do than to answer all your questions. Besides, you really need to be in school, so I hope you decide to obey me.

"You'll have other days when you can hear this new rabbi. Another thing—before tomorrow you had better think about what the consequences will be if you skip school again. And *there will be consequences!* Your grades, your teachers, your homework, and especially your dad and I will all have things to say about your skipping school. It had better not become a habit."

Coming in from outdoors, my dad added, "Zach, you are now considered a man, so it's time to realize that when you make decisions and then act on those decisions, there are consequences that will follow. For example, one consequence for your action today: you are grounded for two days. If there is a second time, it will be for a week! Is that clear?

"Yes, Father, very clear."

Mother said, "There can also be positive consequences when the action you take has positive effects. A positive consequence could be that you can have some time off from chores to go fishing with Andy, your buddy."

You know, I guess all parents are cut from the same cloth. Andy says his mother is the same way—forever warning him that boys are to be seen and not heard, and that you reap what you sow. I think parents are always figuring out the worst things that can possibly happen if we disobey them.

"Okay, Mother. When will you realize that I am fourteen years old and able to take care of myself? So stop worrying. I'll be just fine."

However, I decided that I could not stay away from Capernaum tomorrow. I needed to see Jesus, Andrew, and Philip, and find out if those guys were for real. I also wondered if Andy could go with me tomorrow without telling his parents.

Andy couldn't go. He was practicing his running again. He told me that his teacher said he stood a good chance of coming in near the top of the class. I hope he does. Maybe he and I will have more time to spend together to study for exams and play some brain games, and do some extra fishing, too.

I think you probably know what happened the next day. Right! I skipped school another day. It was just a little walk around the north side of the lake over to Capernaum. Capernaum is next to Bethsaida and is a slightly larger place than our little town. I joined the crowds that had already gathered to hear Jesus. I felt more at home on this second day and searched for Andrew and Philip. They both recognized me. It surely felt good to know that I was not just a nobody to them. I don't think that anyone is ever a nobody to them or to Jesus, either. I heard someone saying that on a recent day she had seen Jesus pick up a little child, hug him, and say that no one could enter the kingdom of God until he became as a little child. That made me feel really good to know that Jesus said that. Kids are not very important to some people in our community. I wanted to look for signals today that would tell me even more about the kind of person Jesus really was—the kind of person he was down deep inside.

Andrew and Philip were talking about their fishing adventure last night out on the Sea of Galilee. The wind came up, as it often does on the lake, and the large waves kept them from rowing back to shore. The two of them talked about the storm and the surprise they had when Jesus walked on the water toward them. *Another miracle!* They told me a little more about the scary experience and their relief when Jesus stepped into their boat. That settled it for me. This man was for real!

In Capernaum, it was another busy day for Jesus with the crowds clamoring for another miracle. Some of them were asking the question I was starting to form in my own mind: "What do I have to do to do the work of God?" The answer Jesus gave seemed rather simple: "The work of God is to believe in the one that God has sent."

I asked Andrew and Philip later that day if it would be possible for me to be a Jesus follower with them as soon as I finished school.

"Sure," Philip told me. "But it won't be easy."

"According to Jesus," Andrew added, "it will be similar to running a race with all kinds of obstacles, but Jesus says that it will be really worth it. We will be in on the beginning of a completely new world in which God's love for all people will be the most important part of our lives. Zach, you will be a most welcome addition to our group. Just don't neglect your schooling. We will need all the smarts you can bring with you."

I had to deal with my parents again that night. I paid the price for my disobedience by being grounded for a week and doing extra work at school, too. I told my parents about my hope that I would someday join Andrew and Philip as a follower of Jesus, or as they came to be known, followers of the Way. I hope I can convince Andy to join with me as a follower of the Way. I know we'd make great partners in helping other people find the Way.

My parents had another talk with me about how I make my decisions. In addition to suggesting I think about the consequences of my actions, they talked about thinking of the options or alternatives I needed to explore before making a decision. Dad asked me what other action I could have taken other than skipping school. I told him that I figured I could have found out when Jesus would be back in our neighborhood again and plan to take a non-school day to go and be with my new friends. Dad surprised me by saying that he thought I was really growing up and becoming more mature.

Looking back now to those two great days, I don't want ever to forget them. However, so much has happened since then that I need to tell you the rest of my experiences.

Over the next year, I kept in touch with Andrew and Philip They kept me up to date about the problems that Jesus had down in Jerusalem during Passover and the ultimate sacrifice in his crucifixion. When Jesus and the disciples were here in Galilee after his resurrection, I found out about what had happened on that first day of the week: Resurrection Day.

When they came back to Galilee, I saw Jesus again and was so excited that he still remembered those two small fishes and the five barley loaves of bread that my mother had packed for my lunch and that he had used to feed all those people.

I've told that story to many groups, especially after I had finished school, as well as on the missionary journeys some of us took to parts of the Roman Empire that I had never expected to see. I still get goose bumps when I think that those loaves and fishes were just the beginning of how Jesus would use my small contributions to his work, and how he is still using my contributions even though he has gone back to his Father in heaven. His love has filled my heart and flooded my life like the overflowing baskets on that day of feeding the hungry crowd. I will never forget that.

When I decided to follow Jesus and walk in the Way, I had no idea of the unbelievable consequences of *that* decision. My life has not been easy, but it has been rewarding. Many people, including my loving parents, considered their options and decided to follow the Way and are now living an abundant life. One of my greatest moments came when Andy also decided to be a part of the disciples' group encouraging people everywhere to be as hungry and as filled with God's love and kindness as the crowd on the Galilean hill was filled with nourishing food. In this kingdom feast, there is no limit to the amount of love a person can have, and the baskets will always be full.

Biblical reference: This story is built on the experiences of the boy who gave his lunch to Jesus on the hillside in Galilee. The story adapts the account in John 6 to include the possible thinking and actions of that young boy, probably a teenager. The boy is not a creature of the imagination of the story's author, but only assumes who and why the real boy was on that hillside and not in school.

Scripture: John 6:5–15 (Other gospel accounts: Matthew 14:15–21, Mark 6:34–44, Luke 9:12–17)

Discussion possibilities:

1. How would you have responded to a son or daughter who made the decision that Zach made about his future?
2. If you had been Andrew or Philip, how would you have counseled Zach about his future?
3. How would you counsel your own teenager about a future with the disciples?
4. Do you think teenagers can think about consequences and alternatives in situations that are problems for them? How can we help them to think this way?

On the Edge of Murder

Voice of a Synagogue Attendant

I could hear the villagers as they greeted each other out on the road and the children as they shouted back and forth to their playmates. It was just a typical Sabbath day—nothing particularly special about the day. That is, nothing more than the usual, and that's because the unusual had not yet happened! Of course, every Sabbath day has something special about it. There's always a sense of community and celebration when we meet together in our synagogue, as well as the knowledge that we are in a sacred place. We see each other daily in the markets and at school, but the Sabbath day has something that is very important to us. As usual, the families were coming into the synagogue and choosing their seats, the men sitting on one side, and the women and children on the other side.

Nazareth is nothing special in itself. We are a small village, a blip on the map, if we even are on a map. There are at most five hundred of us in the village, and we are crowded into about sixty acres of land. Our synagogue is small as synagogues go. You see, in our tradition, there must be at least ten men in a village before we can establish a synagogue. We barely qualify since husbands seem to die much sooner than other members of their families, leaving families with mothers providing for them. So, having ten men in our small village can make it difficult to organize a synagogue. Death is a constant reminder to us of the Psalmist's words: "Men and women don't live very long; like wildflowers they spring up and blossom, But a storm snuffs them out just as quickly" (Psalm 103:15–16).

My wife died shortly after we married. I want to marry again, but my track record, so far, is not so good. Romantically, I'm striking out in attracting another woman even to consider me as a prospect. I had hoped that at least some woman's mother might see me as a good catch since I am the attendant at the synagogue. I blow the trumpet from the roof of the synagogue three times before each service. That makes me a synagogue official and puts me in the public view. However, the Yenta in Nazareth only works for mothers, but not for lonely bachelors. I heard, too, that I was getting a poor reputation for asking too many questions and for casting doubts on people's beliefs, established theories, and common practices. Doesn't that make it sound that I'm almost a subversive? Yenta mentioned to a neighbor that I was not a good prospect for marriage. (Busybody!) My friend Hiram told me more than once, "Caleb, keep your brain quiet and your mouth shut if you want to find a wife." I responded without thinking, "I can only say what I believe when I'm asked a question. I can't help it, Hiram, that's just the way I am." Enough of my problems. Let me tell you about the problem a visiting teacher created by simply reading our scriptures and then commenting on what he had read.

Whenever we have a visiting teacher, we invite that person, usually a rabbi, to read the scripture for the day. I assumed this particular teacher was in our village to visit his family, who were faithful members of our synagogue. This young rabbi had been gathering fame in the cities of Galilee and was getting quite a reputation among the villagers. People had been praising him as a new teacher with an important message about the imminent coming kingdom of God. Of course, the miracles he had been performing had strengthened his reputation and popularity. From what I'd heard, he had restored a blind man's sight and cured a person of leprosy. You can be sure that such miracles quickly catch people's attention. However, this was not the first time in Israel's history that we have had a teacher who appeared to perform miracles. I think I'll just reserve judgment until I gather more facts and analyze the data.

When he stepped up to the front of the synagogue, this visiting rabbi asked me for the Isaiah scroll. He unrolled it almost to the end until he found the passage he wanted to read. He chose the passage in which the prophet Isaiah wrote about what the Messiah would do when he made his appearance to our nation.[10]

Some members of the rabbi's family were in the synagogue that day. I couldn't help but think of the pride they must have felt because one of their own was in a place of such prominence. However, they also may have had some concern, hoping that he would do them credit, but uncertain about what he might say. After all, he was getting a reputation for being outspoken and sometimes even being critical of our Jewish authorities.

The passage he chose to read was familiar to us:

> God's Spirit is on me;
>> he's chosen me to preach the Message of
>> good news to the poor,
> Sent me to announce pardon to prisoners and
>> recovery of sight to the blind,
> To set the burdened and battered free,
>> to announce, "This is God's year to act."
>> (Luke 4:18–19) [Quoted from Isaiah 61:1–3]

Initially, the congregation's response was very complimentary. I heard comments such as: "Such a nice young man." "So well spoken." "So gracious." "Isn't he one of our hometown boys?" "I think he went to school with our children." and, "Isn't this Joseph's son?"

After he had handed the scroll back to me, he followed the typical custom and sat to talk about the passage he had just read, and to give us the meaning that he attached to it. He began by explaining the true mission of the coming Messiah. That mission was to be a spiritual mission: to be a friend of the poor in spirit, to be the physician of diseased hearts, and to be the deliverer of souls in bondage. As Jesus explained it, the message was not to destroy Rome or its power over us but to minister to the needs of others. However, I knew the congregation wanted to hear that the Messiah would destroy Rome! This had almost become a mantra in our nation: "Destroy Rome. Destroy Rome." However, we whispered our sentiment for fear of the Romans and even of our own Jewish leaders, whom we suspected were in league with the Romans.

What happened next was like nothing I had ever seen or heard in Nazareth. The words that followed were enough to drive the congregation almost crazy. He calmly sat there and claimed himself to be the anticipated Messiah, saying that he was the fulfillment of that scripture. He might as well have lobbed a projectile into the middle of our synagogue.

I am certain that this was his first announcement that he was the Messiah that the prophets had promised. Now to a small group of average people—farmers, carpenters, mothers and fathers—this was nothing less than blatant blasphemy of the worst kind.

The mood of our small congregation suddenly turned ugly. I could not believe how quickly a few words from this popular teacher could turn people from feelings of pride and admiration to feelings of disdain and hatred. In years gone by, our people had killed prophets who had claimed to have this same authority from Jehovah. Within minutes of his declaration, the men of our congregation rose up in anger, and drove him out of the building, down the road, and through the village to the edge of the hill on which our founders had built Nazareth. I think they intended to murder him by edging him over the cliff. However, when the men returned, they reported that Jesus seemed to disappear as though magically. However, I felt sure that he was not like one of our popular magicians who could perform tricks that "fooled the eye." He seemed to be too authentic and transparent to play us for fools.

A few observers told me that the rabbi just walked through the crowd and continued walking until he was out of Nazareth.

I never did learn how his family reacted to his messianic claim, but I felt certain that his words split and hurt the family. Oh, I heard many reports about what various people had said. But there were so many discrepancies in the reports that I thought it would be better not to repeat them. I once heard from someone who investigated crimes that witnesses to a crime are rarely good witnesses because each witness will have seen the same scene from a different perspective. What I felt was appropriate to do was to continue to be friendly to the family. I just don't want his family to be hurt because of the incident at the synagogue. Maybe I can help by being friendly.

I was shocked by how quickly the congregation was split into two factions. From where I was standing, most of the people were on the hateful, ugly side of the split leaving very few that understood his declaration and accepted it.

However, I felt something else was going on here, and I had to find out what it was. I decided at that moment to keep my eye on this man to see what he would do next. He was young, about thirty, I guess, and there were several things about him that attracted me to him: his intense eyes, his apparent self-confidence, the way he spoke with authority, and mostly, the way his words spoke to my heart. I had a strong feeling that I had not heard the last of this young rabbi, and I intended to follow him from a distance so I could learn more about him and his revolutionary ideas. I knew his family, so despite what had happened on the Sabbath day, I figured that Jesus would be in and out of Nazareth with some regularity. I thought that someday I might, even in spite of my shyness, work up enough nerve to speak with him privately. I guess you could call me introverted, or as the few young people we have in Nazareth would say, "a chicken."

After speaking in our synagogue, Jesus was next seen again here in Nazareth at the home of Simon Peter, where Simon's mother-in-law was suffering from a fever. The family asked Jesus to help. He immediately commanded the fever to leave her, and the next thing they knew, she was out of bed, out in the kitchen, and helping to serve their meal. I think you probably know what happened next. After Jesus healed Peter's mother-in-law, a flood of people started bringing their ill family members and friends to Jesus so he would heal them.

I don't want to be sarcastic, but apparently some people were able to set aside their hated and anger when there was the possibility of getting a loved one healed! It seems that if there is a benefit to be gained, some people can forget their anger and hurt quite easily and quickly.

On another Sabbath the young rabbi went over to Capernaum, and there he healed a demented man who was possessed by an evil spirit. It seemed that everywhere he went someone was healed, given their sight back, or their hearing restored. The word was out on the street about this man. News spread quickly from village to village and had everyone talking about what this man was doing and saying. People kept asking each other, "What is this teaching?" and "He speaks with such authority and power so that even the evil spirits obey him." The conversations about

Jesus were not so much about the miracles, but more about his teachings, which were heard by some as radical and by others as fulfillment of prophecy. His ideas seemed to generate a split in our community.

Apparently, Jesus did not act or speak differently in other villages than he had when he was in our synagogue. My interest was piqued even more. Did he seem as authentic as he did here in his hometown? How did other people react to his teaching—favorably or unfavorably? Now I wanted to hear reports from the other places where he had been preaching and compare them with what I had seen and heard with my own eyes and ears right here in Nazareth.

It wasn't long before he said that he had to leave Galilee, go south to the cities of Judah, and "preach the good news of the kingdom of God, because," as he said, "that is why I was sent." Now that stumped me more than just a bit. He was sent? By whom? What did it all mean? I knew then that it was more important than ever that I keep track of him until I had answers to all my questions about him. This man was beginning to fascinate me so much I was having difficulty keeping my mind on my job.

The next thing I heard was that he had asked several men to follow him after they had been fishing all night on the Sea of Galilee but had caught nothing. Jesus told them to go back out and try again. After a brief argument, they reluctantly did as he said. I'm sure they were tired and were not happy about getting advice in their own area of expertise from this man, who was not even a fisherman but a carpenter of all things!

However, the fishing experts did what Jesus said and they caught so many fish that the nets began to break, and the boats began to sink even as the expert fishermen tried to get all the fish into their boats. I learned that the outspoken leader of the small group was Simon Peter and his two partners were brothers, James and John, and a third guy, Andrew, was also with them

Jesus had told them, "Follow me, and from now on you will catch people." I wondered what it meant to follow this Jesus. Where would they be going? What would happen to them if they followed this new teacher? How would they feed their families if they gave up their fishing business to follow Jesus? You can imagine my surprise when I learned that they just left their boats on the shore and followed him. To catch people? Now what did that mean?

I tried to keep tabs on Jesus, but it was difficult. I couldn't afford to pay a messenger to stay with him and run back to Nazareth every Friday to let me know what was happening. We didn't have a national news source such as a *Main Lane Journal.* Maybe someday someone would find a way to keep in touch with other people faster and cheaper. My fascination with this man, Jesus, increased as I kept hearing more about him. I suppose I could have dropped what I was doing and joined his group. However, the thought of doing that made me very nervous. After all, I was young, about his age, and younger than some of his followers. I also thought there might be a dark downside to being too close to him and his followers. Our people in the past have rallied around prophets, and then later turned their backs on them when those prophets turned out to be phonies, and the situations became tenuous and difficult. If anything like that ever happened to Jesus, I might lose everything if anyone ever connected me to him. It would only give Yenta more ammunition for warning mothers against me.

"Cautious Caleb" was not a nickname I could deny.

I kept getting reports from a growing number of friends in the villages and cities. Jesus continued to perform all kinds of miracles, and he continued to speak about the coming of the kingdom of

God. Just as I had thought, there were mixed feelings about who this Jesus really was. He was creating a division between some of our people and our own Jewish authorities. The authorities were increasingly on the defensive against him *and* his followers. To many of us, it seemed that the temple rulers wanted to be rid of Jesus. They seemed to be concerned that the Roman government might view him as a threat to the Roman occupation of our land. That is just how influential our Jewish authorities thought Jesus to be. He could be a threat to the Roman Empire? To Rome, no less? *Give ... me ... a ... break!*

As you may know, our priests and Jewish rulers won. They crucified Jesus at our Passover time. I was in Jerusalem once when the authorities ordered a crucifixion. I had never seen such a gruesome, horribly inhumane practice. This Passover crucifixion must have been an unspeakable experience for Jesus, his followers, and his family, especially for his mother.

I found myself crushed by the news of his death. I had been putting off my decision to follow Jesus, thinking I had plenty of time to make that choice. After all, it had only been three short years since I first met him at our synagogue in Nazareth. Hiram chided me until I was tired of hearing him, "How can you be so equivocating? Cook, or get out of the kitchen!"

Then I heard the great news. It seemed almost too good to be true: he rose from the dead on the first day of the week following Passover. It was then that I realized that it had not been in Jehovah's plan to sacrifice Jesus in Nazareth three years ago when the cliff could have become an early death: a cross or gallows for him. Three years ago in Nazareth was not on the divine timetable. The time to reveal his true destiny was to be at Passover and the place was to be in Jerusalem, at the center of our faith for centuries.

The additional piece of news I heard was that the risen Jesus would be coming up to Galilee from Jerusalem to meet with his disciples. I lived where they would be, and I would have a chance to meet him again. I couldn't wait for him to get here. I planned what I would say to him, and then I'd do what Peter had done on the day they hauled in that net-breaking, boat-sinking catch of fish. I'd fall on my knees and ask him to make me one of his disciples. I was sure that I was ready for the next phase of my life as a teller of the good news of the Holy One of God.

However, I'm very bothered now as I look back on my last three years and realize how hesitant I had been to follow Jesus even after I became convinced he was all he said he was. I had heard his words. I had seen his miracles and had watched other disciples following him. Most importantly, I felt that longing and hunger in my heart to be a part of his kingdom. It was a longing that I could not stop! Why had I been so reluctant? What had held me back? I remembered what my friend Hiram had told me about my love to question everything. Maybe I was just too analytical, too obsessed with data, too cautious about taking risks, and too slow to move on my intuition. I really had known what I should do and what I *must* do. I guess I thought that I needed to wait until someone answered all my questions. I finally realized that not all of my questions would ever be answered unless my brain stopped working.

Most of my questions were, now that I think about them, only excuses and a very weak rationale for delaying my decision. I know that I'll still have questions, but as one of Christ's followers, the answers will be revealed, as I need to know them. Now I understand that as I commit myself to follow him, I will learn more about his purposes for me.

Maybe, too, I was also overly concerned with what my neighbors and friends would think about the changes from my usual, careful, and objective demeanor, to the person that I have become: a careful, thinking, and rational follower of the Christ. I guess you could say that Jesus *"edged"* me into his group of disciples. My decision to be a part of the community of Christ-followers has brought a great purpose into my life as well as a great challenge. I now feel that I am alive in a way I had never been alive before. In fact, I feel as though I have been given a new life. But in this new life … I'm still single! Oh, well!

Biblical reference: This story about the beginning of Christ's ministry expands the gospel record to include the fictional synagogue attendant's role in the account. It also inserts the ordinary events customary for a Sabbath Day in that time in history.

Scripture: Isaiah 61:1–3 and Luke 4:16–21

Discussion possibilities:

1. What held this synagogue attendant back from following Jesus?
2. What other reasons could a person use for not being a disciple of Jesus?
3. What would happen if just 25 percent of Christ's followers wanted to tell others?
4. Discuss the damage that hatred creates in a religious setting or in any volunteer organization.
5. Discuss how splits happen in religious communities.

Extreme Exclusivity

Voice of a Supposed Rival

There I was, just doing what I thought I was called to do: throwing out demons from people who were being tortured by their demons. These people were badly hurting themselves, were being discriminated against by neighbors and relatives, were denied usual and common courtesies, and were not welcome at religious services where they might have received some help and sympathy. When they came to me in faith that I could help them because I was calling on the name of Jesus to heal them, they became my friends for life. The more of these hopelessly friendless people I saw, the more intense I felt about bringing them to the healing grace of God. No one else in this district of Galilee was bothering with them except to try to keep them away from their families and others in their communities. They were simply and profoundly both an embarrassment and a threat to everyone else!

One day, I heard that some of the followers of Jesus had come to our district to teach, and I was anxious to meet them so I could learn more about this phenomenal person whom I had heard preach in Galilee about a year ago. When I met them, I discovered that I had some brothers who loved Jesus as I did, and had committed themselves to follow him wherever he led them. I also discovered that they each knew some of the same people that

I knew in the villages in Galilee. We shared some wine together as we talked into the evening hours before tiredness got the better of all of us, so we retired to get some well-earned sleep.

Someone banging on the door of my simple home awakened me early the next morning. A strange man was howling, swearing, and causing a disturbing ruckus. I don't know how my guests could sleep through the racket. By the time I threw on a robe and opened the door, there he was staring me in the face—a man who was obviously possessed by demons and needed to be healed. My newly found friends, the followers of Jesus, were still in their beds, so I went outside to talk with the possessed man. There was no talking to him. He screamed, "Get these demons away from me. They want to kill me. If you don't help me, I'll kill myself."

What was I to do? I put my hand gently on his shoulder and calling on the name of Jesus, commanded the demons to come out of him. The demons protested loudly, but with even more noise and drama, they left the demented man. The poor man almost collapsed. I had to hold him up until he could stand on his own two feet so I could walk him back to his own place.

I was exhausted and only had one thought: I just wanted to go back to my bed. I too could hardly stand up by myself. However, before I could get back to bed, my new friends woke up and appeared in the room. John asked, "What was all the noise about? It sounded serious. Are you okay?"

By the time I had explained about the demented man and the healing that I had been called upon to do, these men who had been friendly began to turn very unfriendly. Their new demeanor was not a slow, gradual change, but was almost cataclysmic. I was shocked at their harshness as they ordered me to stop my healing ministry. Their friendliness was gone, and in its place was scorn and what sounded to me like rage. It became apparent that I had more than just upset them. It was beyond rage, significant enough to cause me concern. Knowing that they were going back to Jesus, I wondered if they were planning to report that I had done something that would also enrage Jesus. I couldn't think what that might have been, but it had been quite some time since Jesus and I had talked together when he had empowered me to heal sick people.

To end the matter with his followers, I simply told them, "No, I will not stop, and until I hear from Jesus, I will keep on doing what I am doing."

That really ticked them off. Enraged, they left without even having something to eat. I saw them shake the dust off their feet when they arrived down at the road. (That must have some meaning that I'm unaware of.) Now don't get the wrong idea— what I do is not an everyday occurrence. Thanks to all that is good, these demented people will not be taking over our district, not very soon anyway. There are not very many of them around here. The one man that pounded on the door this morning was the first one that I have dealt with in many weeks.

I didn't hear anything from Jesus or from any of the disciples until after a few months had gone by, so I assumed that nothing had come of the report they made back to Jesus. Then I had a visit from John. "Oh, oh, now what?" He seemed to be the follower who had a more sensitive heart and who may have been closer to Jesus than the others were. John told me he was in the neighborhood and thought he would stop in to see me. I offered him some water to drink and a footbath for his dusty feet. After the amenities were finished, we had a cup of wine and sat down for a visit. I found his company refreshing and pleasant. I think I could really learn to like this guy. He listened without interrupting me. He seemed to be open about his own experience with Jesus and his fellow followers, and asked me about my life without judging me for my mistakes. To me, that is what friendship is all about!

I started to think that maybe John was not going to tell me what I needed to hear. I finally asked him what Jesus had said when they reported back to him what had happened when the demented man almost tore down the door demanding to have the demons thrown out of him. John was a little apologetic for the way they had reacted to me at that first meeting. I figured he had something to tell me, but it was like pulling teeth to get him to talk about what had happened when the group told Jesus about their experience with me. I especially wanted to hear what Jesus had said about me casting out demons. John told me what they had told Jesus and the response that Jesus gave them: "Don't stop him. If he's not an enemy, he's an ally" (Luke 9:50).

I can tell you that answer was music to my ears, but I suspect that it was discordant to the followers, and did not set well with *their* ears. Jesus simply told them that he and I had talked about a ministry that I wanted to have. At times, we have a similar disturbance in our district. It must be the water we drink! To make sure I heard correctly, I repeated back to John what Jesus had told the followers about me. I assured John that I was very much in sync with him and the rest of the followers of Jesus. I hoped he would take my response back to them. For what seemed more than just a minute, we sat there thinking about what that response might have meant or would mean in the future of the work of the followers.

John suggested that his entire experience with Jesus seemed to him to be more than just a relationship with a great teacher. John had the distinct impression that this was the beginning of some new world order in our faith. If so, Jesus had just set down a basic principle of how the followers and disciples of Jesus were to treat others who might seem to be different from the rest of us in the details of their beliefs and the actions that would result from those beliefs.

John began to tell me about his friends who were also followers of Jesus. Some of them seemed to me to be outspoken and maybe not actually opinionated, but what you might say as not open to new ideas. I was interested in John's comments that he felt that some of them were learning from Jesus to be more open to listening and open to changing their opinions and ideas about his teachings. He also said that Jesus kept talking about the kingdom of God and that something big was on the horizon, but that Jesus seemed to be pushing them because he had to go to Jerusalem first for a major event in his life. John said they had no idea what that "major event" was. Jesus also told his followers that they would be doing greater things than he had done. This was all very mysterious, and John was not sure what to make of these words of Jesus. We spent a little time playing a little game of "suppose it was this, or suppose it was that." John convinced me that whatever it was, the event was going to be a major event in the life of Jesus as well as in our lives.

The only history we could bring to bear on the possibilities for the future was our *own* history as a nation. From our earliest days going all the way back to Abraham, Isaac, and Jacob, our forefathers, we were a nation of a people with many disparate notions of how we should live, worship, and govern ourselves. We have had many, many divisions and sub-divisions in our life as a people. Several hundreds of years ago, we even divided into two separate nations: Israel and Judah. We had good kings and evil kings; good prophets and false prophets; and good outcomes and disastrous outcomes from many of them. Sometimes it seemed as though being intolerant of the ideas of others was a prized quality in our small world. We had more than enough intolerance to keep the factions in our society verbally at war probably for as long as we would survive as a people.

Sometimes, John and I would have a good laugh at ourselves

with the old saying: "Sometimes wrong, but never in doubt." However, that statement was only valid for those who held other opinions than our own. For instance, the Sadducees said there is no resurrection from the dead. They had their followers who were convinced that death ended everything, and that their belief was as solid as the rocks in the Negev Desert, on the southern border of Judea. The Pharisees took exception to the Sadducees' intolerance of anyone who disagreed with them. However, the Pharisees were as intolerant in their teachings as the Sadducees were in theirs. It seemed as though everyone had an opinion that had become solidified as a basic principle of life. Moreover, woe to anyone who disagreed! We had more than enough intolerance to go around to all of our twelve tribes and then some left over for the rest of the world.

I finally got up my nerve to ask John, "Why did you guys take such a hard line with me when you told me to stop throwing out the demons from these unfortunate wretches?" After all of our conversation about tolerance and intolerance, John finally told me that as they traveled back to Jesus, they had confessed to each other that they had admired me for sticking to my principles and for refusing to be cowed by their prohibition to me. He finally admitted that their unsuccessful prohibition was simply because, "I was not one of your group" (Luke 9:49).

Probably more loudly and strongly than I meant it to be, I scornfully said, "*That was it*? I was not one of you? Really? *I was not one of you?*" I stared at him in dumfounded disbelief while neither of us said anything. After a few minutes, John spoke first and was obviously and extremely embarrassed, and asked for my forgiveness for their elitism and pride. A warm hug was the healing touch that brought us together again.

Wow! I guess Jesus had straightened them out on that score. We realized that we were now going to be expending a lot of our energies and minds to overcome the natural intolerances of people to new ways of thinking about God, without battling each other on minor issues or the finer points of belief and life.

John and I made a pact just before he left to return to the followers that we would do our best to be open to the spirit of Jesus in dealing with each other and with those with whom we differed. We vowed to keep reminding ourselves that he that is not against us is for us. I could foresee more than a few difficulties ahead for the followers of Jesus over similar opinionated attitudes. Look what it almost did for just the two of us, John and me.

Biblical reference: This unusual story is from the account of a meeting of some of the disciples of Jesus with one man who assumed he was doing "God's work." Jesus enunciated a major principle of doing the work of God by way of this story in Luke. Many of the divisions in the life of the church can probably be traced to the low priority of this "Jesus principle" that grew out of the confrontation between the disciples and this committed healer of people.

Scripture: Luke 9:46–50

Discussion possibilities:

1. How and when has this kind of intolerance been repeated in Christendom?
2. How connected to this intolerance of ideas is the intolerance of religious leaders?
3. What were some of the possible issues for a few or our denominational differences?
4. In your experience of discussion of "religion" with others, do they end up with a hug?
5. How often is there agreement after such a discussion? Do you end up as friends?

Looking for the Lost Coin

Voice of a Minor Miser

Where did you go, you little piece of silver? Come on now, I don't have all the time in the world to keep looking, but I will. You are important to me—although you are not really mine, you belong to Jehovah. You were the tithe for the Sabbath. You were here yesterday, right here, and now I can't find you. Let's see. Did you fall out of my purse on the way home from the store? I was talking with my neighbor when I thought you were in my hand. I'll check with her to see if she remembers if I dropped it in her yard. Now I remember—I'm sure you were in my hand while I was talking with her. On the other hand, maybe you dropped out of my hand when I was reaching for my key to the house?

She doesn't remember even talking with me yesterday—some neighbor she is! Just my luck to have an absent-minded person living right next door to me. I hope she remembers that she invited me to have Sabbath meal with her. Oh well, I'll keep looking if I have to tear the house apart to find you. It won't be the first time I've misplaced something in this house, and it probably won't be the last. If my husband were still alive, he'd find you. I could always count on him.

Let's see. I'll take one room at a time. I know you can't be very far. You're probably in plain sight—things usually are when

I lose them. My mother used to say, "Deborah, you'd lose your own head if it weren't attached to your body." I never appreciated her comment, especially when she said it so often. I never realized that I lost stuff so much, but I guess I did. Maybe it's just a girl thing. My daughters were always begging me to help them find their lost whatevers. It can't be that—my sons were not much different. Maybe it's just a human thing. I think that's it—it is a human failure. We even get ourselves lost sometimes. Isn't it a blessing that Jehovah always knows where we are? Moreover, that he knows how to find us and bring us back home?

Where is that broom? Don't tell me I've lost it, too. If you were as big as my broom, I'd find you fast, and hey, if you were the only coin—one of many that I have lost, and I find them all, I'd end up being quite rich. I hope my neighbor doesn't stop by to tell me she remembers inviting me for Sabbath meal. She'll see that I didn't get my housework done before Sabbath, which begins in about an hour. Swoosh, swoosh, swoosh. Talk about getting housework done quickly. Almost done! I know you'll be in the last place I look. Funny how that happens, isn't it? The house is almost clean. Ah ha! There you are, you little piece of heaven. I knew I'd find you. Now we can both go to synagogue together. I'll pray and listen, and add you to the offering box, where we'll both be happy to know that you will be helping others who are in more need that I am.

I'm not going to make a fool of myself by running down the road telling the world that you are found, but I feel as though I should be doing that. Now, I have a great story to tell my friends and neighbors after synagogue tomorrow. Of course, my neighbor next door won't even remember that I lost you! You can be sure, however, that she'll remember to stop by and celebrate with me about finding you.

I learned, from the rabbi that God's angels throw a great party every time a lost soul turns to God. Hallelujah!

Biblical background: This brief story is an adaptation of a parable told to many people who were hanging around Jesus. The Pharisees and religious scholars were not at all pleased that Jesus took in "sinners and ate meals with them, treating them like old friends." Their grumbling prompted this story found in Luke. Eugene Peterson's translation, *The Message*, is a source for some of the story.

Scripture: Luke 15:8–10

Discussion possibilities

1. What is different in the lost coin parable from the lost sheep and from the lost boy/man parables?
2. Which of the three parables most impresses you? Why?
3. Did the original listeners of these parables understand the meaning of them? How do we know they did know or didn't know?
4. Do you thank God often enough for finding you?

A Lot of Work for Just One

Voice of a Sheep Owner

I was probably asleep at the switch when I got the word from one of my shepherds that a sheep of the flock was missing. What was wrong with me? I am usually awake when I'm doing the books. Maybe I was too tired to hear correctly, but I'm sure that's what he said, "One is missing—gone." I had to ask, "Which one? Was it one of the new little lambs? Oh, it *was* a lamb? Where were you when you realized the lamb was gone? Did you search for it? Where did you look?"

I had plans made for the rest of the day and early evening, too, and some other reasons why this was a bad time for this to happen. However, a guy's got to do what a guy's got to do. No way around that, or so my dad always told me whenever something went wrong. Dad is gone now, but his words still ring in my head. I guess I'll never get his voice out of my head. There are times, though, when I just want to be able to think an issue through on my own without my parents' advice in my head. I suppose my son will someday have similar experiences—my voice will be ringing in his head. I'd better be very careful of the words I put into his head!

Enough of this daydreaming! I should be out there looking for my lamb right now instead of merely daydreaming. A lion could be stalking it now for its dinner. Who knows what other dangers she could be in? Oh, I know it is just one lamb of the many that were born this spring. But she is special! Sure, you tell me, they're all special, but this one is extra special! I was with her when she was born. Her mother didn't live through the birth, so I bottle-fed her, then watched her grow. It wasn't long before she was gamboling all over the pasture.

I had to give her a name, and not being very creative, I decided to simplify and just call her Lambie. I'd call her when she was playing with the other lambs. She would stop, look at me with what I'm sure was a questioning look, and then quickly run to me. Now she's gone, lost, and probably trying to call *my* name.

I put on my heavy coat, took my walking stick and a club to fight off any animals that might be attracted to a good meal, and headed out to the last place my servant had seen her. Night was falling fast, as it does in our hills, but the hills are rocky and difficult for walking, let alone for running. I was soon at the place where Lambie had disappeared, so I started calling her, "Lambie, I'm here. Come to me if you can. I don't want you to be hurt. Do you remember when I used to bandage up your hurt places when you were smaller and I'd rub soothing oil on those hurt places?" I probably sounded strange to anyone who might have heard me. But a lamb is precious and worthy of all the care I can give it.

Wait just a minute. I couldn't believe I was actually calling to a sheep. Am I nuts? Would she recognize my voice? Would she be able to get out of the brambles if that's where she was? Maybe she was injured—oh, no, I didn't bring oil or anything to use as a bandage. All I brought was my love and concern. But would that be enough? I was not so sure it would be. However, I thought it was a start—it got me up in the hills in the brambles where she was probably caught. Love makes us do radical things similar to going out in the night to find a lost lamb.

I started wondering why she was lost. Why did she run away? Was she frightened? Was she merely curious about the big outside world and felt she needed to discover for herself what she was missing? On the other hand, did she talk with one of the other sheep who had run off by itself, and my lamb heard some stuff that sounded tantalizing and exciting? Since Lambie is a little ewe, maybe one of the young rams may have promised to go with her and then "chickened out" and let Lambie go on her own. I'll never know why. I can only guess. But that isn't important now—I must find her and bring her back to the sheepfold, where she'll be safe and loved.

Then I remembered what it was like when I was younger and had some of the same thoughts and inclinations that I was ascribing to Lambie. Did I forget what it was like to be safe in my dad's "sheepfold?" What had seemed so attractive about life that I didn't know? I remember hearing the other guys talking or bragging about their escapades and finding them exciting and alluring. I thought that maybe, just maybe, it would be more fun to try it on my own. Then, someone told me a story about a lost son, who begged his dad to give him his inheritance so he could run away and live life the way he thought life should be lived. It was a disastrous experience for that guy. He ultimately came to his senses and returned to his dad, and to his home, where he was welcomed, loved, and cherished. It took a while for him to realize what his experience had cost his dad in worry, gray hair, and sleeplessness.

When I first heard that story, I asked my dad if he thought the story I had heard could actually be true. "Would you accept me back the same way if I took off even if I didn't have your money to finance my dream? Would you accept me back the way the storybook dad did?" He told me with a smile on his face, "Oh, I would, son, I would. I'd hug you just as the storybook dad did."

I told him that I decided not to put him through that ordeal of worry, sleeplessness, and gray hair. (Yes, I did mention his gray hair.) I started to feel quite proud of my decision, until I realized the storybook dad was, in a sense, my Jehovah God, who wanted me to come back to Him even more than I wanted Lambie to come back to me. That's when I realized that Jehovah loved me so much that He would personally come looking for me wherever I was and whatever I had done to disappoint Him.

Just as I was thinking through the theology of this experience, I heard a very weak, "Baa," and I knew I was close to a lost sheep. It was almost totally dark and I couldn't see very well, but I heard another "Baa" even closer this time. I strained my eyes to see where Lambie was. There she was stuck in some brambles, just as I thought she'd be. I knelt down and held her while I untangled her from the cruel but binding thorns and strong weeds that held her tightly. Her little heart was beating fast, and her bleating sounded weak and tired. As soon as I had released her from her prison and held her in my arms, I remembered the joy that Jehovah had when He found me—*His* lost sheep.

I had one hundred sheep. Only one was lost, but it didn't matter whether it was Lambie or another one. I am sure I would have felt the same way and would have spent all the time it would take to find her. Every lamb is precious to a shepherd! Then I realized that God saw me as a precious son who had wandered away from Him.

I put her gently around my shoulders and headed back to the sheepfold, talking to her all the way home. I knew I needed to check the safeguards we had around the pastures, and I promised her that I'd do that tomorrow. I also told her about the big, bad animals out there that would threaten her if she ever did that again. I guess all my talking was more for me than for Lambie. You know how that is. I again remembered my dad's little sermons about the dangers that could threaten my safety if I ever decided to go it alone before it was time for my independence. I tried it just once and found out that Dad was right.

I shouted all the way home to everyone I saw that Lambie was shaken up but was alive and fine, and that I would throw a big party the next day to celebrate Lambie's return. Some of my neighbors looked askance and with a question in their eyes—a *party for a lamb's return*? "You *are* kidding, aren't you?" That was the typical question. All I could say in response was, "Let's celebrate—God is just as excited and happy when one of us turns to Him in faith and lets Him take us back to his sheepfold" (Luke 15:7).

Biblical background: This story is an adaptation of the biblical account in Luke, one of three parables that Jesus told about the joy in heaven when one sinner is reclaimed.
Scripture: Luke 15:1–7
Discussion possibilities:

1. Talk about what radical things love makes us do.
2. What would be the difference today for a parable about something lost, rather than Lambie? Compare with the stories of the "lost coin" and the "prodigal son."
3. Nothing is said in the parable about the feelings of the lost lamb upon its rescue. If you had been the lamb, how would *you* have felt? Why?

Possible Hymn:
"The Ninety and Nine," music by Ira D. Sankey, 1874, Words by Elizabeth C. Clephane. 1868. Words in the Public Domain.

Note: Ezekiel describes a "good shepherd" and an "evil shepherd" in chapter 34 of his book in the Bible. Ezekiel is the seventh book after the book of Psalms.

The Runaway Son

Voice of the Prodigal Son

I really get upset when I think back to those years—so upset that if I could, I would kick myself. Mostly, I just get upset with myself, but also more than a little upset with my brother, Jacob, but maybe not so upset with my father. I really don't want to relive those days, but I think it's important for me to understand what was happening with my family and me.

When this story became reality, I realize now that I was just a boy-man, eighteen years old. By the time the experience was over, I was twenty-three, although somehow I lost track of time and events. In those few five short years, I learned a lot, except I'd want to forget some of what I discovered about myself. However, I doubt I ever will forget some of the stupid and tragic experiences I had. How could I have been so stupid? But there are at least a couple of things I came to realize, and they were probably some of the most important lessons I have ever learned—the lessons were about the power of love and the value of my family.

I'm not sure when my troubles began. There's no question in my mind that they probably began two or three years before I did anything about the concerns I had. Even though my father had hired several servants to help with the animals, the pastures, and the grain that we grew, there was still more work to do than

I'm sure my brother Jacob and I could handle. From the time we sowed the seed until the time we harvested the crops, we were busy day and night in the barns stacking hay or in the fields plowing dirt. Actually, the busy times started before we even sowed the seed. In the spring, lambs were born to the ewes, kids were born to the nanny goats, and even though we had only a few cattle, cows gave birth to calves. From early spring to late in the fall, our lives were pretty much controlled by the birth cycles of animals and the growth cycles of seeds. In the other months, we repaired our tools and mucked out the barns and stables.

In the busy spring and summer months, it was not unusual to be awakened in the middle of the night and told to get to the barn to help deliver a lamb, a kid, or a calf. That kind of schedule can really interrupt a young guy's fun times, parties, and especially his social life. The last thing I wanted to hear in the middle of the night was Jacob's voice: "Aaron, wake up and get out to the barn. I need your help."

The one positive about my story is that my father was very wealthy—at least, at the time I considered that fact as a positive. We had everything, and I mean everything that we wanted, except the one thing I thought I needed most—my freedom. My life was in a dead-end circle (if that is possible), and it seemed as though my future was already determined. In other words, I felt depressed beyond anything that my friends ever expressed about themselves. I spent much of my time obsessing about my restrictions because of the rules, schedules, and requirements laid on me by my father and even by my older brother. Jake was my bigger problem. Yeah, he was always on my case, and it didn't take much to get him upset with me. He noticed every little fault and every infraction of the rules or schedules that I was told to meet. Every time he thought I had failed to hold up my share of the jobs we were assigned, Jake was angry. For instance, he went ballistic if I didn't muck out the barn to his satisfaction. Mucking out the barn was about the last thing I wanted to hear while eating my dinner. That's when he reviewed my day—every day!

The final straw made me so angry I could spit mud: Jake made up the schedules, the rules, and the job assignments. I didn't have the right, or so it seemed, to have even one word to say about them. That was okay, I guess, when I was younger, but not after I had become a man. He still called me his "little brother, Aarie," when he would talk about me to his friends or neighbors or even to our Father. It also seemed to me that my dad didn't help the situation. Rarely did I ever hear a good word from Dad or a word of caution to my brother, Jacob, about the way he treated me.

So I often spent much of my waking time thinking about ways to get myself out of this situation and into a place as far away from here as I could get, and the sooner, the better. If you haven't figured it out yet, Jake and I never got along—we never hit it off. There was a constant battle going on between us over everything we did. I sometimes thought Jake hated me, and I was beginning to think I hated him. We spent a lot of time arguing, and when we were not arguing, we were not even talking to each other. It was similar to a war! There was no way I could continue to live this way when I knew there was so much more of the world to see just waiting for me out there. The rest of the world started looking better and better every day.

When I had my plans all worked out and Dad seemed to be in a good mood, I dropped my plan on him. "Dad, someday when you die I'm going to get my share of the estate. How about dividing it up now between Jake and me?" I probably didn't say it exactly in those words, but more like this: "Dad, someday I'll get my share of everything, so why not now? I need to get away from here, try life on my own, and take on responsibility that I choose.

I really don't want to fight with Jacob all the time either. So, give me your blessing and my inheritance, and I'll be out of your hair."

Dad easily went along with my plan—too easily, I thought. Maybe he was happy about me leaving and heading out on my own. I was not sure what that meant about his love for me, or even if he did love me. I knew this for sure—Jake would not be sad to see me go. He'd be all smiles now that I would soon be out of his hair so he could do everything exactly the way he wanted to. But I bet he'd miss having me to boss around!

My dad really surprised me when he easily agreed to my request and split the money between Jake and me. I packed my bags and took off for another country, any country, thinking to myself: *I can now live the way I want to. Jake and Dad can't tell me what to do, when to do it, or what happens if I decide not to do it. This the way I've always wanted to live!*

I had very few problems on my great trip. No robbers attacked me, and I stayed in some very fine places. Along the way I met some fun people who introduced me to some exciting, new experiences that I would never have known back home. My brother would never have approved of some of the people I met and partied with, and I would never have heard the last of his scolding. Occasionally, I met up with some other travelers and found their company to be much better than Jake's sour disposition. Of course, it would never have taken much for anything to be better than Jake's company.

However, I found out that things don't always work out the way I had planned or the way I thought they should have worked out. Did I put my money into stocks and bonds or in a bank vault? Of course not. After all, money is meant to be spent. I went through my inheritance almost as fast as I could think of ways to spend it. I always wanted to be the big man in town, and with all this money, I became just that: the big man in town, the party guy who could pay for everything—in cash! Before I realized what was happening, the money was gone! You know what happened to all my newfound friends, right? Like my money, they were also gone. To make matters worse, there was a famine in my new home country, so I couldn't buy food even if I would have had some money. My landlord kicked me out of the room I had rented and told me that he didn't want to see me coming around there even for meals. However, I was hungry, and to my way of thinking, I was probably starving. I was in a bad way, with:

- no food
- no money
- no job
- no friends
- no place to sleep
- no one who would even have cared if I lived or died

I don't remember how, but somehow I heard about a farmer who needed help taking care of his pigs. As much as I hated the thought of practically living with pigs, I landed the job, even realizing that as a good Hebrew, pigs were despised and forbidden. Believe it or not, the food that the pigs ate started looking pretty good to me. The pod that they ate was a kind that grew on certain trees in that country and was the main diet of the animals. The animals had no problem scarfing them down, so out of desperation, I tried the pods. At first, they tasted terrible! But they didn't kill the pigs, so why not? I found out quite quickly that hunger could drive a person to eat just about anything that would fill up his stomach. It worked that way for me.

Amid all this self-made mess, I began to have a strong inner compulsion that I needed to go home. I started thinking that it was just my current situation of being hungry and alone that was causing this feeling, but the feeling was stronger than anything I had ever felt about anything in my life. I tried to analyze what was taking over my brain. I couldn't sleep without dreaming of Dad and home. When I was awake, I couldn't think without seeing Dad everywhere I looked. Even Jake didn't seem such a bad guy in my mind. Where was this powerful drive coming from? I knew I had to do something—and soon, or while I could still function.

I finally came to my senses and thought about all that home represented: The servants had food, more than they needed, while I was starving to death. But could I really go home? Would Dad take me back? Would Dad ever forgive me for my stupidity?

Yes, I finally admitted to myself I was stupid!

In spite of all my questions, eventually I made the decision to start for home. I was surprised that it was a more difficult decision to make than it had been to decide to leave home in the first place. But finally, I found that I could not suppress this compulsion any longer. I'm still not sure what all was involved in my decision to turn myself around and go back home. If I ever got home, maybe Dad would help me figure it all out. I hope so! I could not stop longing for home and for the closeness of my dad. I realized that I missed him and wanted so much to hear and see him again.

However, now I had big problems—very *big* problems!

- How much should I tell my dad?
- How would I explain what had happened?
- Would he or even could he ever love me again?
- How could I possibly face Jake, and what would I say to him?
- Would he still hate me?
- How would I face my old friends?
- Would they throw my stupid decisions and bad choices in my face?
- How would I convincingly tell my dad that I did love him and be real about it?

After all, I had told many people in that strange country that I loved them. I think I missed my mother much more than I realized, and I guess now that I may have been looking for her in the strangers I met. On other occasions, I may have been searching for a loving father or a caring brother. Oh, I don't know, it's all a blur in my mind. I know now that what I felt for those people wasn't love but just the need for some attention and the search for a significant attachment to someone, to anyone. Maybe it was a yearning for a replacement parent—I just don't know. Now I miss everyone from home. I miss them all, especially my family. Well, Dad anyway. Jake? Maybe—Jake, not so much!

I started walking home since I had sold my horse. I had no luggage, and there were no good-byes from anyone, and no tears shed at my departure. I realized I had a long walk ahead of me, but I hardly cared.

Tired? No, I was exhausted. Worn down? No, I was totally worn out. There were times when I thought it would be better for everyone if I just laid down and ended it all in the desert where no one would ever find me. I realized, however, that was the coward's way out, and I couldn't do that to my dad, so I trudged on, thinking my journey would never end, but also hoping that it would never end. That sounds confusing to me too. What do I wish?

So, on and on I went day after day after day. I thought I was in turmoil back when I had been living and eating with the swine. But during the long days on the road I realized that my turmoil now was even greater than it had been when I lived with the pigs.

I felt as though my head and heart were at war with each other. My heart was saying, "Go home, man. It's the only place where you will find peace." But my head was afraid that I'd be told, "Go away. We don't know you, and we don't care who you are."

The turmoil in my head kept accusingly raising these questions:

- What would Dad say?
- Would he even recognize me?
- How could I possibly explain why I left?
- Would he forgive me and accept me back?
- How could I say strongly enough, "Dad, I'm really sorry"?
- Would he believe me?
- What if he didn't accept me?

I had a plan B, but that plan included the farmer and his pigs, and it, too, had failed. I think I must have used up all my plans. I only had a Plan C, and that meant to go home. Somehow, I managed to survive—sleeping in ditches or in abandoned sheds and barns, eating what I could find of scraps and any animals I could catch, and trying to forget my whole wretched, wasted five years.

Eventually, I realized I would have to say something to Dad—if he were still alive. These words seemed to fit the need: "I've sinned against God, I've sinned before you, I don't deserve to be your son. Take me on as a hired hand" (Luke 15:17–20). The more I said this to myself, the more I realized it was true—so very true.

After walking for days and weeks or longer, the landscape began to look familiar: there were barns and houses I thought I could remember. Once in a while, I saw someone I thought I recognized. Some of the villages I passed through reminded me of those I had known as a teenager. However, no one greeted me or even acknowledged my presence. In fact, most people seemed to move out of my way to avoid me. I think most people probably thought I was just another crazy, old man who smelled like he lived in a pig sty and was dressed in torn and dirty rags.

The sun was almost directly overhead when I thought I saw my childhood home. It was still far off in the distance, but I was sure that it was my father's house. However, I wasn't sure that I dared to call it my home because I think that along with everything else in my past, I had rejected it, and I was afraid it might have rejected me. Now all the questions I had been asking myself about how I would be treated began to hit me like the hard desert rocks that I had to walk over.

I tried not to blink my eyes because I just wanted to take in that wonderful sight and remember what it was like and what it would be just to be home again. *Then I saw him!* He was standing in the middle of the road with his hands shading his eyes from the sun, leaning forward with his hand on a long walking stick. I am sure I will never ever forget that sight. Suddenly he dropped his walking stick and held out his arms to take me into them. I tried to run, but my legs wouldn't move. I was filled with a sense of joy but also a greater sense of fear for what might happen next.

What happened next? I saw my dad crying. I realized that I was glad to see him crying. I think that meant that he wasn't angry with me, but that he was glad to see me. I couldn't understand everything he was trying to say, but I think he was telling me that he loved me, that he had missed me so much, and that he was glad I was home. I heard that word *home*, and it was a word of healing to my soul. There really *is* a balm in Gilead!

I just couldn't move fast enough. When I finally came to the place where he was standing, I fell into his arms and began sobbing. I was overcome with so many different feelings that it is difficult now for me to remember all the feelings that I had: heartbreaking guilt, over-whelming sadness, but also unbelievable thankfulness just to be home.

I started to say my practiced, but true words, "Father, I have sinned," and so on, but Father cut me off. I never even got to the part about being one of his servants. I am his *son*! The seemingly unstoppable war between my head and heart was over.

Dad broke into my apologies and instead called one of the servants, gave him some orders, and threw a big barbecue for everyone. Before the party, I had a long soak in a tub, had a beautiful robe put on me, and had a special ring placed on my finger. Even Jake, my brother, showed up for the party even *if* a little late, but what else is new, but he didn't seem very happy or pleasant about everything that was happening.

He will tell his story and Dad will tell his story a little later after I get some sleep and rest my weary bones. I am just relieved and glad to be home, forgiven, and accepted, at least by my dad. As I went to sleep in my own bed, I realized that it is possible to come home again, and that home is where I belonged. I fell asleep knowing that I was forgiven for my stubbornness, my willfulness, and my selfishness, and that my father's love for me was greater than all the wrong I had done to him. His love overwhelmed me—it was as if I had never done those terrible things to my dad or to anyone else. Dad told me that's the way God works with us: "though our sins be as scarlet, they shall become white as snow.[11]" Dad used the word *redemption* whenever we talked about my experience.

I am redeemed!

Biblical background: This story is an adaptation of the parable of the prodigal son in Luke. It is one of the three parables in which Jesus compares the joy in heaven when a lost person comes back to God to the joy of human beings when we find a precious object or person who returns home or is found.

Scripture: Luke 15:11–30
Discussion possibilities:

1. Describe Aaron's probable thinking before and after his absence from home.
2. How typical is his self-centeredness?

3. What were the promptings that propelled him to go home?
4. Describe Dad's role in this family. Any similarity to some modern families?
5. How does it feel to know *you* are secure in God's family?

The Lonely Father

Voice of the Prodigal's Father

(A dialogue between the father and the prodigal son starts on page 271.)

I love my boys very much. I had better start with that—they are my life. I'd do anything for them, and sometimes it seems to me that I do everything. I think that their mother may have favored the younger of the two, Aaron. After all, he was her younger, her baby. She seemed to stick up for him most of the time and criticized me for what she called my lack of faith in him. Some of my friends tell me the same story—the youngest child is often the favorite of the mother. I have two sons, the younger one, Aaron, and the older one, Jacob. They are radically different from each other. Not one of my friends nor I seem to understand how to deal with those differences. You'd think that one of us would have some answers to this problem. What we probably need is someone who is trained to help us understand what makes other people tick, especially our kids. That'll never happen in our lifetimes!

Boys fight over what jobs I give them to do, which one is responsible for taking care of the sheep, and who should be able to be in charge of even simple things, such as who's going to clean up the barn after shearing the sheep and in which field we should put the sheep after a round-up.

It is usually Aaron, the younger one, who comes running to me to complain that Jacob won't listen to him, or that Jacob is being obstinate, etc. It seems as though no matter how much I try to be reasonable with them, nothing works. There are times when I want to give up, but I can't. After all, they are my sons!

It all came to a head one day when Aaron found me alone and asked if I had time to talk. My first thought was, *Now what? More of the same? More griping about Jacob's this or Jacob's that? Aaron is eighteen or nineteen years old. Shouldn't he be getting past this stage of his life?* I feel sometimes like saying, "Aaron, just suck it up and get on with your life." But I don't say it.

"Of course I have the time, Son. What is it you want to talk about?"

"Well, Dad, I've been thinking about my future."

"That's great, Son. I hope you and this farm will share that future together. I've always had a dream that you and Jacob would share this place when I pass on. I have it all worked out."

"Dad ... *Dad*, just *listen* for a minute, okay? That isn't exactly what I've been thinking. I think I need to be more independent: a chance to try out life on my own; to experience life in another culture; meet new people; and try my hand at some other occupations. Know what I mean?"

"No, Aaron, I don't know what you mean. This is quite a shock. Does this mean you don't want to be a part of the inheritance of the farm, the herds, and all we've built here?"

"Not ... exactly ... Dad. Yes, I do want to share in my inheritance, but I want to have my share now so I can finance my own future—where I want to go and what I want to do. The inheritance will be mine someday anyway, so why not now? I don't think that will put a strain on your finances or budget. Of course, I don't know since you never share any information about money with us. You seem to have a lot of money available for just about anything we need around here. I really want to get out on my own, experience life as a young man, and try out my skills in other situations."

"Have you discussed this with your brother, Jacob?"

"Are you *kidding*, Dad? Naw, he wouldn't understand. I think he's satisfied with being right here for the rest of his life—doing the same old thing day after day and probably year after year. Dad, I think you are stuck with him forever!

"Well, Dad, what'da think? I'm kinda in a hurry to get going. I know you have to get my share of the inheritance ready, but maybe you could pull some strings and get something going … soon … maybe *now*?"

"Aaron, how can you be sure that this is what you want? You're still young, and there is so much for you to learn right here. I'd be glad to spend more time with you so you can learn the business end of the farm, our market possibilities, and I can learn your ideas for growing our business even bigger. We could become a team here to develop this place into a showplace for the neighbors to come and learn.

"Why not wait for six months before you definitely decide what you want to do while you, your brother Jacob, and I start planning for bigger things for our farm, animals, and crops? In the meantime, if you care to, you can start planning on where you can go and find suitable work, your transportation, and what and who you will need to take along with you."

"No, Dad, I've done all the planning I need to do. I'm ready now. I'll just plan my trip as I go along. I'll be just fine. I don't need anyone else to go with me, and I don't need anything but basic supplies. I can get what I need along the way. I want to go *now*! I can't wait for six months!"

I wanted so much to ask him, "Why, what went wrong?" but I couldn't take that personal risk.

"Okay … Okay! I'm very disappointed, but I'll check and see what the banker has to say, but I think I will be able to get it all wrapped up soon. I hope that fits with your schedule."

Only a parent can understand how I felt. The bottom of my life seemed to drop out. First, it was my wife's death, and now Aaron, my little boy, the baby of the family wants to leave me. I felt so alone with no one to talk to, no one to share my desolation with. Even Jehovah seemed so far away. I knew He would understand, but I couldn't bring myself to share my heartbreak even with Him.

The banker put the money together although he seemed shocked about Aaron leaving. He didn't approve of my dividing the inheritance now, saying that there would be more for each of the boys later as my account accrued interest over time. I tried to explain this to my son, but he either *couldn't* or *wouldn't* try to understand. He obviously had only one thought in mind, and that was to get away from here or from us as soon as possible.

I asked Jacob about his thoughts on his brother's leaving, but he seemed to think that his brother was just a headstrong kid who was bored with the quiet life around here. I thought I was lenient enough on him, but Jacob seemed to think that Aaron couldn't live under my rules any longer. Jacob thought that I wasn't hard enough on his brother and that I had always let him get away with too much. Apparently, it was easy for Jacob to overlook the times he also fell short of my expectations for him. Maybe so, but I just don't know. I'm both frustrated and confused.

This was a tough situation for me to consider. I wonder how many parents have realized too late what went wrong between them and their headstrong son or daughter. Now I have sleepless nights wishing I could go back and correct those things I had mistakenly thought were the important factors in running my business. I have another son, Jacob, who probably won't take the same way out of his difficulty with me, but I'm sure that he is also bothered by some of the same issues that bothered Aaron. Maybe I wasn't appreciative of their work or wasn't friendly enough.

However, I have been making an effort with Jacob, and it *is* an effort, to be more encouraging, more interested in his concerns by listening to him, I mean … *really* listening, and in general, just being more pleasant and collaborative. I've been trying, although it isn't easy, to let him know how much I appreciate him and love him. I think it will take longer than I realize for him to believe that I do want to change. Only Jehovah knows how much I need to change. To this point, I haven't noticed any difference in my relationship with Jacob. I guess it will take a long time for him to believe that I am really going to change. Maybe he will be more relaxed after Aaron has been gone for a while.

Where did I go wrong? Since sleep is avoiding me, I have had the dark hours to think about the answers to that question. After too many sleepless nights, I may have come to some answers. I realize *now* that all my attention has been on the farm, the crops, the animals, and the production numbers. My attention has not been on the most valuable, but non-renewable resource that Jehovah had given me: my sons. Somehow, I began taking them as a given and not as a gift. I stopped appreciating what they did, and saw only what they did *not* do. What they heard from me were the errors they made, the tasks that they forgot to do, their failure to keep my timelines, and their increasing carelessness about keeping accurate records. Oh, yes, they heard from me, but as I thought about my conversations with them, I can only remember a few times, but only a *very* few times, when the words where pleasant, encouraging, or loving. I had just assumed that most of the time they knew that I cared. After all, I was their dad, and don't all dads care?

I think I have come to a conclusion about why Aaron may have run away. He left because of me, not because of the work or of his brother. As he thought about the way things had developed, he probably could see no possible changes in me or in the way I treated him. He was not ready to waste his time trying to deal with the way I dealt with him. He had the required stamina and fortitude to take his chances, possibly feeling that some other place couldn't be any worse than it was here. So, he followed his heart.

Well, he's gone! All I could think of this past week was, *Will I ever see him again? If I only knew where he is going, I could go and bring him home. What if he gets into trouble and wants to come home? Will he waste his money or be robbed?*

Even after all the sleepless nights when I think I have figured out the reasons why Aaron left, there are still those nights I can't get to sleep worrying about him. As soon as the darkness gives way to the sun, I keep looking down the road, thinking that maybe he will be there returning to us, but I live in constant disappointment. Jacob keeps telling me, "Don't worry, Dad. He's a big boy now. Let him find out for himself what life really is. He'll be back." But I'm not so sure. I wonder if other parents have been through this same situation. Oh, how I wish I could talk with someone who could help me deal with it, but I'm embarrassed to let anyone else know that I'm having these concerns about my own son, my little boy.

I guess eventually my heart and mind became accustomed to the idea that this was going to be my life—without him. Sleep comes a little easier, the work is getting done, and Jacob seems more pleasant now that his brother has gone. I have even become more accustomed to Jacob's compulsions, and out of sheer exhaustion, I let him have his own way on some of his crazy ideas. I find I am always reminding myself of my need to be more appreciative, listen *more*, criticize *less*, and show him how much I do care. But it is difficult to change my way of handling things after so many years.

Then, one day as I stared down the road, I saw a man walking slowly toward our farm. He was almost limping. He was alone, no camel or horse, and not carrying anything that even resembled a traveling bag. Could this be Aaron? No way, I put it out of my mind, assuming again that my mind was playing tricks on me. I've been seeing this apparition too many times for it to be true today.

But I couldn't stop looking. There was something about his walk that took me back to my little boy. He had that odd little step that was unique to him. One foot was just a little slower to move than the other foot, so his walk looked a little bit similar to a skip, although now a very slow skip. Then I remembered how that happened. He was racing some of his friends when he tripped and badly hurt his ankle. And now, by the time I had watched his feet for a while, he was closer, and I could see that the man's face looked familiar although dirty, unshaven, and scarred. His clothes were also dirty and torn. He looked more like an old man than anyone I recognized.

Hesitantly, I softly said his name, "Aaron?" A second time I said it, but a little louder, "Aaron."

It was Aaron, my son, my boy! He was coming home! Faster than I thought I could, I ran to meet him, threw my arms around him, hugged him close to myself, and kissed him as only a father can kiss his wayward but home-again son.

Then the words poured out of him. He said, "Father, I have sinned against God, I've sinned before you; I don't deserve to be called your son ever again …" (Luke 15:21).

It sounded to me as a prepared speech, but I interrupted him. I called for a couple of servants, "Quick, bring the finest robe in his closet, a jeweled ring for his finger and sandals for his bare feet." I forgot to say anything about a bath, but I am sure that they understood how much he needed a bath. He smelled horrible!

I told some other servants to get the calf we had been saving for a neighborhood barbeque and get it ready for a celebration tonight. One of the servants looked at me as though I had lost my mind. I could see in his eyes the question: "*Why?*"

"*Why?*" I responded. "My son is here—given up for dead and now alive! Given up for lost and now found!" (Luke 15:24).

So, in just a few hours, the party began. The music was loud, so loud that Jacob, who was working in the field, could probably hear it.

Sure enough, Jacob heard the racket and hightailed it back to the house, I guess to find out what was going on. He must have met a servant on his way back to the house who told him the story of Aaron's return, because when he confronted me out behind the house, he was angry. *Very angry.* I won't go into the details of our conversation. I'll let him tell that part of the story later.

I told him the same thing I had earlier told the questioning servant. "My son is back from the dead; he was lost but now is found."

Jacob apparently could not understand how I felt about this joyous event, just as he couldn't understand my feelings on the day Aaron had left us. I only hope he never has to live through something as heartbreaking as a son of *his* announcing that he is leaving home. In those situations, all the tears come from a parent's eyes.

We had the celebration. Aaron was so appreciative, and I was overjoyed over one boy who had returned to the home where he was loved and cherished. Love *does* win out! Jehovah taught me that love is not conditioned on a child's behavior. I don't love him because he is good or dislike him when he is bad. I love him because he is my child! God doesn't love me because I am good, but He will make me good because He loves me. Jehovah has been so good to me because I am His child. The prophets called it grace—just because I am His. Someday Jacob will also come to know what grace is as he sees Jehovah's grace living in me and through me.

Biblical reference: This story is an adaptation of the parable in Luke 15. The father's role in the story is critical to the outcome of the story. The story's words are taken from a modern translation of the Bible, *The Message. The Bible in Contemporary Language.*
Scripture: Luke 15:11–32
Discussion possibilities:

1. How close to reality is the dad's experience with Aaron, the prodigal son?
2. What is the possibility that a parent could or would share his agony with a church group?
   Why? Or why not?
3. Why is it so difficult for Dad to change his behavior?
4. How can we minister to parents who are in pain because of their children's lives?
5. What does it mean to "come home"?
6. Why does it take so long for people to believe we have changed our behavior?

The Angry Brother

Voice of the Prodigal's Brother

I'm the *other* son—the one my little brother tried to upstage with the money scam he pulled on our father and me. Aaron, now my *big* baby brother, never liked me, and the feeling was mutual. I'm only about three years older than he is, but that difference was huge in his mind, and maybe in mine, too. We lived with our dad, a very successful man who had pastures with sheep and goats and the fields of hay and grain that were necessary to feed our large herds of animals. There were so many animals on our acreage that dad had hired servants to help do much of the work. I always thought my dad was a wise and good man until the episode with my spoiled little brother occurred.

I guess Aaron was about nineteen (a big baby!) when it happened. He had never said anything about it to me, but I should have guessed something was going on with him. He and I rarely discussed anything, much less his plans for his future. He just spouted off, and I just pretended to listen—as most older brothers do, I suppose. It was complain, complain, complain! Here are just a few of his complaints that I heard almost every day, but it seemed that I heard them endlessly!

1. I have to work too hard.
2. I always get the toughest jobs.
3. Even tougher than the servants' jobs.
4. Dad *never* thanks me for what I do around here.
5. You get *all* the easy jobs.
6. Jacob, I am *not* going to take it much longer.

That last statement was a clue I didn't catch and hadn't really heard: "Jacob, I'm not going to take it much longer." You know how it is. After a while, I just stopped listening to Aarie's griping and bellyaching. The servants had heard the same words, but they didn't tell me that he ever talked to them. I guess they didn't much care for him either. I know that he didn't treat them very well. There were times when I overheard them complaining that he treated them as though they were dirt, and that he expected them to pick up after him as though they were his slaves. I never put myself out for the servants, but I would never have made my thinking and feelings public, certainly not to them or to our father or to little Aarie, either. (I enjoy calling him Aarie. It really gets to him and makes him simmer, and reminds him, I hope, that he is not number one around here.)

One morning I overheard my little brother talking to our father about getting his share of Dad's fortune. He didn't want to wait until Father died to get his portion of the estate: he wanted it *now*. I guess he didn't know that was not the way things worked. When it comes time for the heirs to take over an estate, the heirs receive their portions but not until the father dies. Since I was the older, I would get two-thirds of the estate,[12] and little brother, Aarie, would get the one-third that was due to him. It was as if my brother couldn't wait for Dad to die. I was furious at Aarie and even more so at Dad. How dare they make this deal without consulting me? I felt as though I was treated as one of the servants!

I stewed over this for months, reminding myself of all the good things I had done and that I did not deserve this slight and neglect. Certainly not from this kid, this punk brother of mine.

I'm quite sure that Dad broke with tradition and the law and offered the kid one-half of the estate now. I'm sure Dad felt as though he was getting slapped in the face, and by his own son.

Aarie kept his word. As soon as he took "our" money, he left Dad, the farm, and me and headed off to some other place where he could "find out who he was!" Maybe it was worth all this mess just to be done with him. Hurray, he's gone! He's gone!

I hoped that I'd never see that kid's ugly face as long as I lived. It was all I could do to look Dad in the face after he had betrayed me with his deal with the little brat. That kid was always able to get whatever he wanted. He was popular with other kids his age and could talk Dad into giving him transportation to go wherever he wanted to go with his friends. Somehow, I managed in spite of the wrong they had done to me. I was *angry* and I didn't care who knew it.

Good riddance! He left without tears or good-byes from me or the servants. Although, I think Dad took Aarie's departure pretty hard. I didn't see Dad around for a few days, and when he did show his face, he looked very haggard and had aged considerably.

He began to go out to the road every day and stare, apparently watching and waiting to see if his prodigal son would return. You can be sure that *I* didn't look down that road! But my life was much quieter and more relaxed, with no arguments, no tension, and no worries about what might happen next with that kid. I've never been so happy to have someone gone. He's *gone!* Now I can give my orders to the servants without being second-guessed by a know-it-all little brother!

However, what happened five years after my brother had left home was even worse than the fast financial swindle that he pulled, if anything could be worse than having your own brother pull a fast one on you. It seemed to me that five years was a long time to try and "find out who he was." Then one day while I was out in the fields, I heard music—party music that was happy, not sad—I couldn't imagine what was happening. The music was loud, and it was not the kind of music that Dad preferred. I realized that I had better get myself in there to make sure Dad was okay. As I walked closer to the house, I met one of the servants, who filled me in on what had happened.

Dad, as was his usual daily custom, had been watching the road that the kid had used when he left home. On this particular day, the servant was sure Dad had seen Aaron when the kid was still a long way off. It wasn't enough that he was waiting for the kid to show up, he actually *ran* down the road to meet the crazy kid. Worse yet … he hugged and kissed him. Ugh, I don't know how he could stand it. It was as though he had never left—all was forgiven.

Can you believe it, forgiven and welcomed back even with love, *love*? Dad must have flipped out and forgotten all that the fast talker had done to both of us. Dad called one of the servants when the two of them finally got to the house, and told the servant to go in and get one of the finest robes, put it on the kid (I hope they gave him a good bath first!), get out one of the precious rings for Aaron's finger, kill the calf that was in the fattening stall, and make a great celebration for everyone.

I wanted to throw up! I vowed I was not going to that party no way, no how. How could Dad *do* this to me? To expect me to accept my clever, sly brother back as though he had never done anything wrong. I think not! I told Dad that, too. "Go ahead and party. That's all your son has been doing for as long as he has been gone, and you expect me to be happy to see him. I'd rather die than admit that I'm glad to see him, because *I … am … not …*

happy ... I'm *angry.* He was a self-possessed, self-absorbed boy when he left, and I'm sure that the only reason he is home now is because he ran out of money—some of it was my money—and has come to the end of his rope." (I can't believe that the rope didn't hang him!)

I couldn't believe what Dad said when I exploded and told him that this flagrant boy had probably wasted Dad's fortune, and spent all that money foolishly and sinfully on some of the worst people on earth. The worst I saved for last: He left us in the lurch with this huge farm. We are a family business and he walked out on both of us and the farm, causing us both to work our butts off. I reminded Dad that on the other hand, "I spent all my years doing what I was supposed to do, never neglected any of your orders, but have never been given even one calf so I could have a party with my friends. But just as soon as this wastrel shows up, you turn everything inside out and upside down to make him welcome. I just don't understand what all this means, and how you could *do* this to me. I just don't get it!"

Dad's response didn't help make matters any better. He told me "Son, you don't understand. You're with me all the time, and everything that is mine is yours—but this is a wonderful time, and we had to celebrate. This brother of yours was dead, and he's alive! He was lost, and he's found. Not only lost as a sheep might be lost, but he lost *himself.*"

That was supposed to make me happy? Are you kidding? I am supposed to be happy that this ... wasteful ... immoral ... and degenerate man lost himself and then decided to come home?

I don't think I can ever forgive Aarie for doing what he did. He'll have to work very hard to prove himself to me, even if all it took for Dad to forgive him was to hear him say, "Father, I have sinned, and am not worthy to be your son ..."

I told Dad that his son can't just waltz back in here pretending to be sorry. "Sorry" just doesn't cut it with me. Anyone can say, "I'm sorry," and even toss in some tears to make it sound and look real. As far as I'm concerned, such a person can go to—well, you know where—and I'll never cry.

Right now, I'm not sure if I can *ever* forgive either one of them for the dirt they piled on me. After all, a person can only take so much! The ball is in their court now. Let them sweat it out. It wouldn't surprise me if in a couple of years, he'll decide to travel again. He'll approach Dad and want some more of our inheritance money. Dad has worked hard to rebuild his fortune, and that caused both Dad and me to sweat and work extra hard. I'll keep my eye on him—he can't make a move without me checking him out, and he better not louse up again, or he has had it with me *forever*. And for sure, don't bother talking to me about Jehovah, forgiveness, and the grace and mercy of Jehovah. I don't believe in all that stuff—not after this mess.

Biblical background: This story is based on the story of the Prodigal Son in Luke 15, one of the three stories that Jesus told about the joy of finding a lost article, a lost sheep, and a parent's joy of having a lost child find his way home.
Scripture: Luke 15:11–30
Discussion possibilities:

1. How was the older brother *also* a "prodigal son"?
2. What would be your ideal ending for the older brother's story?
3. Are there Christians today similar to the older brother? How should *we* deal with them?
4. How and why do some Christians and others hold the past over the head of their prodigal son or daughter?

Hijacked on the Road to Jericho

Voice of the Good Samaritan's Patient

I *know* this road is extremely dangerous. I've heard all kinds of stories about people who have been robbed and hurt, and some who have been killed going from Jerusalem down to Jericho. It's a very desolate road, only about seventeen miles from Jerusalem, but each mile can be treacherous. The road is physically challenging—it is very steep and difficult for travel. Even though it is not far to Jericho but in just those few short miles the road precipitously plunges about thirty-five hundred feet to the valley below Jerusalem.

I had been in Jerusalem on business and was now on my way back home to the lush hills of Judea, anxious to get home to my family and friends. I had done quite well up in Jerusalem, and was bringing back some trinkets for my children. They get so excited when I walk in the house after being gone for a while because they know that their dad has been to Jerusalem and has brought a toy or two for them. My National Rent-a-Donkey was in the "preferred aisle" and was a better model than the one I had rented to go up *to* Jerusalem—the saddle on this one was highly polished leather, and the saddlebags were large enough to carry everything that I was bringing home. The rental agent gave me the best beast with the very *latest* equipment available.

Since there was a well-worn donkey track down the hill to Jericho, I gave the donkey free rein and let it pick its way around the rocks and other obstacles in the track. The donkey was almost self-driving, requiring very little help from me. Relaxed, I let my mind wander, thinking back to the good deals I had made up in Jerusalem. If all goes as planned, this next year should really be a profitable one as far as my business is concerned. There is so much good news to tell my wife when I get home that I know she will be thinking and planning the next improvements on our little home. Maybe I'll be lucky and they will only be new curtains.

Suddenly, I was jolted awake with shouts and commands: "Get down and give us everything you have with you." I don't know where they came from, but there they were holding sticks and big rocks, with very evil looks on their faces. I tried to talk myself out of what I knew was going to happen. I had heard all the stories, and I just wanted to get out of this situation alive so I could get home and be with my family. The bandits pulled me off my rented donkey and as I protested, they began to beat me unmercifully. I told them, "Just take it—the donkey, my goods, and anything else that you want." One of thieves hit me so hard that my last thought was, *This is it.* I must have rolled over and looked as though I were dead, and the beating mercifully stopped.

I don't know how long it was before I felt or heard footsteps coming toward me. I laid there very quietly, trying not to move thinking that the robbers may have come back to see what they might have missed. But I kept one eye slightly open and saw a rather well-dressed man coming toward me. He was wearing a long and expensive priestly-looking robe with the required scarlet, purple, and blue yarns woven into it.[13] Silently, I prayed to God, thanking him for my deliverance. I don't know how long it had been since the brigands had stripped me of my clothing and all my luggage, but I hope you can feel the joy *I* felt knowing that a religious person, a man devoted to God and to serving God's people, was here to rescue me. Then just as quickly as I heard the footsteps approaching me, they began to go away. I couldn't even stand up and scream, "I'm *here*, I'm *here*, please don't leave without me." But I was too sore, achy, and bleeding that I dared not even move my hand to wave. All I heard from him was, "Tsk, tsk, why doesn't someone do something about the crime on this road?"

I think the shock of seeing this religious man moving away from me was almost as great as the shock I felt when the thieves surrounded me. Hopelessness consumed me. Now I knew for sure that I was a dead man. I began to blame myself for being so foolish as to think that I could make this trip by myself. Why didn't I wait for others who would be going this same way to their homes north of Jerusalem? Everyone knows that there is safety in numbers. Why did I let my enthusiasm to get home run away with my rationality?

While I was mentally rolling around in self-pity and blame, I thought and felt I heard more footsteps. Could this be possible? I assumed that more thieves were coming to finish me off. But I had nothing left to give them. *Nothing*! The footsteps seemed to slow down as they came closer to me. I was so weak that I couldn't even tremble. But Jehovah be praised! It was another religious person. From what I could see, it was a Levite, a man dedicated to being a legal expert. I hoped that he would be more caring than the priest. He would know that the law *required* him to help me or anyone else when that person was in need. Even though I was in pain, inwardly I chuckled thinking if anyone was in need, I was. It would be impossible for him not to see my need. Out of the corner of my swollen eye, I caught him glancing down at me, and then moving away from me and continuing his journey down the steep road toward Jericho. I think I heard another, "Tsk, tsk!"

This can't be happening to me, I silently screamed. *Why, why*

*did these men who had committed themselves to God simply walk
around me and leave me here? Did they think I was just a decoy for
more thieves? Or were they just too rushed to take the time to fulfill
their religious responsibilities?* Did they calculate the time it might
take to deal with me and figured they didn't have that kind of
time? Or did they assume that I would soon be dead, and they
would have wasted whatever time they had spent on my needs?
Maybe they didn't want to tell whoever was waiting for them at
home that they had stopped on this dangerous road to minister
to a broken person. It must have been easier to walk by me than
to figure out in their heads a good enough story. Whoever was
waiting for them at home would understand the dangers of this
road and could be very critical of them for taking this way to
Jericho. After all, there were three ways to get to Jericho from
Jerusalem. This was just the most direct one. But now I'm out of
luck. What are the chances that another religious person will pass
this way? My guess is—none! So far, the odds certainly haven't
been stacked in my favor. If I can't count on leaders in the temple,
a religious person, or a legal expert, who can I count on? In my
confused mental state, I searched my memory to try and think
if I had ever reacted poorly to a needy person in the same way I
had just been treated.

I wish there was some way to let my family know what has
happened. If even one of the two who just passed by had stopped
and asked if there was anything he could do, I would have asked
him to notify my family when he arrived down in Jericho. Now
I am resigned to just being a statistic—another missing person in
the "lost but *not* found" files.

I felt myself getting weaker and weaker so that I could barely
keep my eyes even partially open. But my ears must be working.
I think I hear someone else approaching or maybe it's a donkey.
Yes! It is a donkey. I just heard a "hee-haw" close by. I don't think

it's another band of robbers since I don't hear people talking. Wait! A person just said, "Whoa, boy." He is stopping and walking toward me. I must let him know that I am alive even though I may look dead.

He has knelt down beside me and is looking at me so closely that I can see his face even through my blurred vision and he is asking me something. From his speech, I can guess that he is not from Judea, but possibly from Samaria. If he is a Samaritan, I know I am supposed to hate him. But please, Jehovah God, don't let my national racism and my own or his prejudice stop him from helping me.

Oh, *no*! Please God, *no*! He's walking away. He must hate me in the same way that my people hate them, the Samaritans. But wait a minute. He's walking back toward me, and holding my head up a little so that I can drink a swallow or two of wine. Now he's opening an oil skin of olive oil and gently pouring it and some wine on my cuts and bruises. I wish I could tell him how wonderful it feels to have someone who cares close by me and helping. He is asking me something about my ability to move and to walk. As best as I can, I shake my head and try to say no. Oh, he's walking away again, and if I could, I would cry, "Please stay. Don't leave me alone to die in this God-forsaken place."

All he was doing was bringing his donkey closer to me. He stooped down and gently put his arms under me and lifted me to put me on his donkey. The pain was excruciating, but my joy was greater than the pain. I was rescued, and if I lived, I would soon be going home. I don't know how long I sat on that donkey's back, but it really didn't matter. Someone cared, and I might live and be okay.

This may be difficult for others to believe, but on this entire road from Jerusalem to Jericho there is only one building, and it is a traveler's inn. I can't imagine that it will be here very long

VOICES from THE WORD

since from my personal experience most of the travelers seem to be thieves and robbers, along with a few non-caring religious people. At any rate, this good man pulled up to the inn, carried me in to the innkeeper, and asked him to put me up for the night. My savior stayed long enough to bandage up my broken body, and then *he* stayed for the night. The next morning, he asked the innkeeper to feed me and to care for my wounds. He gave the innkeeper some money, actually two day's wages, and told him that he would pay any other charges when he returned. I didn't sleep too well that night because I couldn't stop thanking God for my newfound neighbor, my Samaritan rescuer, for his kindness to me. This is probably beside the point, but I also can't stop thanking God for that man at the rental counter who encouraged me to take out a "full coverage" insurance policy on the donkey.

I may be only one voice in all of Judea, but I will never, ever speak badly of a Samaritan again. If anyone were to ask me which one of the three men that I met on the road to Jericho was a neighbor to me, that would be one of the easiest questions I could ever answer. My Judean neighbors will probably be shocked at my answer, but when they hear my story, I think they will be convinced. I only wish that all my neighbors were as kind as the Samaritan was.

It's easy to say what someone should do about a person in an unfortunate condition. It's quite different not only to talk about the situation, but the test of friendship and neighborliness is found not in the talking, but in the helpful, loving action of a true neighbor.

What I will never figure out and understand is: why was the Samaritan on that disastrous road? What caused him to take the most dangerous road to Jericho when there were two other roads to get there? I started to wonder if God is that concerned about just one insignificant person: me—that he would send a Samaritan man, a hated enemy, to rescue and save me.

Do I *really* know who God is?

Biblical background: This story is based on the biblical account (a parable) in Luke 10 that the caring actions of the Samaritan will be evident in the lives of all the readers of this story.

Scripture: Luke 10:25–37

Discussion possibilities:

1. What is your personal experience with a "good Samaritan"?
2. What motivated the Samaritan to minister to the traveler?
3. What was the danger to Jesus for telling this story to the legal expert and to the crowd?
4. How does racism and prejudice affect our neighborliness and care-giving?
5. In what other ways can we express our Christian compassion to hurting people?

My Two Sisters

The Voice of Lazarus

It's the same old story day after day. When you're a guy living with two sisters, there is always something you wish would start, or stop, or just go away. But it doesn't! If anything, it just seems to go on and on and on. And I am usually right in the middle of it all. Some of you know exactly what I'm talking about, don't you?

I don't know when I first realized that life was going to be like this: being in the middle of family squabbles. But I think I was able to keep it quiet so the neighbors never tumbled to the real situation. I didn't want *everyone* to know that we couldn't get along. I guess I assumed that most families lived through this kind of problem between siblings and managed to keep it quiet. So I think I have managed it quite well.

But now there was a problem—a *big* problem. You see we had a visitor, a fairly regular visitor who usually brought with him a few other fellows. We just called the visitor Rabbi or Master, and the other fellows were rarely the same ones. Sometimes it was Peter, James, and John. Other times it was Phillip, Andrew, and Nathaniel.

Of course, that meant cleaning the house, sometimes even *after* they arrived. Then there was cooking and baking to be done, too. When it came to house chores, my one sister, Martha, was a possessed woman. She usually said something like this, "Everything has to be perfect, and I mean, perfect and flawless, or impeccable, if you prefer that word. I don't want my reputation in the neighborhood lowered. Everyone knows how well we keep this house, how perfect the table looks when it is set, and how the food we prepare is always considered indescribably delicious."

Does that give you a sense of what Martha was like? Fussy and fuming and even worse, a worrier. It isn't easy living with such a perfectionist. But some of you know all about that, I'm sure.

Now it's Mary's time to get in the spotlight. She is the younger of my two sisters. She is so much easier to live with than Martha is. But there are issues here too. While Martha is compulsively cleaning, cooking, or baking, Mary can be seen in the backyard strolling around the garden talking to her flowers, or selecting some veggies for a salad. It seems to me sometimes that she purposely chooses to stroll around her garden about the same time that Martha gets out the dust cloth, broom, or wash-bucket. Of course, I have never made that observation verbally, within the hearing of either of them. At least I hope I haven't.

I have tried to analyze the two of them and figure out why they are so different. I have concluded that their sense of who they are is different. Martha is an A-leph (Alpha) kind of person while Mary is a Beth (Beta) kind of person. Sisters, but of two different natures or persons. Martha sometimes seems obsessed with her tasks, while Mary is much more relaxed about hers. I usually know where Martha is coming from, but Mary is more private, and doesn't often give signals about her intentions or her feelings.

I startled them both the morning that Jesus turned up. "Mary, Martha, Jesus will be here in an hour or so. Are we going to be ready for them?"

"You gotta be kidding," Martha replied. "There is no way that I can get everything done that needs to be done in that short time.

Maybe if Mary would stop gossiping with the neighbors and help in the kitchen, I could *almost* get everything done."

Playing my usual role as peacemaker, I went out to the garden and interrupted a conversation to warn Mary that all was not going well in the house, and that she was needed in the kitchen. "Oh, all right. Tell Martha I'll be right there as soon as I hear the rest of Miriam's story."

Martha gave me her exasperated look, "I don't know how I put up with her as well as I do. She can be so provoking sometimes, it's a wonder I don't blow my top!" I thought to myself, *Sure, and you would* never *do that,* would *you? Ha!*

In his good time, Jesus and some of his followers arrived, tired and thirsty. I had no sooner given them some water to drink, washed their feet, and put out some cushions to sit on, when Mary left the kitchen and sat down with us and started asking Jesus questions. "Are you sure, Jesus, that you are going to be all right in Jerusalem when the temple authorities see you? We have heard rumors here in Bethany that they want to arrest you, and try to stop all your sermons about the kingdom of God and what it could mean to us on earth as well as in heaven."

I have to say this about Jesus. He is so *patient* with us. He doesn't get upset when we quiz him about something he has already told us. It seems as though he wants to repeat over and over again his message of what the kingdom of God is, and what we must do to be a part of that kingdom. A couple of years ago on a mountainside, he first told us what being a part of that kingdom would be: "We'll be humble, we will show mercy to others, we will have pure hearts, we will be peacemakers, and we will be hungry and thirsty for righteousness. When you become that," Jesus said, "you will be happy and blessed, you will receive mercy, you will see God, you will be called God's children." I hear him say that as I go to sleep at night. Just imagine, we are to be called God's children! God is not a far, distant being, but is as close to us as we are to a father.

There we were, listening to Jesus reminding us of our status as God's children, when Martha marches into the room, and right up to Jesus and lets go with her common complaint, "Master, don't you care that my sister has abandoned the kitchen to me? Tell her to lend me a hand" (Luke 10:40). Talk about putting a damper on a good conversation—that did it. I was embarrassed and so was Mary. I was ready to tell Martha something rude when Jesus saved me from myself. He kindly said, "Martha, dear Martha, you're fussing far too much and getting yourself worked up over nothing One thing only is essential, and Mary has chosen it—it's the main course, and won't be taken from her" (Luke 10:41–42).

That more or less put Martha in her place, but Jesus said it kindly, and Martha didn't seem to take offense at his words. I wish I could say things like that to other people so they wouldn't get mad at me. Jesus meant that making a meal was a good thing, but being attentive to the word of the Master was the best thing that anyone could do. It took a while for us to get beyond the embarrassment of the moment.

You know how it is—we sat there without saying a word until Jesus broke the silence with, "What were we talking about?" He accepted the gifts of hospitality and generosity so easily. I wish that I could do that without being embarrassed and feeling the need somehow just to give back or make light of the moment. I need to learn how to accept the graciousness of the person offering the gift without sensing that I must return in kind something of value to me.

Little did we know then that this may have been the last time Jesus would be in our home. I still wonder what we would have done differently if only we had known that in just a few months he would be crucified. I think that even Martha would have sat at the feet of Jesus as he quieted all her fussiness and obsessive-compulsive needs and just *listened* to our Master.

After Jesus and his followers left the next day, I couldn't help but think about what had happened the day before. I realized then, if I never had realized it before, that we rarely appreciate a gift when Jehovah sends us a gift. Sadly, it is often after the event has happened that we come to our senses about the good gifts of God to us and for us. I tried to explain this to Mary and Martha. I think that Mary "got it," but I'm not sure that Martha did, but I think and hope she did. Both of my sisters had good gifts that Jesus appreciated, and I also appreciated them. But I had to learn to express more appreciation to them than I have in the past. The three of us learned how to flex our own behavior to complement the ways and customs of other people, even of the people to whom we are not close, or even count as friends. Together as a family, we realized we needed to figure out our priorities. So, together we sat down and we did that just as soon as Jesus left us that day.

Biblical background: This story is based on the visit of Jesus to the home of Lazarus, Mary, and Martha as found in Luke 10. There is more about Lazarus and his resurrection in John 11.
Scripture: Luke 10:38–42
Discussion possibilities:

1. Do the relationships in this family sound unique to you? How and Why?
2. Discuss Lazarus's way of handling the conflict between Martha and Mary.
3. When is it time to be busy, and when it is time to relax and take it easy?

From Fisherman to Missionary

Voice of Disciple Andrew

I've had my life turned upside down more than once. You've probably had similar experiences. Not just your life, but your entire world—upside down. If I had known then what I know now, I don't know whether I would have gone the way the arrows pointed. But I didn't have a clue what the future could *possibly* hold in store for me. And now, I can't believe what it actually *did* hold for me.

I started out as a young man with a very successful fishing business with my brother Peter, and two good friends, James and John, who were also brothers. We lived in Bethsaida up near the Sea of Galilee and north of Jerusalem, a distance of about forty miles. I guess I should say that our business was very successful, but there were some nights when we would have dumped it in the sea, or sold the business in a flash. There were times when we just didn't *know* where the fish were holding school. We needed a magic tool that could tell us if we were over or even near a school of fish.

We heard about a new prophet who was dipping people into the Jordan River. He called it "baptism for repentance." Others who had seen and heard him told us that he didn't mince words when he spoke. He called a pig a pig and called some people in our religious circles snakes and even worse. Anyway, John and I decided to go have a look for ourselves. Peter, my brother, said that he and James could handle the business while we were gone. He told me, "Andrew, take care that you don't get involved too much. Our people have been fooled so much in the past by prophets who were just out to make a few shekels from easily fooled people. You know how sympathetic you can be when you hear a good line from a fast talker who is really just after your money. So, please be *very* careful."

So John, one of my fishing partners, and I took off for the Jordan River down near Bethany. We heard John the Baptizer preach and saw him baptize people in the dirty Jordan River. Some of the leaders in Jerusalem sent a few priests and Levites to question John the Baptist to find out who he *really* was. Some people thought he might be Elijah or the promised Messiah. He quickly set them straight on that but said that one would soon be here and was, in fact, standing here among us now but we couldn't recognize him.

I think John and I were ready to accept the baptizer's message. It didn't seem possible that right then and right there the Messiah would be present. But the very next day, John the Baptizer called out, "Here he is, God's Passover Lamb! He forgives the sins of the world!" (John 1:29–34). John and I looked at each other in disbelief. Could it possibly be that we were there when the Messiah, who had been promised for centuries, was made known to the world? While we were still trying to get our heads around this good news, we felt ourselves being pulled to follow this person who was called by John "the Lamb of God!" We got up and followed this Lamb of God, asking him where he was staying. We were convinced after a long talk with him that night that he was the Christ for whom we had been waiting so long.

I could not wait to get back to Bethsaida and tell Peter what had happened. I am certain that John felt the same way about getting back to James, his brother. I don't know what John told his brother, but I know that all I told Peter was, "We have found the Messiah." That's when I led him to Jesus. I suspect that John said something similar to his brother, James.

Peter and I grew up together near the Sea of Galilee, where we first learned to fish. Everyone in the neighborhood knows us as inseparable brothers. In fact, some of them assume we are twins since we share a house together. I don't know how they could think that because Peter is bigger, bolder, and more outspoken than I am. He often speaks before he thinks about what he wants to say, while I am more hesitant and deliberate about what I have to say. I love him just the way he is, and I know he always comes to me to help him get out of some of the scrapes he gets himself into—his mistakes or errors in judgment. As the kids say, we have each other's back! As fishermen, we get along swimmingly. Some of my friends figure I am jealous by letting him always take first place, but that isn't true. We worked that out as teenagers. When I need help, I know I can count on him. When he needs help straightening out his problems, he knows he can rely on me. It's funny, but when people introduce me to someone, they almost always say, "Oh, you know, this guy is Andrew, *Peter's* brother."

So, it was the most natural thing in the world that when I met Jesus, I had a strong need to get to Peter as soon as I could to tell him we had met the Messiah. Because you see, in school we learned that the Messiah was not only prophesied to come to this world, but that he was expected to come fairly soon to rescue us from the Romans. What we *didn't* know was *where* he would arrive and *what* would be his purpose. Our hope was that he would assume control of things and free us from the hated Romans.

As John and I listened to the Baptizer preach, we learned that the Messiah came to be among us as the Lamb of God. We knew almost instinctively that when the words the "Lamb of God" were mentioned in our Scriptures, a sacrifice was not too far away. I know

now that we didn't give *that* theological concept much thought. Our personal dreams for a Roman-free life seemed so real that sacrifice was not even considered in our thoughts as even a probability.

As I think back now, I realize that neither John the Baptist nor Jesus ever said anything about overpowering the Roman government and its minions. I guess it just takes a long time for something to really sink into our consciousness, especially something that was so contrary to our way of thinking. We would never have thought of the Messiah as being concerned with sacrifice and service. Here we were, two young men with ambition and strength as natural elements in our lives being faced and challenged with concepts that were strong enough to shake us, our worlds, and all of our futures. We had choices just as everyone does when confronted with dynamically powerful options. We could turn our backs on this new data (new data, that is to us, at least,) or we could run with this new information and see where it would take us. The only people around to encourage us were John the Baptizer and the newer guy on the block, this Jesus whom the Baptizer was introducing to us.

John, the fisherman, and I became good friends. He was so easy to talk with, and I guess he wanted to remember some of the events in my life that he considered significant. They didn't seem that way to me, but then, I never was one to push myself out front. I remember one time when we were all with Jesus by the Sea of Galilee just before Passover. There was a large crowd that had followed Jesus to listen to him speak and to see him heal people. It was getting to be late in the day, and Jesus asked Philip, "Where will we buy food to feed these people?" Philip, always the practical "data-guy" in our group, was quick to say, "More than a half year's salary worth of food wouldn't be enough to feed each person to have even a little bit." I don't know how he could figure that out so quickly, but he did.

Quietly, I told Jesus that there was a young boy here, a teenager, I think, whose mother had packed him a lunch of five barley loaves and two fish. I added, "But what good is that for a crowd such as this?" I had the absurd thought that, just maybe it would encourage others to share what they had brought. John who was standing by, gave me a slap on the back as he said, "Andrew, there goes your sensitivity again." Of course, I laughed as I slapped him right back with a, "Yeah, yeah, do you always listen to everything I say? What are you planning to do, write a book about me or something?" Maybe a book. But back to the hillside, Jesus took the fish and the loaves, blessed them and gave them to us to distribute. The baskets were full of bread that tasted as though it were newly baked, and the buckets were full of tender, healthy fish. Everyone had all they could eat. That day there were five thousand hungry people on that hillside—and we fed them all.

When we cleaned up the place, there were twelve baskets of food left over. Jesus realized that the people were beginning to think that this miracle-worker could be the prophet that was promised in our scriptures, so Jesus took off for some time alone on a mountain. He needed a place of refuge.

John reminded me of another event in our lives together when some Greeks sought out Jesus. This could have been a serious situation for our group to handle since we were not the most welcoming of people, especially, the pagan Greeks who had temples to more gods than you could throw a stick at even in our *own towns*. They figured that Philip, whose name was Greek, as was mine, might be of assistance in their search for a bright new star in the heavens. Then I was in the picture again. Philip came over to me and explained the situation. "These foreigners want to see our Master." If Samaritans were not acceptable to us, Greeks were even less welcome. We vehemently oppose everything Greek.

But after Philip and I talked together, I took them to Jesus. But these Greeks may have been different. After all, they *were* here for the Passover, so they may have just been curious, or they may have been proselytes to our Jewish faith. I don't know, but I don't think it really matters. Again, John took note of this.

However, to a good Israelite, foreigners are always suspect. We've been treated poorly, to say the least, by foreigners even before we were slaves in Egypt. We have tended to forget that early in our life as a separate people, God Himself, challenged us many times when He was giving us directions for living. God told us in the book of Numbers that His directions and laws are for all of us as well as for "foreigners or native born"[14] living in our midst. It would appear that God thought of us and anyone living with us as equals under the same laws that bound us to God. God, Himself, said, "You and the foreigner are the same before God" (Numbers 15:15). I feel sure that this will always be a difficult concept for us to live with, as it will be for any group of people who live with foreigners and immigrants in their midst.

As I thought about this situation later, I began to think that their reluctance to approach Jesus directly was probably more of a concern to *them* than *our* concern about taking foreigners to Jesus. After all, we were the majority group here while *they* were in the minority. I have a feeling that someday we may well be in *their* boat, the minority. I hope we will remember how that feels—being in the minority.

Philip and I stepped back as the Greeks moved toward Jesus. As we considered what had just happened, we assumed that Jesus would be encouraged by these Greeks seeking Him out when He had been rejected so many times by our own and His people and especially by our religious leaders. I'm sure that John had something to say about this also, but for the life of me, I just can't remember what he said. But knowing John as I do, I'm sure that he was kind and encouraging to both Philip and me. He's just that kind of guy!

I never did get around to asking Jesus what happened as a result of the conversation that he and the Greeks had. But I know that Jesus always had time or took the time to meet with those who sought him out. The courage that it must have taken to ask us to help them "see Jesus," could not have done anything else but open the heart of our master to their cry: "We would see Jesus." We did hear Jesus talk about the necessity of a seed dying before it would bear life. At the time, we didn't understand what that was all about. In just a few days we *learned* what he meant and were devastated when we finally figured it out.

As Philip and I talked later about this event with the other followers, especially with John and Peter, we were reminded that there were foreigners, the Magi, at the birth of our Lord, and now at the close of his ministry, foreigners are again at his side. Our questions of each other were about the future of our own ministries: Will Gentiles and foreigners be involved and included?

Biblical reference: We don't know much about Andrew, but his story may be similar to our stories. Being Peter's brother, he may have been second fiddle for most of his life.
Scripture: John 12:20–26
Discussion possibilities:

1. Talk about the "second place" position of Andrew. What does it mean to be in "second place"?
2. How does this fit into your concept of leadership?
3. What is the difference between the Jewish feelings about the "Greeks" and current attitudes about strangers and foreigners or anyone else who is different from the majority?

From Watcher to Writer

Voice of John Mark

There I was standing behind a tree trying to get some idea of what Jesus was doing and saying. When he left my mother's house with a couple of his followers, he looked solemn and more than a little distracted. Before they had even finished their Seder meal, I had decided to keep them in my sight and to attempt to understand the mystery of their behavior. I had helped serve the Seder meal to the group, and then some other ritual that I couldn't figure out.

During the meal, Judas had rushed out, looking determined to do something, but not saying a word to anyone about where he was going or what he was planning to do. Now, it was my time to try to unwrap what was behind all these strange events with these different players in what to me seemed similar to a drama. Little did I know just how dramatic it would turn out to be.

It was a strange night with strange events happening. In our culture, a servant is supposed to wash the dust off the feet of visitors. Strange event number one, *Jesus* washed the feet of his followers, and then ate the Seder meal with them. Then strange event number two happened. He took a loaf of bread and asked for a fresh tankard of wine for a curious ritual. This was a new one for me. I had never seen anyone do this strange ritual. Naturally, I wanted to find out what all of this meant. Off I went to the kitchen to ask Mother but she couldn't tell me, so I guess I had to find out for myself. I couldn't help but feel strangely attracted to this man, who seemed to be very much in charge of events. Even though he was visibly distracted, he seemed to be a different kind of leader than those we have had in our synagogues.

After I finished serving the group, I was so tired that I thought I'd just close my eyes for a couple of minutes. Before I knew it, I woke up and realized I had been asleep and didn't know they were leaving until I heard the door loudly close. I hurriedly grabbed one of my mother's hand-woven linen robes to wear while I ran after them, leaving Mother and the servants to clean the upper room and the kitchen. Mother called out, *"John Mark*, where are you going at this hour of the night?" I purposely didn't answer her. It is never good to stay and question or answer a mother when she uses both names to get your attention (both names—not good!). I didn't think she sounded anxiously concerned anyway—just a mother-kind of thing.

It was not easy to follow Jesus. He hurried along the dark streets with his followers trailing along. I had to run up some alleys so no one would see me, dressed or undressed as I was. To me, it seemed as though it must have been for him a life-or-death decision. He walked as though he was possessed with a purpose that only he knew.

The small group went east out of the city across the Valley of Kidron up to the Mount of Olives where from the top of the mount you could see the city of Jerusalem. The Mount of Olives was also known as the Garden of Gethsemane. Oh, by the way, since there was often a cool breeze up there, it was a place where people would go to get away from the scorching heat of the city. Jesus told his three followers, Peter, James, and John, to stay where they were—part way up the Mount, and to watch and pray. I couldn't get close enough to hear *why* they were to watch, or for what. Except he told them that his soul was crushed by sorrow to the point of death. He went farther up the hill and fell down. I thought maybe he had tripped and hurt himself, but he started talking with someone. That was obvious to me even though I was hiding close to him but behind a tree. I hope I never see another person in such agony—it looked as though the agony alone could kill him.

I didn't see anyone near him but I heard him say, "Father, Father!" Then something about his will and his Father's will. He asked that something would pass from him. I realized that there was so much I didn't know about him, why he was here, and saying what he was saying. I need to talk with my mother about him and see if she knows why he was distressed. I think she knows more about this than she lets on. (Just a mother's thinking. Mothers think that way. They often keep things to themselves when they don't want their kids to know something.)

At one point, he checked back with his followers and found them asleep. He did this two more times, and they were asleep each time. I guess he gave up on them, because he said, "Let's go, oh … wait … my betrayer is here."

Things started happening quickly at this point. First, there was an armed mob with swords and clubs, no less, and there was one of his followers, Judas, leading the way. It seemed strange to me that a *follower* was now the *leader*. Now I remember—he was the follower who had left the supper early. What in the world is going *on*? Then unexpectedly, Judas ran forward, gave Jesus a big hug, and planted a kiss on his cheek. This was going way beyond anything I could imagine. Something very strange was happening right before my eyes, and I couldn't figure it out, but I thought the best thing I could do was to stay hidden and watch. Besides, I was only a teenager—what could I do against what looked to me something similar to a small army?

The noise of the small army must have awakened the three

sleepyheads. Peter rushed forward, took his short sword, and cut off an ear of a servant of the high priest. Yikes, this was real drama. *It was turning into a blood and guts night!* The three followers took off running, leaving Jesus alone with the mob. There I was, however, still watching from behind the tree. It looked as though the mob might find me, so I took off too. In fact, they *did* find me. One of the soldiers grabbed me, and in struggling to get away from him, my robe was caught on a tree branch. I ran off, running even faster than before. I now had to run home naked without my mother's linen robe, but it was late, so most people would be in bed. I just hoped I could get home without anyone seeing me. I was so embarrassed, I wanted to find a shallow hole and spend the night out of sight.

How can I explain this to my mother? She will be furious and I am sure she won't understand, first, for running out without telling her, and then about the naked bit. Maybe I can just slip into the house without anyone knowing. It is almost midnight so I hope no one is still awake in the city or at home. At least, I hope that not one of my mother's friends is looking out a window to see this strange man fleeing as though from a robbery. The same for my friends as well. If they do see me, I will never live this down.

I don't think anyone saw me before I made it home, found clean clothes, and went out to see what was happening. By the way, this "following of Jesus" is not an everyday kind of easy thing to do—at least, it wasn't tonight!

Well, I lived through the experience, but Jesus did not. I am sure you know the story: The high priest's officers led him away, and he was brutally questioned in a kangaroo court. (Somehow, I'm not sure where I heard about kangaroo courts!) They condemned him to death, but they had to get the governor's approval for a death-sentence judgment. The next few days were horribly tragic and in a way even despicable, making me ashamed to be an

Israelite. Pilate gave the okay, and that same day they conspired to crucify Jesus. On Golgotha's height, they nailed him to a cruel cross and left him there to die. I had followed Jesus through the city, but I stayed on the edge of the crowd, too embarrassed to be seen. I was worried that someone who was there may have seen me the night before running through the city lanes and alleys.

I heard about most of these last events from Peter, one of the followers of Jesus. Peter confessed to me that he had denied knowing Jesus that night when a servant girl suggested that he was a follower of Jesus. Oh, did I tell you that Jesus was now *alive*? That's right, he rose from the tomb on the first day of the week, just a week from the day he had entered Jerusalem on the back of a donkey while people shouted "Alleluia" and sang psalms. A week later, they shouted, "Crucify him! Crucify him!" They even said "We'll take the blame, we and our children after us" (Matthew 27:28).

Years went by while I finished school and took my place as the eldest son in our home. A cousin, Barnabas, took me under his wing, and I began to think seriously on the teachings of Jesus and their meaning to my life. Finally, I just gave my future over to his will and his intentions for me. Peter helped me in the decisions I made—he had become like a father figure to me. In fact, he called me his son in the first book he wrote,[15] and he was like my spiritual father. While I was still quite young, in my early twenties, I traveled with Paul and my cousin Barnabas up to Asia Minor on a missionary journey. I guess I was like a "go-for" for them. However, while we were there, something came up at home, and I left Paul and my cousin and went back home to Jerusalem. That really upset Paul, who said I could never go on another missionary journey with him. My cousin defended me so well, I guess, that eventually the disagreement was ironed out.

The Roman authorities put Paul in jail in Rome because of his missionary endeavors working to convince the Romans (Gentiles) to follow Christ. By the way, those endeavors were very successful. We didn't keep figures, but Paul and the other followers of Jesus had huge crowds when they preached in some places, and many churches were established wherever they went.

I went to Rome to be with Paul during his first imprisonment. I also spent time with Peter and then with Timothy. Later, Paul was again in prison and wrote to Timothy, asking the younger pastor to come to Rome and to bring me with him. As Paul wrote, "bring Mark with you because he, Mark, is useful in my ministry."[16]

I consider myself very fortunate. I was able to see and hear Jesus during his human lifetime. I saw the birth and growth of the Christian church and personally knew most of the greatest of the early Christians. They told me many of the events of the Messiah's life, but I was *personally* familiar with the last days of his life.

I hope that those who read the book I wrote come to know Jesus, too. I also pray and wish for the readers that each one will find ways to serve the risen Christ, not necessarily in Asia Minor or in Rome, but in their own communities. Following Jesus is difficult sometimes, but the rewards are fantastic. Follow him, but don't lose your hand-woven linen robe or nightshirt. However, if you do, don't run naked through the streets at midnight! Find someplace to hide!

Biblical background: This is an adaptation of the biblical account in Mark's gospel of the last days in the life of Jesus before the resurrection. The author of this story injects some additional words that fit in with the story and with Mark's young life.

Scripture: Mark 14:43–52

Discussion possibilities:

Try to picture the events though Mark's eyes, and talk about what it means to "*follow Jesus.*"

It's Tough Being a Servant

Voice of Miriam

(A dialogue between Miriam and Peter begins on page 260.)

This place was a madhouse that night. The later it became, the crazier it seemed to get. The confusion just kept building and building until I thought I just might go crazy myself. People were running around, yelling at each other, ordering me around, and standing in corners of the rooms in small groups whispering to each other. I was sure they were conspiring to do something evil. The whole day was the kind of day that would make a person want to change jobs. After all, I was just a servant girl from Galilee working in the house of the high priest, Annas, and his son-in-law, Caiaphas. Everyone knew these two men were appointees of the Roman officials. Oh, and by the way, those two had been in the high priest function longer than any other family had been. Anyone that had those kinds of connections with the Romans, and was, in fact, appointed by the Romans, received much of the same disdain and hatred that we had for the Roman authorities.

One of my issues with them had to do with my name. Sometimes the priests and their political appointees called me by my name, Miriam, but usually it was, "Hey you." If I didn't respond immediately to whatever name they called me, they just yelled, "Hey you," louder. However, they made sure to let me know that I was in fact a no-name nobody.

It was Passover time, and during the preparations for the Seder feast, a strange man came to the door demanding to see Caiaphas. I didn't know whether to let him enter or not. He seemed more than just a little strange, as if he didn't quite know what he was doing or why he was even there. I thought he even looked a little dangerous. Even so, I let him in and he and the priests talked for just a little while and then he left. In one way, he seemed to be quite happy, but in another way, he seemed like he was being torn apart inside. I could only see one difference in him when he left. He was carrying a small bag that jingled. He didn't have that bag when he had come into the house. Maybe it was money. Money never seemed to be in short supply around here, especially for one of the pet projects of the priests. That is, until I needed some of it for shopping. Over time, I had learned about their money sources. They had locked up the rights to run the sales booths in the temple. They had the approval of the Roman officials for the franchises used for changing money into the appropriate currency with the usual interest rates, and for selling doves for the sacrifices. These franchises brought in a lot of "pocket change" for them.

However, later that night that same strange man was back again, but this time he seemed more crazed than he had been earlier in the day. After more secretive conversations, he and a large group of men left together. It was late—actually, it had been dark for several hours. It was obvious to me that something suspicious was going on. I was sure Judas, the man who'd been here earlier, seemed even more upset then before. He was so upset that the priest had to speak harshly with him to get him moving. I was glad to see them leave so I could breathe again, but I was uneasy because I was sure that tonight they were not up to any good! I couldn't help it—something was wrong about whatever they were planning. But much that this group was involved in often made me uneasy.

Finally, there was some peace and quiet around here. I expected them to be gone for several hours. I was just hoping that whatever they had been planning was over, and that life around here would return to normal, whatever normal *could be* in the home of this high priest.

When they returned, some of them came into the house laughing and saying, "Well, that's done. We got him, and now it's up to Pilate." I didn't know what they meant by "that's done," but I was certain by this time that I knew who the "him" was. That man was in danger, and I hoped he would get away from them. My grandmother used to talk about feeling things in her bones. That night, I could feel in my bones the evil in the house. These religious people were often filled with hate, and more concerned about their unbearable rules that demanded more of others but demanded very little of themselves. Their hypocrisy was obvious every day to anyone who had to deal with them. They talked about their sacred rituals and proper ceremonies, but they did not practice what they preached. These priests seemed to have *no* mercy, *no* grace, and showed *very little* forgiveness for anyone. Their concerns were more often than not focused on punishing those who had broken the endless laws rather than finding ways to forgive such people.

When Annas, the high priest, came into the house with the group, he seemed to be in a very positive mood, but when I heard what he said, I could not believe my ears. This was unbelievable. It was the worst thing that could possibly happen. This proved to me just how evil someone could be to think and plan such a thing. Now, I was totally convinced that people have the capacity to be worse than evil. Then I saw them drag Jesus into the house as though he were a common criminal. As I listened to them talk,

I picked up on what had happened while they were gone. Judas, the crazed visitor, had led them to the Mount of Olives up to the Garden of Gethsemane, where he identified Jesus, his leader, to the high priests and the soldiers who were with them. Judas had told them that they would know which one was Jesus because he would kiss the wanted person.

By the time the priests and the soldiers had gotten back to the house, the Sanhedrin, made up of seventy men who served as a court, were ready to investigate and interrogate Jesus. It was almost daybreak when the priest called the court into session. These men were often called together to pass judgment on the rest of us for our unfortunate failures to keep all the laws of our people. When they weren't finding fault with some of us, they did a lot of fighting among themselves. However, on that particular night there was no fighting among themselves. Jesus was the focus of all their anger, which they seemed to delight in directing at him. Our history has had many men just like these Jewish authorities, men of whom we are rightly ashamed. They asked Jesus many questions about who he thought he was, and by whose power he did his miracles.

By this time, the house was full of people since the word had spread around quickly that something big was going on. In spite of the large crowd, when the priest asked witnesses to come forward and testify against Jesus, the crowd was silent. At least, no one stepped forward. No one said a word. Nothing! Finally, two men came forward and testified that Jesus had said, "I am able to destroy the temple of God and rebuild it in three days." I thought the court would have apoplexy. It was no longer quiet. The noise became unbearable. For the second time that day, people were yelling and screaming at each other and this time as well, at Jesus.

I remember Jesus saying something like that earlier in the week at the temple when I had gone to market to shop for the

Passover food. On the way back from market that day, I had stopped by the temple. Jesus was there, so I hung around for a few minutes. I didn't dare stay very long even though I wanted to stay and listen some more. He seemed so sincere and caring. He wasn't bragging when he said that about destroying the temple and rebuilding it in three days, but it seemed like he wanted us to know that he lived in the power of Jehovah. I knew that if I were there very long, a priest would be asking me, "Where have you been?" I'd be in big trouble with him.

You see, I had been listening in on some of their conversations about Jesus as I served their meals, and I had the impression that there was trouble between Jesus and these temple authorities. I can tell you this: if I hadn't needed this job, I would immediately have joined the group that followed Jesus. On that day in the temple, I saw a loving spirit unlike anything that I had ever experienced around here from a house full of religious people. These priests and their cohorts were hung up on their own words and their laws, but they just laughed at the loving actions of the rest of us. They seemed to know all the right religious words, but their actions were anything but religious. I couldn't help wondering if something happens to people when they get power over other people, or *think* they have that power. What happens to their humanity?

That day when I was coming back from the market, as I said, I walked by the temple and I saw Dorcas, a poor widow. She climbed the steps and threw two small copper coins into the temple treasury. As I watched, I heard Jesus remark about her two coins being of more value than those of the rich people who were very openly putting in their money. I think they wanted to make sure that others saw the larger amounts they were putting into the treasury. At the time, I didn't know what Jesus meant by that remark about the value of those two coins. That's where I heard Jesus say about being able to rebuild the temple in just three days. I must've looked surprised, and even though I didn't say anything, I had the feeling that Jesus knew what I was thinking. He turned toward me and smiled. He even held out his hand to me and touched my shoulder. I knew then that he was a very special person, a person who really knew Jehovah in a way that I didn't know him. I thought at the time that it was strange that I felt like that, but I did. I envied those who were around him,

That's when I saw Peter for the first time. Right away, I knew that Peter was devoted to his leader, Jesus. I took one look at Peter and thought that if any man would be my hero, it would be a man like Peter. He was handsome, rugged, and I thought he was probably one of the leaders of the group of people around Jesus. "That's the kind of man I want for a husband," I fantasized.

I'm sorry. I think I was distracted from my story by talking about Peter. Back to that night and the mock trial of Jesus. I didn't like the way they were treating this good person who seemed as if he could see right through all of us, and that he understood where all of this was going. Then my hero entered the house. I was positive that Peter would say something in defense of Jesus. Peter seemed like a forceful man who didn't take much nonsense from anyone. I asked him if he were one of the disciples, hoping that my question would make it easier for him to say, yes.

Now, I had heard about Peter from some of my family up in Galilee. People up there knew Peter as a businessman, with a good fishing business, but who gave up much of his fishing time to be with Jesus and the other followers of this popular rabbi. If anyone would speak up for Jesus, I figured that Peter would. However, he said, "I am *not* one of his disciples." In fact, at least three times during that night he denied even having *known* Jesus. How could he say that? I have so often been disappointed in men, but I thought Peter would be different. But he wasn't. I decided right then, that even if he were not married and asked me to marry him, I would never marry such a coward.

This was starting to take on some heavy overtones. What was going on? What could be so critical about this sort of trial? That's when it hit me; they were planning somehow to stop Jesus from teaching about a spiritual kingdom of God. They wanted him out of their hair and out of their sight. I think they were afraid that he might uncover their money-grubbing activities and their political alliances with Rome. We common people might revolt against them if we found out all about Annas the high priest and Caiaphas, his son-in-law, and their cohorts, the Sanhedrin. From what I had heard, Jesus had already had a ruckus during the week with the money-changers in the temple. He had tipped over their tables and opened the cages to release all the sacrificial doves.

I was right there, so I could see and hear everything that was going on, and it was so easy to see the differences between Jesus and the Sanhedrin. This unofficial court that night seemed intent on pinning something on Jesus so they could charge him with criminal activities to make sure he would suffer, maybe even die. Their hatred of him was so obvious. That hatred was certainly in sharp contrast to his quiet, peaceful responses to their questions, and he was anything but defensive. I had the feeling, in fact, that he had the whole world in his hands. After all, I had felt his hand on my shoulder, and it had soothed my spirit. I'm sure that anyone who was heavily troubled, burdened, and weighed down with care would find rest and peace if they came to know him.

In synagogue services, we had learned just a little bit about the coming Messiah. As I remember, it was Isaiah who wrote about someone who would appear in the future and would be badly treated, but would not open his mouth in his own defense. Isaiah had written, "Like a lamb taken to be slaughtered and like a sheep being sheared, he took it all in silence" (Isaiah 53:7–9). Could this

Jesus be that person? He certainly caused an uproar in this house that night. When Jesus said, "From here on, the Son of Man takes his place at God's right hand, the place of power" (Luke 22:69), the high priest Annas, went crazy. He tore at his clothes, and the trouble really began. The worst thing they could say about anyone was that the person had blasphemed God. Blasphemy was judged in our system to be worthy of death. I didn't think that what Jesus had said was blasphemy, I felt sure that he really was the Messiah. But would anyone listen to me? No! They would not, and they *did* not.

They slapped him, laughed at him, spit on him, beat him, condemned him to death, and finally decided to send him to Pilate for the legal charges. They planned to ask Pilate to crucify him. You see, they themselves could not carry out a death sentence. I hoped that Pilate would have more sense than these crooked men had. Talk about justice! In the future, I hope someone writes about these events to clarify just how unjust, immoral, and probably illegal this court and trial had been.

I decided on the spot that I had to get away from Jerusalem, from this house, and from these people. I had had it up to my eyeballs when what I had needed was for someone to tell me more about Jesus, and his love for people like me. I was sure that there must be some followers of Jesus who would take me in and help me to see him. I planned to go home to Galilee and find someone there who would fill me in on the whole story of Jesus. My parents had told me once about a boy who lived in Bethsaida. One day he had carried his lunch to a large outdoor meeting that Jesus had held. My father had told me that the boy, Zach, was telling other boys what he had learned about Jesus. But I don't know how to ask a boy for information—that just isn't done among our people.

Maybe *you* would tell me.

Scripture: Mark 14:53–72
Discussion possibilities:

1. Who in your life is or was in your life that is like the servant girl, hungry for God, but didn't know anyone who could help her or him find a way to God?
2. What would you need to do to help that person satisfy his or her hunger for God?

Man on the Third Cross

Voice of a Thief

What a racket! I had no idea that half of Jerusalem would be out here today on this cursed hill. I wonder what the attraction is and why there are so many people—I'm sure they are not here to watch *me* die. Everyone is watching the man next to me. I wonder who he is. I've never seen him or heard about him from any of my pals. He certainly isn't Barabbas, but that old crook was *supposed* to be here today, not this guy.

I had heard that they were going to crucify three of us today: Barabbas, me, and the man on the other end of this three-cross drama. I wonder why the Romans changed their plans and substituted this stranger for Barabbas. The last time I saw Barabbas was on the road down to Jericho where we robbed a man. In addition to the loot, we also stole his donkey. Yeah, I remember the donkey—it was a young one and well outfitted with all the latest gear. That man won't need the donkey any more. We were sure we had killed the businessman, but now I'm not so sure of that. I thought I heard a moan as we were leaving him beside the road. We had to leave in a hurry because a priest was coming up the road toward us.

Oh, well, this is probably the last drama I'll ever see, so I might as well watch and see what's happening. Although, who knows, someone could still swoop down and save me from this murderous crowd. As if anyone is about to do that!

The younger guy in the middle is saying something. I don't even know who he is so why should *I care* what he says, but anything to take my mind off this pain. Oh, God, it's *excruciating!* Just let me die. But wait a minute, what did he just say?

> "Father, forgive them; they don't know what they're doing" (Luke 23:34).

"He said *what*? *'Forgive* them'? Didn't he mean to say, 'I forgive them,' or 'please forgive *me*.' But, not *'Father,* forgive *them.'"*

How can anyone forgive these sons of dogs for what they are doing to us? This man must be crazy to want anyone, let alone his father, to forgive *them*. But wait, I don't see a man down there who *could* be his father. There are only a couple of men there with those women. Wait … a … minute! He was looking up to the skies when he said that. Could he be calling Jehovah his father? Who does this guy *think he is*? I don't know much about prayer, but I certainly don't think of Jehovah as *my* father. I don't think I have prayed since I was in school, and that was a long time ago. A prayer certainly didn't help me in my exams or anything else, so I don't think Jehovah would be interested in anything I have to say to *Him*. But why would Jehovah forgive these religious rascals? *Religious?* Not when their actions speak so loud that their pious prattle is meaningless.

But how dare this guy next to me, who is hanging on a cross as I am, call Jehovah his father? That sounds a lot like blasphemy to me. Saying something like that would be enough to be kicked out of synagogue school for at least a week, or more likely for a year.

Now who's talking? "You'll have to speak louder. With all this noise, I can hardly hear you over here. I don't think that we even know each other, do we? Obviously, you are a criminal just like me since we are both hanging here on these Roman crosses. We've got this guy hanging between us—I don't know who *he* is or anything about him. What'd you say over there? Get real! Does that make any sense to you? You called him 'Messiah?' Is that your opinion or just something you read in the paper? But you made a joke of it and threw it in his face. 'Some Messiah you are! Save yourself! Save us" (Luke 23:35).

Oh, yes, I did hear some people down there also saying something like that. "He saved others; let's see if he can save himself if he is the Christ of God, the chosen one." Did they say that he saved others? I seem to remember some of those synagogue school lessons about a servant of Jehovah who was to come to Israel sometime. But, *now?* Could he be here hanging on a cross just like we are, and *now?* ... *Now?* ... On a *cross?* ... How can that be? ... How can you be sure?

"Hey, hold on there, fella, you know very well that we are getting exactly what *we* deserve. But if he is who they say he is, he hasn't done anything wrong. Is this the prophet they say went around healing the sick, even lepers, raising the dead, and doing all those other miracles? He is? *Oh ... my ... God!* He is!"

"Jesus, remember me when you enter into your kingdom." (Luke 23:41)

I can't believe what he just said. He promised me, "Don't worry, I will. Today you will join me in Paradise" (Luke 23:42).

Now, Jehovah, oh God, let me die in peace ... Wait, don't I need a sacrifice, a lamb to die in my place? Or is *he* the lamb that Isaiah spoke about? The lamb that was led to the slaughter? He took the punishment, and that made us whole. Through his bruises we get healed. But it was *our* sins that did that to him, that ripped and tore and crushed him—*our* sins (Isaiah 53:7–9). Did Isaiah really *mean* all that?

This "lamb" said other things too, before both of us died. I guess one of those women is his mother. He told one of the men in that little group to take care of her as *his* mother, and to his mother a similar word—that she was to see him as her son. Can you *believe* it? To be dying on a cross in horrible pain and to be concerned about his family? I guess so—after all, he took the time to listen to me, to forgive me, and to promise me life in his kingdom. He didn't save himself, but he made sure to save *others* in spite of what those rulers and the crowd had to say. Why didn't I know all of this a couple of years ago? My life could have been so much different, and I know my life would also have been much better.

It was only the middle of the afternoon, but something frightening was happening. It got very dark, almost like a moonless midnight. The pain was dulling my senses until suddenly I was jolted back to life again because in just a minute, or so it seemed, he screamed, "My God, My God, why have you abandoned me" (Mark 15:34). I have never heard such anguish, such torture, and such aloneness all wrapped up in one scream. The soldier and the other men in charge didn't know what to do so one of them ran, dipped a sponge in some vinegar, and held it up to his mouth. As soon as he took a taste, he cried out, *"It's done ... complete"* (John 19:39) and then he cried again, *"Father, I place my life into your hands"* (Luke 23:46). And that was it! Suddenly, I knew this was all there would be, and that when I woke up I would be with him. *With him!*

Some of his followers didn't stick around to see all of this. Although some of them were at the back edge of the crowd when this entire horrid event had begun, but only a few women and I think just one man, maybe two, stayed with him for the entire time. I overheard someone say that they were his disciples who had counted on Jesus to rescue our nation from the Roman rulers. He didn't do that, but he *did* rescue *me*. Oh, I know that before the sun comes up tomorrow I'll be dead, but I know where I'm going—to be with him in Paradise. I hope I can live long enough to tell all of this to my partner in crime on the other cross so that he can be rescued, too.

What did that centurion say, he who seemed to be watching the other soldiers and us? I just heard him say, "This man was innocent! A good man and innocent!" (Luke 23:47)

I have just seen what I think was a world-changing death; at least, I know it changed me! I can leave this world now knowing that these hours on this cross have been the most important hours of my life.

Scripture: Isaiah 53 (Emphasis on verse 12: "numbered with the transgressors" KJV) and Luke 23:44–49

Discussion possibilities:

1. Identify some of the issues in this scene that stand out for you.
2. When you meet the redeemed thief in heaven, what do you think you'll say to him or ask him?

When All Hades Broke Loose

Voice of the Guard at the Tomb

Lucky me, I pulled *easy* duty tonight. Even though I had thought I was going to be on the crucifixion detail today. I really hate that duty. The last time I had to be a guard at a crucifixion, my heart almost broke. My best friend, Justus, was called up for today's crucifixion duty. He told me when he stopped by after our evening meal, "Quintus, it was the most terrible day of my life."

It had started in the morning when, even from the soldiers' quarters, I could hear the noise from the nearby governor's palace. The soldiers were called to order and told to report to the palace grounds because there might be a crucifixion. The temple authorities were ready for them and had spread the word that there *was* to be a crucifixion that day. There was something about such an appalling event that seemed to bring out the worst emotions of a crowd. The hordes of people crowded into the palace grounds where the religious leaders worked them up into a frenzy. The leaders encouraged the crowd to yell, "Crucify him, crucify him" over and over again. It seemed to my friend Justus that Pilate was almost *forced* to give in to their demands, if you can imagine a Roman ruler being forced by the public to do *anything*. Although he wasn't sure, Justus was there checking out the entire procedure as well as the temple authorities. He seemed to think that the man they wanted to crucify might have been framed by those same temple authorities. Pilate gave in to the crowd, and after going through some guilt-saving ablutions, he sent them on their way to Golgotha, the place of the Skull, giving them the power to conduct a crucifixion.

Justus said that the criminal was a mild-mannered man. Even after being nailed to a cross, he seemed more concerned about his mother and the thief on the next cross than he was about himself.

My captain called me for tomb duty, an easy job compared to crucifixion duty! A servant of the chief priest took me to a beautiful garden owned by a wealthy man who had made a cave into his personal burial place. The Jewish authority told me that this was the criminal's secure burial place. Talk about security— it was *secure*, all right! There was a huge stone rolled in front of the cave opening, a thin yellow rope around the stone, and an official-looking seal on the stone. I heard this had been done so that the criminal's followers wouldn't come and steal his body. Duh! Why would anyone want to steal a dead man's body, let alone the body of a common criminal? The Jewish bigwig told us, "Just keep an eye on things and let us know if you see anything strange happening." That was the only charge to the few us on duty at the tomb.

After dinner, I had shuddered while Justus was telling me about *his* day. He noticed my shuddering. "Quintus, you're just not cut out for this kind of work. Let's face it, you're not a killer yourself, and you are much too sensitive and kind to be involved in anything that includes killing people." For me, it seemed that some soldiers thrived on these crucifixions and death marches. *I don't*! I just hope it is a quiet night so I can get some sleep, but that will be possible only if I can shake off the images left by Justus's account of *his* day. Tomb duty, oh yes, bring it on!

The other guards and I were just settling down for some good rest when all hades broke loose. It actually did feel as though hades *itself* had surfaced to this world, and that demons themselves would surely claim all of us.

First, a horrendous shaking began, an earthquake so powerful it rolled the huge stone away from the cave's entrance, breaking both the rope and the seal. I thought the earth was collapsing in on itself. I found that I needed to quiet not only *my* fears, but also those of my fellow soldiers who were also trying to get some sleep.

At the same time, a person in white clothing appeared on top of the stone that had rolled away, while some others in white clothing walked right into the now-open tomb. We were so frightened that we all fell down as if we were dead, but we still couldn't stop shaking from fear. When I fell, my body rolled to one side, making it possible for me to see and hear what was going on, all of which was difficult, if not almost impossible, to believe.

After the initial explosion and earthquake, some women showed up at the tomb. Surprised that the stone was gone, one of them said to the others, "The stone was here yesterday when he was buried." The women said to someone, "We are here to anoint the man's body for burial." As they walked into the tomb, one of the men in the white clothes asked them, "Don't be afraid. I know you're looking for Jesus the Nazarene, the one they nailed on the cross. He's been raised up; he's here no longer. You can see for yourselves that the place is empty. Now—on your way. Tell his disciples and Peter that he is going on ahead of you to Galilee. You'll see him there, exactly as he said" (Mark 16:6–7). The women were just as shocked as I was. Shocked is not *nearly* the right word of how I felt, and I was just the guard, but it is the only word I could think of at the time. Thinking back now some other words come to mind: horrified, terrified, frightened could also describe how I felt.

Some of the other guards ran into the city to tell the authorities what had happened. Such *obedient boys!* Would you believe it? The authorities gave them *money* to lie about the night's events. Later I found out that the temple authorities promised they would tell the governor something to keep them out of trouble. While they were cashing in on the story, I stayed at the tomb. Something told me that what I had seen and heard was probably as significant as anything I could or would ever experience in *ten* lifetimes. I could *feel* something happening to me inside. I didn't know at the time what it all meant, but I knew it was *big*, even *humongous!*

In what seemed like just minutes, some men showed up to check out the story they had heard from the women who had already been there. Obviously, they didn't believe the account the women had told them about *their* visit to the empty tomb. I heard someone call one of the men Peter. The others said that Peter had actually run all the way from the city. (He was one fit guy!) He was perplexed when he saw the strips of linen lying where the body had been. He and the other two followers seemed to *want* to believe what the men in white told them, but it seemed to me as though they just could *not* believe. I couldn't decide if I should tell them what *I* had seen and heard, but I didn't. The guards that had gone to the temple told me that the authorities at the temple told them that we were not to say *anything* about what we had seen and heard. In other words, "Keep your mouths *shut!*"

I was still there when sometime during the early morning hours, a woman stood beside the tomb crying and asking the men inside where they had taken Jesus. That's when another man showed up. I think she thought he was the gardener and that he would know where Jesus had been taken. When she asked him, the man just quietly said, "Mary." She apparently recognized the voice as that of a man called Jesus because she called him "Teacher." I was right there, heard them talking, and was so close to both of them that I could have reached out and touched his robe. I didn't, and I'll kick myself every day of my life until I finally, if ever, see him face-to-face again.

When I told Justus about my night and morning, he told me that he had been standing near the cross when the criminal, Jesus, had died. He had heard everything that Jesus had said, and he became convinced that this person was not just an *ordinary* man, but was an *innocent* person and was God's Son. Justus reminded me that Jesus had seemed more concerned about the men on either side of him than he was about himself. In fact, he promised one of the two men that on that very day, the criminal would be in paradise with him. With *him!* Can you *believe* that? Justus also confessed something to me that he said he'd never tell another soul except me. He said, "I looked up into his face, while he looked at me, and I know I saw the face—the very face and eyes—of God looking down at me. It was so real—it changed my life. Quintus, I'm not sure I can be a soldier in this kind of army. We seem to do the bidding of the people we dominate and end up killing people who, like this Jesus, was not a criminal but a teacher from God."

Justus had always told me that *I* was a softie. However, I couldn't help it, I broke down and cried because I really wanted to see and hear this Jesus. I wanted to see *that* face, and look into *those* eyes, and feel the *love* that Justus saw in that same look.

I almost asked the followers if I could tag along with them when they went up to Galilee to meet with Jesus, but I knew I would get into a lot of trouble with my commander if I took off for Galilee. I told Justus that I had to meet this man who could promise paradise to a criminal, ask God to forgive his killers, and then rise from the dead. Then walk right by *me*. What was I thinking? I should have spoken to him when I saw him. I know he would have welcomed me and probably even asked me to follow him. I won't rest until I meet him and ask him what I must do to be one of his followers.

I know now that I was wrong about *one* thing. I should had said, "All *heaven* broke loose" that day. It was heaven, *not* hades, invading our known world that night and ultimately, changing our lives and everything around us. I know now that he had come to make me his follower.

Biblical reference: This story is an imaginative recounting of the events of Resurrection Day, Easter, as the guard at the tomb might have told it. The essential facts and events are taken from the accounts in the gospels and adapted to this story. This author is certain that the emotions and reactions of the "tomb watchers" and the disciples as related here were more real to them than they could possibly be described.

Scripture: Matthew 27:57–66

Discussion possibilities:

1. How do you think you would have reacted if you had been by the tomb standing in the soldier's shoes and experiencing the same events?
2. How do *you* think the story ended? Did the guard meet Jesus and become a follower? Why or why not? What would have happened to you if you had been Quintus, the guard?
3. Think about the difference between the songs, "Away in a Manger," and "The Hallelujah Chorus," as representing the birth of Jesus and the death and resurrection of Jesus. What does that difference mean to you?
4. What if the "gardener" had called *your* name instead of "Mary" as he did? How would you have reacted to him?

Hand Signals

Voices of Cleopas and Companion

There we were on the road from Jerusalem down the seven miles to our home in Emmaus. My buddy and I had a lot to talk about considering all that had happened over the weekend. "I have never had such a gut-wrenching experience in my entire life," I said to my friend. The reply was a simple, "Cleopas, I can only say ditto."

We got into quite a heated discussion about some of the details of the weekend from the crucifixion of Jesus to the news of his resurrection. Being human, we had not seen all the events in the same way, so we had different interpretations of what all of this meant. We didn't agree very often on what we believed had been happening during those three excruciating days. My friend had heard some of the statements that Jesus had made, but I had become separated from my friend and saw and heard other events. There were probably as many different views of the events as there were people who saw them. Moreover, we were sure that everyone *had* seen them, or had at least *heard* about them unless they were living under a rock somewhere.

We had met Jesus only a year ago but didn't get to know him very well, since we lived in Emmaus and didn't get up to Jerusalem very often. We also had learned from some of his disciples that he and they had spent most of their time up in Galilee. However, this was Passover celebration, and we, along with most Israelites, went to Jerusalem for the remembrance of our freedom from the Egyptian captivity a thousand years or more ago. This Passover was certainly different—*radically* different from any others we had attended. Passovers are always crowded, but the crowds this year were larger, or seemed to be larger, and certainly much more vocal. The Roman officials were also involved more than usual. They were always there to prevent riots and even the insurrections that the Zealots were always fomenting. Someday, we both agreed, something would tip it over the edge, and there would be Lucifer to pay for that.

Seven miles is a long way to walk. But since we are great friends, the time seemed to fly by. It was about a two-hour walk if we stepped right along, and that's what we did. Besides, we have always believed that walking is great for keeping our weight down.

Then suddenly, someone walked up to us and joined us in our conversation. It was the first day of the week after the Passover Sabbath, so there were many others walking to their villages from Jerusalem after the big services. To have someone join us just seemed like a natural part of a long walk. It happens all the time and seems to shorten the time.

This particular stranger was not familiar to us, but that was not too surprising since so many people were going in our direction and probably many of them continuing to go north up to Galilee. He must have noticed how intensely we had been talking to each other, because his first question was, "What are you guys talking about? I assume something important must have happened because you seem so involved. I'm not sure you even realized I had joined you."

"Well, hello," I responded. "No, we hadn't realized you had joined us. We were just sharing with each other our recollections of what we had seen this past weekend. Were you also in Jerusalem for Passover?"

The new companion replied, "Yes, I was. However, as I listened in on some of your discussion, the two of you seemed more than just a little agitated about those recollections. What happened that has you both so upset?"

"*What happened?*" we both said rather loudly, I'm afraid, as we both looked in amazement at this stranger's apparent lack of awareness of the events of the Passover. "Are you the only one in all of Jerusalem who hasn't heard what's happened?' (Luke 24:18).

"What happened? Were you even in the city this weekend? Were you in hiding? How could you *not know* all the things that happened?"

"What things?" the stranger asked, as he must have seen the shock on both our faces.

"All the things that happened to Jesus the Nazarene," Cleopas said. "He was a man of God, a prophet, dynamic in work and word, blessed by both God and all the people" (Luke 24:19). "We figured that he was the one to deliver our nation Israel from Rome, but our chief priests and leaders handed him over to Pilate, to be sentenced to death, and they crucified him."

Then I broke into the conversation, saying, "Everything we have been talking about happened in just the last three days. Where were *you* when all this was going on? You must have heard some of the shouting. But that's not all, there's more. Some of the women in the group of his followers told us an addendum to the story that still has us stunned.

"Early this morning the women went to the tomb Joseph of Arimathea had lent to Jesus's followers, but his body wasn't there. Can you imagine? The body *was* not there! They came back to the city and told us they had seen a vision of angels who told them that Jesus is alive. '*Alive,*' they said, if you can believe that! So some of the closest followers who were with us took off running. Well, at least Peter ran to check up on what the women had said. They found things just as the women had told them. And *they* didn't see Jesus either. That's what we have been discussing all this time. I don't think either of us can believe you haven't heard anything about all of this. You must have slept through the whole thing."

We were still recovering from our shock at this stranger's lack of knowledge and information about these recent events when the stranger began to speak. We want you to know that what he seemed to lack in information about current events, he made up for it in his understanding of our scriptures.

"So thick-headed! So slow-hearted! Why can't you simply believe all that the prophets said? Don't you see that these things had to happen, that the Messiah had to suffer and only then enter into his glory?" (Luke 24:25–26). Then he began to explain all that was written in our scriptures about our Messiah, starting with Moses and going right through to the last of our Prophets, pointing out everything in the scriptures that referred to him.

All of a sudden, we realized we were in Emmaus, home again. I couldn't believe the time had gone so quickly. I think this must prove something—when conversation is about something that is important, we become so engrossed in it that time seems to fly. I must try to *remember* that when I am in a discussion with my teenage son!

Now, we had an issue to resolve. We found ourselves between a rock and a hard place. It seemed to us that the stranger was planning to go on farther, maybe up to Galilee, but we didn't know. So how do we balance courtesy to the stranger, and yet accommodate our own needs to check on our families and see about having food in the house? My companion blurted out, "Stay with us. It's getting late, and we have room for you here. So come on in and at least have a meal with us." I am sure that my friend was trying to be polite, and was probably even hoping that the stranger would want to continue on his journey. We were so impolite anyway that we hadn't even asked where he was going or where he would spend the night.

Much to our surprise, he took our invitation and stayed for supper. What happened next was the biggest surprise of the entire journey from Jerusalem to Emmaus. Actually, it was more than a *surprise*, it was a *shock*. We sat down around our table, the stranger took the loaf of bread, gave the blessing, and then the shock hit us. It was as if a stone wall came crashing down on us and knocked us silly. As the stranger took the bread in his hands and broke it, *we saw the prints of the nails in the palms of his hands.* Our eyes were opened, and somehow we knew it was Jesus who had been lying in Joseph's tomb *this very morning.* He was the same one who had been raised sometime in the last eighteen hours and had spent much of the last two hours with us. While we were still in shock, Jesus left the table and disappeared.

We couldn't contain the joy we felt in ourselves. My friend said, "Didn't we feel on fire as he conversed with us on the road, as he opened up the Scriptures for us?" (Luke 24:32). All I could say was, "Amen." Now, what were we to do? We had no other way to let the disciples know what had happened except to start back to Jerusalem—all seven miles! Only this trip was uphill much of the way. But we headed out immediately, and I think we arrived there in record time—like running a marathon. We found ten of the followers still talking about what they had seen and heard for themselves and the witness of the women who were the first to reach the empty tomb.

We were so excited that I know we had difficulty describing what had happened to us. The other disciples kept telling us to talk slower and try to talk without using our hands so much. They sounded like our parents when we were young and trying to explain what had happened when we won a contest at school.

We were embarrassed because we didn't have a chance to tell

Jesus that we were sorry that we were so slow to understand what he had been telling us on the road. We also wanted to know his plans for the future. It was about that time when suddenly he was *there with us*. His words were His familiar welcome, "Peace be with you" (Luke 24:36), but we were terrified thinking we had all seen a ghost. However, he calmed us down and showed us his hands and feet, and asked for some food. Someone brought out a piece of baked fish, which he ate right there so we could see that he was for real.

Jesus then became the teacher again to all of us as he had done with my friend and me on the road to our homes. He reminded us that he had previously told us that he must suffer, die, and rise again on the third day. We then were told that we were to preach in his name to all nations, and to tell everyone that He had died so people could have a change of heart and have the forgiveness of their sins.

Would we ever forget what had happened on *that* first day of that week? *Never!* I don't know how many times we repeated what we had heard and seen to everyone who would listen to us. I think you'll believe me: there were many who seemed hungry to hear our stories about the risen Christ.

Why did this all happen to *us*? We were common, ordinary, hardworking people, who struggled like everyone else to keep body and soul together. And now, we were charged to witness to the whole world of the greatest miracle of all time.

Every time we eat the bread and drink the cup, you can believe that the two of us will see Jesus sitting at *our* table, praying, breaking the bread, and revealing his scarred and wounded hands. That table became *his* table that night. We both trust that you will experience the same excitement we felt on that busy day in Emmaus every time you sit at *his* table.

Biblical reference: This story is based on the biblical account in Luke, the account of the two disciples walking to Emmaus from Jerusalem after the crucifixion and resurrection of Jesus. After their seven-mile walk, we can be sure they would have been hungry to eat and relax, but supper postponed any plans they may have made.

Scripture: Luke 24:13–35 or to verse 49 if time permits

Discussion possibilities:

1. Try to imagine what was going through their minds as they walked with this stranger.
2. Put yourself in their sandals, what would have been your reactions at supper?
3. What did they talk about on their return walk to Jerusalem from Emmaus?

Suggested hymn: "Be Known to Us in Breaking Bread"
   "Be known to us in breaking bread, But do not then depart; Savior, abide with us, and spread Thy table in our heart."

Music: *Day's Psalter* (1562); Tune: St. Flavian, CM; Text: James Montgomery (1825)
(This story works well as a triad with Jesus being the person accompanying Cleopas and his companion. "Hand Signals," begins on page 281.

Who Is That Man?

Voices of Thomas and Other Disciples

Entr'acte

He doesn't say much, but what he does say is powerful. Even in our small group, he is on the quiet side when he could possibly add to the conversation. I have only known Thomas for a little over three years, and it has only been in the last year that I feel I have really come to know who he is and what he's like. And then, just when I think I have him figured out, he comes up with a strange question or statement that throws us all for a loop.

We were back in Jerusalem again where every time we turned around, the temple authorities badgered us—at least, it seemed that way. So far, Jesus seemed to be winning the verbal battles they insisted on fighting with him. Sometimes it seemed as though they were opposed to everything that Jesus did to help other people, such as healing the sick, feeding people, or even speaking and eating with people who needed him. Some of those people who Jesus knew were not listed in the social register and were, in fact, looked down upon by our religious leaders.

For example, out of the blue while we walking up to Jerusalem, Thomas said, "John, what did you say when Jesus asked all of us to pick up our cross and follow him?" John responded, "Thomas, I remember Jesus asked us that, but to tell the truth, I admit I didn't understand what he meant, but I also didn't want to find out the details. It all sounded rather scary." We dropped the subject and never discussed it again. But that was typical Thomas. He would make a statement or ask a question, listen to whoever responded, and then leave whatever was said just hanging out there.

The patience of the temple authorities was wearing thin, and while they were standing on Solomon's porch during the Festival of Dedication (Hanukkah), they bluntly said: "Just tell us in simple Hebrew, if you are the promised Messiah." The answer Jesus gave them did not convince them. We are not sure that *anything* could convince them. "I told you, but you don't believe. Everything I have done has been authorized by my Father, actions that speak louder than words … You don't believe because you're not my sheep … I give my sheep *eternal life* and they follow me. My Father has given them to me, and I and the Father are one heart and mind" (John 10:25–30).

That pushed them over the edge. They bent over and grabbed some stones and fully intended to take matters into their own hands until Jesus stopped them with a challenge, "For which of these acts do you stone me?" (John 10:31–32).

Their response was striking to the heart of their problem with Jesus. "It's not for your good works, but that you are blaspheming by calling yourself God" (John 10:33).

"If I am doing my Father's work, forget the words that I use, and look at what is right in front of your eyes—the good things that I am doing. Don't they convince you?"

That certainly didn't seem to help the situation at all. This time, however, they didn't pick up stones to kill him. They tried to arrest him, but they were unsuccessful in that attempt—he slipped through their fingers.

So what did *we* do? We crossed over the Jordan River back to the place where John had baptized Jesus three years ago, and Jesus decided to stay there for a while. Again, the crowds came out from the city to hear Jesus, and many believed in him. People couldn't get enough of him, but then, neither could we.

Act 1 (John 11:16)

"What? Die with him? Who said anything about dying?" Andrew asked.

Thomas sounded like he was ready to die.

Our buddy, Lazarus, brother to Martha and Mary of Bethany, was very sick. The two sisters had sent word to Jesus to get to Bethany as quickly as possible so he could heal him. But Jesus seemed to take his good old time about getting there. There were some conflicts in Jerusalem with the Jewish leaders who seemed intent on getting rid of this person they considered a real nuisance and a threat to their leadership and authority. They tried all the tricks in their playbook to get him to do and say something they could use to convict him, put him on trial, and ultimately get rid of him. Finally, Jesus decided to return to Bethany to be with Mary, Martha, and Lazarus.

Most of us were well aware that if we went back to Judea or anywhere near Jerusalem, such as Bethany, less than two miles from Jerusalem, the temple authorities would descend on us and attempt to finish off what they had tried to do a few days previously. That's when Thomas said, "Come along, we might as well die with him" (John 11:16). This conflict had its beginning with the healing of the blind man, who had confirmed to many people that he really was the man who had been blind but could now see after he had obeyed Jesus's instructions. The authorities didn't think he should have healed the blind beggar because he healed him on the Sabbath day. After all, they had laws against doing this or anything else on the Sabbath Day that they could construe as work. This turned out to be a real brouhaha that eventually involved even the man's parents and neighbors.

We urged Jesus against going back to Bethany, reminding him that he was a marked man, who had virtual nails in his hands. The opposition wants to kill you, and you want to go back? We might as well have said, "Are you crazy? Don't you understand what this means? Do you have a death wish?" That's when Thomas said that we probably ought to go and die with him.

But back we went in spite of the danger to Jesus. Martha met us and more or less accused Jesus of not caring about what had happened to Lazarus. She acknowledged that Lazarus would rise on the day of the resurrection at the end of time. It was at this event when Jesus made a statement to Martha that I have never forgotten. "You don't have to wait for the end. I am, right now, Resurrection and Life. The one who believes in me even though he or she dies, will live, and everyone who lives believing in me does not ultimately die at all. Do you believe this?" (John 11:25). Martha said, "Yes, Master. All along I have believed that you are the Messiah, the Son of God who comes into the world." I think that most of us quietly said, "Amen."

After some conversation with Mary, Jesus actually wept. Then we all heard the shout, *"Lazarus, come out!"* (John 11:43). As we watched in awe, Lazarus left the tomb with his hands and feet tied and bound. Many of the Jews who watched this shocking event believed, but wouldn't you know, some of them hurried back to the Pharisees to tell the temple authorities what they had seen.

After all these events and after the crucifixion and resurrection of Jesus, Gamaliel, a Pharisee on the Sanhedrin, told us what happened in the in the council chambers after the resurrection of Lazarus. The anger level went up several notches, and the crucifixion fever increased proportionately with their anger. But Caiaphas, the high priest, calmly reassured the council that Jesus would die. "Don't you know anything? Can't you see that it is to our advantage that one man dies for the people rather than the whole nation be destroyed?" (John 11:49–50). The die was now cast, although we didn't understand it at the time.

Act 2 (Mark 14:12–25, John 13:1—14:1–14)

We were with Jesus celebrating the Passover feast in Mary's upper room. The table talk was pretty much centered on the experiences we had all had during the previous year. It was a very strange evening. We celebrated our Seder meal, and then Jesus did some very strange things. He took a basin of water, put a towel around himself, and began washing our feet. A servant didn't wash our feet, *Jesus* did. Of course, it didn't go easily with Peter. Peter objected to having the master wash his feet. We had never seen Peter be so obstinate with Jesus—but Jesus told him that if he wanted to be completely clean, he must let Jesus wash his feet. Now what did all that mean?

During the course of the evening, judas iscariot and jesus had some side conversation, and then judas just left, leaving us wondering what was going on. Shortly after this, jesus told us that he was going to be betrayed by one of us. Now we were really confused. Jesus told us that he was going away but that we could not go with him. We had been with him for three years, so we couldn't understand where he could possibly be going without us. In fact, peter asked jesus, "where are you going?" Peter insisted that he was going to follow jesus no matter where jesus went— even to death. Jesus told peter, however, that before the rooster crowed in the morning, peter would deny him three times.

The response that Jesus gave him was that we must make sure to love one another just as he had loved us. He told us, "Everyone will know that we were his disciples when they see how we love each other" (John 13:34–35). Jesus said it was his new commandment to us that we love each other. Talk about overload. It seems as though events were piling up making us even more confused. It's no wonder that we started to feel as though we were spiraling downward.

It was about this time in the evening that Jesus told us that he was going to prepare a place for us so that when he returned, we could go with him to that place. He told us that we knew the way to the place where he was going, and that we knew the road he was taking. This is when Thomas spoke up. As I said before, Thomas doesn't say much, but when he speaks, we really do listen. I heard what Thomas said as a challenge to Jesus. He said, "Master, we have no idea where you're going. How do you expect us to know the road?" He sounded quite exasperated when he said, "We don't *know* that road!" (John 14:5).

This was when Jesus said something that will probably live down through the ages. He said, "I am the Road, also the Truth, also the Life. No one gets to the Father apart from me. If you really know me, you know the Father as well … I am not leaving you alone, but I will ask my Father to send you a Friend who will stay with you forever" (John 14:14–17 and 25–27).

Thomas really opened up the door for us to see beyond that door and to begin to know and understand Jesus when he talked about our futures even though we didn't fully understand nor believe. It all seemed too far out for us to begin to take in:

- Jesus leaving us
- rooms being prepared for us in the Father's home
- a new ritual with bread and wine
- talk of being betrayed
- Simon Peter's dispute with Jesus over his feet being washed
- Where was Judas going?
- What's with a rooster crowing in the morning?

- Is Jesus for sure planning to leave us?
- Why and where will Jesus go?
- Moreover, what is, or who is this new Friend the Father is sending?

Thomas was right—and some of us went over and thanked him for speaking up, and speaking for the rest of us. We were as befuddled as he was. We hope Jesus will tell us more before he goes to wherever it is that he plans to go.

Act 3 (John 20:24–31)

After the crucifixion and resurrection, Jesus appeared to us on the evening of his resurrection and gave us his blessing. Unfortunately, Thomas wasn't with us that evening. When we did see him, we told him that we had seen Jesus. Did he believe us? Not on your life. So what was his response to our good news? "Soooooo ... you *think* you saw Jesus? Did you *see* him walk in the door? Did any of you *touch* him? Did he *touch* any of you? How did he get *out* of the room? Well, from what you've just told me, I think your imaginations were working overtime, or you were so confused that you'd have believed anything. Let me tell all of you—unless I see the nail holes in his hands, put my finger in the nail holes, and stick my hand in his side, I won't believe it" (John 20:25.)

Wow! He was adamant in his rejection of our news. We weren't sure how to handle his disbelief, so we left any arguments we could have used figuring that if we saw Jesus alive again, Jesus could handle Thomas. We prayed that Thomas hadn't rejected us, and that he would come around again. We hoped that it was the same kind of confusion that we all had when Thomas confronted Jesus about not knowing the way to wherever it was that Jesus was going.

The words of Thomas rang in our ears all night long and throughout the following days. Oh, I forgot, he added this addendum: "Give me a break. You all need some sleep because you are seeing things that aren't there. Get a life, and get over these fantasies. Believe me, I wish with all my heart that your words were true, I really do, but I just *can't*!" As we remember, Thomas wasn't upset or angry, but he said he needed visual proof, as we, too, had earlier that morning when we went to the tomb. After all, resurrections don't happen *every* day. So believing in the resurrection of a body isn't something that we are challenged to believe every day of the week either, is it? In addition, as I recall we would not have believed that Lazarus had walked out of his tomb unless we had been there and had seen it happen. Even then, we weren't sure that he was a ghost or if he had just been ill, but not dead. For sure, the last thing Thomas needed was a sermon about God's power to raise the dead, much less, a recitation of the miracles we had seen Jesus do. He just needed to see and touch the marred and scarred body of his Master.

Remember, this was the same day when some of us had run from Jerusalem to the garden where Joseph had built a tomb for his own family's use. We had seen angels, had heard them talk to us, and we had tried to convince the other disciples that Jesus had really risen from the dead. The others of us had been unsure about all the events of the day, and must have had our own doubts about this greatest of all miracles. Now that we think about it, Jesus had told us on several occasions that he was going to die, but that he would rise again. At the time when he spoke those words, they didn't seem real or relevant to us. I think that we more or less tucked those words in the back of our minds somewhere.

We didn't see Jesus for the next week—we were confused and afraid to show our faces out in public. We had no idea what the priests and scribes had planned for the followers of our Lord—probably death or exile. We figured we were marked men, so we hid.

Act 4 (John 20:26–29)

It had been an entire week after the resurrection—a week of unbelievable discomfort and inconsolable grief. We needed to see Jesus again, and we were not sure that the previous week's meeting had actually happened. Maybe Thomas was right—we had been fantasizing that Jesus had literally appeared to us. We had some meals together when we talked endlessly about all the things that had happened. We tried our best to talk about our futures, but we couldn't. We were so confused that we couldn't think straight enough even to begin to plan our next steps. Were our lives over after three years of companionship with the man who had changed our lives? Our hopes had been obliterated by the crucifixion and the resurrection even though we felt sure Jesus was alive. Now what? Were we going to be content going back to Galilee and restarting our fishing business or could Matthew even *think* of collecting taxes again? What else can a follower of a despised leader do? We couldn't begin to think about that kind of future.

We didn't see Thomas all that week. We were not sure where he was, but several of us thought that he probably was hiding away sulking, moping, embarrassed, and frustrated because he felt left out. I am sure that he was upset deeply by his experiences on the evening of the resurrection when we told him that we had seen Jesus. I realize now that Thomas hadn't denied that the resurrection had happened; he merely affirmed that he would believe if he could see the wounds and the scars on the body of his Lord.

It was now the eighth day since the resurrection and the

evening of that day when Jesus had appeared among us and had given us his blessing. We were in a house again as a group. This day was different and better—Thomas was with us. One of us had probably encouraged him to come back to us, that we needed the clarity of his thinking, and most of all, we missed him and we needed him to hang out with us. Come to think of it, I'm sure any one of us appreciates when someone else shows similar concern for us. It just so happened that Thomas was the pensive, melancholic one of our group.

I felt that tonight was going to be different from last week. Thomas was with us. Suddenly, Jesus was there. What a relief! All of us hoped that this was when Jesus would deal with Thomas's disbelief. All we needed was a word from Jesus to heal our sadness and start us on a path to recovery. The room was electric for all of us, even for Thomas, who stared at Jesus with his eyes fixed on the hands of our Master. Without another word, Jesus looked at Thomas and invited him to examine his hands and put his hand on his side. He challenged Thomas. "No more unbelieving. *Believe!*" (John 20:27).

We were all stunned into silence as we watched this drama unfold. What would Thomas do? Would he acknowledge our Lord? Or on the other hand, would he turn aside and walk out of the door, rejecting Jesus and all of us? I don't think any one of us took a breath while this was playing out. We watched in awe and hope, and then we heard Thomas say, "My Master! My God" (Luke 20:28). That's who He is: our God. No one until now had said this, but Thomas had made this confession calling Jesus, *God!*

We were like dummies. No one said a word. We stared first at Thomas, and then at Jesus. Peter asked, "What did he just say? Did he really say, 'My God'?" James said, "Did he actually call Jesus what I think he called him?"

Now as we think back on it, it seems strange that we were so surprised. It's not as if we hadn't had three years of seeing miracles that only God could have done, or heard insights that could only have come from God.

Surprises? Thomas gave us a few. I'm sure that I haven't told you all of them, but the ones I have told you were the life-changing ones for the rest of us. His commitment to going to the death with Jesus, opening the door for us to understand that Jesus was the way, the truth, and the life and the only way to the Father, and the insistence on the proof of the resurrection of Jesus, and the, "My Master! My God!" declaration. This acknowledgment of His lordship over us sent us on our way to the ends of the earth to spread the news that God, Himself, had invaded not only our *world*, but our *lives* as well. This invasion takes away the sting of death and the ability of the grave to have a victory over us.

Again, Thomas cleared the way for all of us—claiming that this same Jesus whom we had followed for three years was our *God*. This doubter had become in just a couple of words a believer—the first of many who would make the same claim as we eleven had just done.

If only Judas had been here to see and hear what we had just seen and heard!

Biblical background: This story is an adaptation of the biblical account of the four times in scripture when Thomas is actively represented as having something to say about the events in the lives of the disciples of Jesus.
Scripture: John 20:26–31
Discussion possibilities:

1. What do you see in the four pictures we have of Thomas?
2. Describe his faith as we see it in the books of Mark and John.

3. Compare his reticence to *believe* with our own reticence to *act* on our faith.
4. Talk about the nickname Thomas has usually been given as "Doubting Thomas."

A Nice Guy Finished First

Voice of Gamaliel

I was caught in one of the greatest maelstroms in human history. What I saw, and maybe was even a part of, was the beginning of the world being turned upside down and I along with it.

You may not remember much about me, especially my name. Not many guys have a name like mine, Ga-má-li-el. In fact, I don't know any men in my circle or even in Jerusalem with my name. I am in a position to know these things since I am on the Sanhedrin, a group of the top seventy men in Israel. We are the lawyers and the judges for and of our people, the Israelites. I don't need to brag, but all of us are from the best families in Israel. Some of the lower classes call us the elite, and so we are. We have the best seats in the temple and in the synagogues, people step aside when we happen to meet on the street, and some people jump to help us when we need help.

I am one of the Pharisees on the Sanhedrin, and people recognize me as a scholar and Rabban, which simply means, "Our Rabbi." (If you were not Jewish, you wouldn't know that I am the first rabbi to receive this honor. It is a step above rabbi and master. My modesty, however, forbids me to flaunt such plaudits.) By the way, in our history there was another Gamaliel who helped take the census when Moses was running things in our nation. In the

Torah, he was identified as from the family of Joseph and the head honcho of the tribe of Manasseh. In addition, while I am talking about one of our ancestors, let me tell you about one more. The first Gamaliel mentioned in the Torah brought an offering at the dedication of the tabernacle in the wilderness. His offering was stupendous: gold and silver plates and bowls filled with fine flour mixed with oil and grain, several goats, lambs, and a young bull and two oxen.

To our faces at least, we are highly respected, but we know, not by everyone. We hear rumors on occasion that there are some in Israel who think we take on too much authority, and from what some people say, they think we enjoy our positions far too much. One of my fellow members says, "When you have it, flaunt it." However, I don't feel that way. I remember my teachers in school giving examples of men in our history who flaunted themselves just because they "had it." King Saul, our first king, was one that I recall as a tragic example. It seems that many of our kings were jinxed like that. Samson, one of the early judges, wasn't a king, but he was another one who boasted of his good looks, beautiful hair, and magnificent physique. Even David, our greatest king, had a few problems stemming from overindulging himself.

I began to think that when people get that kind of power, unless they can somehow control themselves, they are headed for trouble with their fellow human beings. Most people strongly resent such people because they rarely know when and how to respond to unusual situations except by asserting themselves as the controllers of that situation. This was true in our own history, and I am sure that most nations in the future will deal with those who are not true to their leadership role, but let their personal need for power lead them to all kinds of excesses. This man, Jesus, spoke of some of us as the people who like to stand in public and pray so that everyone can see how religious we are. He warned his disciples to watch out for that kind of religious fakery. This was a part of his training seminar for his followers warning them that hypocrites are not the model for prayerful poses. "Be especially careful when you are trying to be good so that you don't make a performance out of it. It might be good theater, but the God who made you won't be applauding" (Matthew 6:2). "And when you come before God, don't turn that into a theatrical production either. All these people making a regular show out of their prayers, hoping for stardom! Do you think God sits in a box seat?" (Matthew 6:5).

Enough of my philosophizing—my fellow Sanhedrin members say I do too much of that. I tend to take the long-term view of things, and really enjoy seeing possible alternatives and then the consequences of those alternatives and of our actions. You can believe that this quirk sometimes gets me into difficulties with my fellow members of the Sanhedrin. They seem to have very little patience with my long-term view of issues, or of my insistence that we use a rational process for solving problems.

Not long after Passover, there was a growing brouhaha in Jerusalem. It had its genesis after the crucifixion of Jesus, the Nazarene, and his reported resurrection. Somehow or other, the followers of Jesus took on a new life after the alleged resurrection. It was as if they were suddenly reborn from nervous, frightened men into unafraid and courageous witnesses of what they heralded as an earth-shaking reality. The change was both unbelievable but at the same time exciting. Anyway, at our Pentecost celebration the temple was crowded with people celebrating the harvest and the gifts of Jehovah. The crowds are always great since every Jewish man is required to attend, and they come from every part of the known world. There were literally thousands of people here.

Suddenly, a most startling and unusual event occurred. The followers of this Jesus started speaking in a language that was unknown to *any* of us, but inexplicably understood by all of us. The immediate and common response was, "They are drunk with cheap wine" (Acts 2:13). This was ridiculous since we are forbidden to consume any wine before ten in the morning and it was only nine in the morning. So, this man, Peter, stood up and started to speak as powerfully and equally just as believably as I have ever heard anyone speak, let alone a *Galilean*. Everyone knows Galileans are not much more than uneducated country bumpkins.

He defended his group and began to recite from the prophet Joel about God pouring out His Spirit on people. Peter claimed that God had done miracles and wonders by the hand of this Jesus, whom we had crucified. I can't believe what I then saw. Many of the people shouted out, "What must we do?" (Acts 2:37). Now this goes almost beyond imagination. That very day, about three thousand men stepped out, said they believed that message, and were eventually baptized.

This was the start of something big! It almost started a *war*! Not a literal war, of course, but we thought that something like a revolution could be the result. Moreover, we have had many of those in our history. Some nutcase gets an idea that our destiny should be of our own choosing and not that of the ruling nation such as Rome. I won't bore you with our history on that subject.

You can believe it was subject "uno numero" in our hastily called meeting of the Sanhedrin. The consensus was that we had to stop this "revolution" or suffer possible Roman consequences. However, no one could come up with a justifiable way to do it. These Galileans were all the rage in Jerusalem. They had become more important than any popular magician or prophet in our culture. In fact, they had the city in the palms of their hands. They were healing people right and left but giving the glory to God and to their Christ, and not to themselves. This was not like any other revolutionary we had known. In the past, it was all about the revolutionary, and not about Jehovah.

The "revolution" became more intense, not less. The Sanhedrin confronted Peter and John, had them put in jail overnight, and still people believed their message. They added another couple of thousand to their numbers. The next morning my colleagues called in the Galileans to answer the charges we alleged against them. "By whose power did you heal that crippled beggar man who daily sat at the Gate Beautiful?" (Acts 4:7). Then the astounding answer! (Now remember, these are uneducated fisherman and who knows what else.) "It was by the name of Jesus of Nazareth, whom you crucified, but whom God raised from the dead, that this man stands before you healed" (Acts 4:10). It was then that we realized that these men had been under the influence of Jesus. They continued to perform these kinds of miracles until it seemed as though the entire city was agog with them. I began to question my own beliefs:

- Just who was this Jesus?
- How could he have such a hold on people?
- What was I overlooking in this situation?
- Could I possibly have been wrong in my assessment?
- Now what do I do if I have been wrong?

I am having trouble sleeping these nights. My mind is in turmoil, and I can't concentrate on my work. Every time I meet another Sanhedrin member on the street, it's all we can talk about. I began to worry about my sanity and myself. I even have become anxious to talk to people who have been close to this mesmerizing Jesus. I ask them the questions I have conjured up in my head during my sleepless nights:

- What did he tell you that caused you to be so committed to him?
- Did he perform some kind of miracle for you or for your family?
- Tell me what it is about him and his message that stirs you.
- Have you ever had a reason to suspect him of being anything but authentic?

The answers were quite similar in their responses. Before I could put my survey report together, and I didn't think it could get any worse, it did! The Sanhedrin, out of desperation for their own skins, succeeded in finally putting his followers in the public jail. Settled? No way! Some way, the jail bars couldn't hold them. The next morning, they were back in the temple again teaching the people. This time my colleagues quietly brought the apostles back to court, not using force, for fear of the reaction of the people. What a switch! The people are supposed to be afraid of *us*! The apostles didn't change message but again accused us of killing Jesus, and that they would continue to obey God and not us!

This was more than the Sanhedrin could stand. They wanted to kill them all. This is where I think my issues with this whole matter were resolved. "Just a big fat moment here," I said. I asked the apostles to go into the hall while I talked with the others of the Sanhedrin. "Look," I said as I reviewed some of the last few revolutionaries and their demises. "Their revolutions failed. If this one is of God, you will not be able to stop these men; you will only find yourself fighting against God" (Acts 5:38–39).

The Sanhedrin could not stop them. They just kept preaching, and apparently, the populace was hungry for what they had to say. They turned the city upside down! Now that is power—and right in the face of extreme opposition. Again, I was turned upside down. I decided not to fight God anymore, but to accept his grace and love for myself. What a difference the love and grace of God can make in the life of even a person like me.

However, I have one regret. In those years when I was fighting the power of God, I was teaching the Mosaic law to a brilliant student. He was Saul of Tarsus, who had come down to Jerusalem to be my student. I think he sensed my Sanhedrin hatred of what he called all that "Jesus nonsense" and then carried it to an extreme. He became a violent persecutor of the "people of the way" wherever he heard that the apostles had been making converts. However, he finally also did what Peter and John had told the people they had to do: "Repent and believe." He did just as I had done. However, while I was the thinker, visionary, and philosopher, the converted Saul, now known as Paul was out there carrying the cross, bringing Jews and Gentiles together in Christ. The mark of the" people of the way" was their love and the demonstration of that love for other followers of the way. I finally realized that I wanted to be known as a man who loved and not as a man who hated.

You've heard my story. So where are you in this journey of faith? My word of caution: make sure that you are well aware of your own heart's need of God's presence in your life.

Biblical reference: The story of Gamaliel is a pivotal one in the life of the disciples and of the yet to-be-born church. Admittedly, there is some imagination in this author's story, but based on the life and times of the Hebrew religion and the probabilities of such a confrontation, this story is as close to reality as it is possible to be. You can read about the dramatic results of the birth of the church in the chapters of the book of the Acts.

Scripture: Acts 5:17–39

Discussion possibilities:

1. What were some of the influences surrounding Gamaliel that may have led to his seeing Christ and the disciples in a different way than they were viewed by the Sanhedrin? (Look at Acts 5 again for some of the answers.)
2. Whom do you know who may need to come to grips with God's seriousness in sending His Son to be the Savior of his life?

I Can't Eat That Stuff!

Voices of Peter and Cornelius

I can't and don't eat that stuff! It's against my religion to even *think* of such food. I'd rather die!" Shocked, I, Simon Peter, sat up in bed on the flat rooftop of my friend's house after a distressing dream that shook me to my foundations. I had only put my head down for a minute or two and had not intended to fall asleep since I had so much to do that afternoon.

What a dream that was—not only distressing, but disgusting I thought as I stood and straightened out both my clothes and my head. It was warm on that sunny day in Joppa by the Mediterranean Sea coast. I had taken a little time away from my friends to pray and think and must have fallen asleep, and dreamed one of the craziest dreams I have ever had.

You know about my religion, don't you? I am Jewish, and I'm very devout in my faith, obeying all our laws, and this dream was about our laws concerning proper Jewish food. Food is either "clean" or "unclean." *No in-betweens*! It's black or white—no gray! It's either clean or it isn't clean based on ancient laws that go way back to Moses when our forefathers had escaped from Egypt after being slaves there for over four hundred years. You see after their escape, our ancestors were living in the Sinai Desert and wandering around waiting to hear the word that it was okay to cross the Jordan River and move into our new homes in Canaan.

My forebears had griped, complained, and threatened to rebel because they felt their living conditions were not satisfactory. Huh? *Unsatisfactory!* How soon we forget! They were slaves in Egypt—*slaves!* They were beaten, their kids were taken away from them and sold to other Egyptians, they had hard lives, and then they complained because they didn't like their free but nomadic life in the desert. God sent them free manna every morning. Sure, they had to go outside their tents to get it. I know, I know, it's hard to believe human nature sometimes, isn't it? They became so rebellious to Moses and to Jehovah that God decided that He had had enough of their complaining so he decided that those who had been delivered from Egypt could not enter the Promised Land, that there would be no crossing over the Jordan River until all the old folks had died. Harsh stuff, huh?

Are you still with me? Maybe that was more history than you were ready for, but unless you understand the background, the dream doesn't make sense. The dream is what's important in this story. In fact, there were two dreams involved—you weren't expecting that, were you!

Back to my dream: there was a sheet coming down from heaven. It was filled with all kinds of animals including reptiles, *ugh*, and birds. Some of that I could have handled, but that wasn't all. I heard a voice from heaven saying, "Get up, Peter, kill, and eat." *What?*

All I could say was, "You have to be kidding! I have never eaten anything impure or unclean." My mom made sure of that, and now my wife is just as strict as Mom was. Then there was my mother-in-law. She lived with us in Bethsaida and did her best to help us conform. As I said up front, "I just can't touch that dirty stuff." I just hope that God understands!

To make a long story short, God did *not* understand! In fact, His response was rather cutting and went against everything I had ever been taught, and went against the grain of all faithful Jewish people. His response was simply, "Don't call anything unclean that God has made clean." The voice was so insistent that it repeated the command two more times. Just in case I didn't understand or hear it the first time, I guess God was remembering my slowness to hear when Jesus, His Son, tried to get me to understand something—like feeding his little lambs and his sheep.

I became aware that God meant to tell me more than just what food I could eat. However, I didn't understand what the vision meant until a few minutes later when I learned that I wasn't the only person in this dream drama between God and man. God told me to get down to the gate because a small group of men were there to see me and that I was to go with them because He had sent them to see me.

The two or three men told me that their boss, Cornelius, a Roman centurion, had a vision. (Two visions in one day?) The centurion, although a Roman citizen, was a righteous and God-fearing man, respected by all the Jewish people, and he had been told by God to send us here to Joppa and find you, and bring you back to see him. It was almost time for a meal, so against all my principles, I invited them to have some food with us and stay overnight before taking the thirty-mile trip back to Caesarea. I knew I was breaking our law, but what's a man to do? ... I couldn't let them sleep out on the porch! It was a frightening decision on the spur of the moment, but I had trouble sleeping that night for fear of what I had done. What was I doing, taking such a risk, and I was only a fisherman?

The next morning, I set out with the men, but being a cautious guy, I took six of the brothers with me. *"You never know ...!"* It took us most of two days to get there. It took all of my strength of mind to enter his house. Our own laws said that Jews did not mix at all with Gentiles, eat with them, or even go into their houses. They were unclean! I mean, *"Dirty!"* Cornelius told me about his vision in which God had told him "that He had heard his prayers, and that he remembered my gifts to the poor." That's when he told me to send for you in Joppa by the sea. "We're all here in God's presence, ready to listen to whatever the Master put it in your heart to tell us." (Acts 10:33)

What an opening! Wow! I haven't heard that very often from anyone. So I told them the Jesus story, but before I did that, I confessed to them that I now knew that God didn't play favorites but that he accepts people from every nation who fear him and do what is right. Then I told them the Jesus story. I never get tired of telling people about Jesus. I probably left out some of the details, but I told them the basics that I had repeated over and over again. It had started with my sermon on Pentecost when the Holy Spirit came upon all of us, and I hope I never forget that the Jesus story is and will be the greatest story in the world.

However, the big surprise came while I was speaking about our Lord. Suddenly, the Holy Spirit came on everyone who heard the message. It was a shock to me and to my Jewish brothers who had traveled with me from Joppa. We couldn't believe that they, the dirty, uncircumcised Gentiles, had received the Holy Spirit. I was so overjoyed that I said, "Are there any objections to baptizing these people with water?" I realized at last that God does not have favorites. Our amazement and excitement about this sudden change in our faith told us that it was okay to stay with Cornelius for a few more days.

It wasn't over yet, though. I still had to defend them and my actions in front of the Jewish brothers back in Jerusalem. If you ever had to defend anything in front of *the* "brothers" you know it wasn't easy. Traditions are difficult to give up—sometimes impossible to get over them to begin new stories and traditions. It was a difficult step for the church to take, but I'm guessing it won't be the last! Of that, I can be quite sure—not the last and never easy!

Biblical reference: This brief story of two dreams—one to a good Hebrew and one to a Gentile Italian—relates the beginning of the gospel to the Gentiles, like most of us. Its fascination lies in one aspect in that, Peter, a man of strength and conviction is the person to whom the task is given to preach to us, the spiritual followers and children of Cornelius. In this story, there is relatively little imagination. The story is merely a rewording of the account in Acts 10, an entire chapter in this seminal book of beginnings.
Scripture: Acts 10:1–48.
Reading for the meeting: Acts 10:9–23
Discussion possibilities:

1. Identify other instances when God's grace has been apparent as it was in Peter's and Cornelius's situations when there were significant changes in long-standing traditions and/or customs.
2. What are some of the current issues in the Church that call for similar responses?
3. Who have been some of the leaders in sponsoring change in the life of the Christian church since Peter and Cornelius led the way?
4. Try to verbalize how the early church must have reacted to Peter's account when he arrived back in Jerusalem and met with "the brothers."

Shrimp *vs.* Giant

Voices of David and Goliath

(A Dialogue)

Goliath: *[Speaking to the audience as though the audience is the army of Israel.]* Why'd you even bother to send your whole army out here today? This is only the fortieth day I've been coming here, and you haven't found anyone yet who wants put up their dukes and have at me. Am I not enough Philistine for you—you dunderheads? I can handle you guys all by myself—I don't need an army to fight you pitiful bunch of weaklings. You are just the bothersome little boys of your King Saul, who thinks he should be the king over this entire region. This army behind me is just backup for me if your god should decide to defeat me, as if that will ever happen.

Okay, listen up … because these are the rules for engagement. Send out your best fighter, and together we'll see who the best warrior really is. Moreover, if by some lucky chance, your warrior gets the upper hand and beats me, all these soldiers behind me will become your slaves. How'd you like that? Think of the hero's welcome you'll get from all your women folk when you get back from camp with all these slaves for them to boss around. On the other hand, if you should not win … okay, let's get on with it. Send out your best fighter and we'll get to it. I can't wait to see what the guy thinks he can do to me.

[David appears opposite from Goliath, but not *facing him].*

David: My dad, Jacob, had told me to take some cracked wheat and these ten loaves of bread to my three older brothers in the army camp at Oak Valley, and ten wedges of cheese for their captain. Dad said, "I want a full report on everything you learn about them, about Saul, and the army situation with the war." I got up at dawn and left my sheep in the hands of a sheep-sitter and was at the camp in record time. Our army was getting into battle formation yelling their war cry. (More than a little dramatic, I think!) Oh, well, it's their war! What I didn't realize was how wrong I could be about the future of the war! At that time, of course, I didn't realize *whose* war it would turn out to be!

After leaving the food with a sentry, I found my three brothers. All of us were chatting together when the giant appeared across the valley on the opposite hill—wow what a giant he was—the biggest man I had ever seen. He scared every soldier in our army with his egotistical, maniacal attitude and his bravado.

[David steps back or out of the spotlight as Goliath steps in.]

Goliath: "Hey, you blockheads, listen up, I've done all the talking I plan to do. This is the fortieth day I've done this. Why haven't you found *someone* who will fight me? C'mon, let's get with it! You little boys of your weak king. If he wants to be the king of this whole region, then let *him* fight me."

As I yelled at the scrawny army boys across from me, I saw a little, but quite handsome, guy talking with some of his buddies. They were having some kind of an argument among themselves.

I just wanted to get this job done, defeat this little army, and get back home. Why aren't they picking a poor sucker to get out here to meet me? Wouldn't you think that after forty days they could come up with someone to give up his life and get this thing over? What ... the ...

[Goliath steps back or out of the spotlight as David steps in.]

David: I saw the biggest, ugliest guy I have ever seen. This Philistine was across the river while I was asking the soldiers whom they were going to send to fight him. I asked, "What is Saul planning to give the soldier who will dispatch this giant to his grave?" My oldest brother broke into the discussion and angrily changed the subject. "What are you doing here? Why don't you mind your own business! Shouldn't you be taking care of that scrawny flock of sheep back home? I know why you're here— you've come here to get a ringside seat at the upcoming attraction to watch us kill this impertinent hunk of muscle who is nothing but a blot on our nation's honor. So go back home like the good little boy our dad thinks you are and where you belong, and take care of your little lambies!"

Shunning my brother's cruel remarks, one of the soldiers related what the king was going to give to the man who would kill Goliath. "The killer will get a princess as a bride, a large reward, and he won't have to worry about anything for the rest of his life. The soldier's family will have it made, too. How do you like that?"

I found out later that one of the soldiers reported this bit of chatter to King Saul, who then sent for me, but I'm not sure why he wanted to see me. In the conversation that followed, I volunteered to fight this giant blot on our nation's honor. I think this must have been a surprise to him because his response was negative. "You can't do that. You're too young and don't have any fighting experience. This brute has been fighting wars before you were even born."

[David steps back while Goliath takes his place on the stage or the spotlight is on him.]

Goliath: "What's going on over there? Are you all too chicken to fight me? Cluck ... cluck ... cluck! I'm waiting and will be here until someone over there gets the guts to face me. Come on, I don't have all day, and I don't want to lose my voice. Hey, here's an idea! Why don't you *draft* a guy to take the place of all the rest of you—make him a hero to your nation?"

[Goliath steps back, and David takes his place on the stage or the spotlight is on him.]

David: When I responded to King Saul, I told him about being a shepherd when the wild, hungry lions and bears attacked my flock. The lion or the bear would grab one of the lambs for his dinner, and I'd have to do something to save the flock from the animal's voracious behavior. It wasn't easy, but I had to run after the animal and knock it down to rescue the lamb. If the beast turned on me, I'd simply wring its neck and kill it. I can do the same thing for this heathen Philistine pig that has nothing more to do than to yell and taunt our troops. The same God who delivered me from the teeth of the lion and the claws of the bear will not let this Philistine get the better of this army or me. Together we can do this!

I couldn't believe what Saul did next. He called one of his guards and told him to dress me in the king's own armor. Included was a helmet for my head and a sword to put over my armor. The armor, by the way, was so heavy that my short body couldn't walk in it, much less move. (Obviously, they didn't have one in my size.) I'm not used to all this stuff, so they took it off. I'm sure I would look strange standing across from my enemy whose armor weighed about 126 pounds, and whose spear was like a fence rail with a tip that weighed over fifteen pounds. Yikes, I hardly weigh that much myself!

[Goliath steps to his place again while David steps back or spotlight shifts to Goliath from David.]

Goliath: "What's going on over there? Can't you little boys hear, or are you just playing dumb?

"Listen up—I'm talking to you, yes, to all of you! Don't you want to go home to your scrawny wives and little girls and boys? Let's get this over with, okay? I have a big date for the weekend, and I'll catch you know what if I miss this date."

[Goliath steps back while David takes the center.]

David: So, Saul said, "Go, and God help you." At Saul's command, I went down to the brook that separated me from the Philistines, picked up five smooth stones from the river bank, and slipped them into my shepherd's pouch and walked over the edge of the brook.

[David now looks across to Goliath]

There he was—the big man himself, looking even bigger now that he was up close to me. He looked to be twice my size both up, down, and around! Did I just tell the King … King Saul that I was going to kill him? Well, I also just asked Jehovah to honor his pledge to Israel, and I believed that He would take care of this little job with me. Did I say "little"? I know I must have meant a huge job! Oh well, here goes! So, "Help me Jehovah!"

[David steps back, and Goliath takes the center stage.]

Goliath: I took one look at the little boy standing on the other side of the brook and couldn't believe my eyes. They must be joking—they can't be serious. Who is this little red-cheeked, peach-fuzzed squirt? Look at me—I'm not a dog that can be chased by a stick, like this little boy with his favorite toy, I can't believe it. A toy—a slingshot no less.

[To David] "Get your body over here and I'll make roadkill out of you and feed you to the buzzards and the field mice. C'mon, you little pipsqueak. I'll slice you and dice you, and show you just how *weak* your god is."

[Goliath backs away while David steps into center or into the spotlight, but with Goliath still across from David.]

David: "You come at me with a sword, a spear, and a battle-ax. I come to this battle in the name of God-of-the-Angel-Armies the God of Israel's troops whom you curse and mock. This very day our God is handing you over to me. I am about to kill you, cut off your head, and serve up your body to the crows and coyotes. The whole earth will know that there is an extraordinary God in Israel. And everyone gathered here will learn that God doesn't save by means of sword or spear. The battle belongs to God—he's handing you to us on a platter."

As the big guy surged toward me, I took one of the stones out of my shepherd's pouch, placed it carefully in my slingshot, took aim, and slung it at his forehead where it sank in as he fell on his face embedding the stone firmly in his head. I jumped across the brook, with both hands pulled the heavy, mammoth sword out of its sheath, and lopped off his giant head as though I were cutting off a sapling tree in the pasture. The Philistine army ran from the battlefield as though they had bees stinging them in their you-know-where, and killer dogs at their heels. That was that! The end of a huge threat to Israel. "Thank You, Jehovah, for saving Israel and me." Now back to my sheep, or as my big brother would say, back to my lambies.

But not so fast! King Saul wasn't quite through me yet. Abner, the commander of the army, came to tell me that the king wanted to see me. King Saul asked me who *I* was and who my *father* was. "I'm the son of your servant, Jesse, who lives in Bethlehem." That's when I met Jonathan, who became my best friend for life—my number-one advocate and buddy. Eventually, I became Saul's man in charge of military operations and never did return to my job as a shepherd. Little did I know what I was going to face in the future. However, I learned to lean on Jehovah and on my "blood brother" many times through thick and thin in the years that followed the rout of the giant at the hands of God through this little squirt of a shepherd boy.

Biblical background: This adaptation of the battle between David and Goliath is from the account in 1 Samuel 17. David was a shepherd boy but also the future king of the nation of Israel while Goliath was a giant warrior of one of Israel's neighboring enemies. Read more of David's exploits in the two books of Samuel.

Scripture: 1 Samuel 17: 38–54 (Read *after* the story has been told.)

Discussion possibilities:

1. How do you suppose David knew about God and God's protective power of Israel?
2. Why do you think this account is in the Bible?
3. Discuss why David did *not* become obsessed with his victory over Goliath.
4. Read the rest of David's story in the books of Samuel.

Props (helpful, but not necessary):

- An old-type slingshot with a few small stones
- A wooden sword

Presentation suggestions:
This presentation may be done as a monologue with one person taking both roles by stepping over an imaginary line and facing the audience. Only face your opponent when Goliath speaks about the "little boy standing on the other side of the brook," about three-quarters of the way through the story.

If you do this story as a dialogue presentation, the two males need to assume the appropriate attitudes for their roles: braggadocio and anger for Goliath, and carefree but determined for David. If it becomes uncomfortable to step forward and backward as the script suggests, then make sure that it is obvious that there is a stream between the two of you (a few sheets of blue paper, or a long piece of butcher paper colored blue). Try to arrange the paper on a slant so those present will be able to see the "water," and that you make sure to never step *in* the water! That is, until David steps across to cut off Goliath's head. (Fake it!)

Keep the dialogue moving with limited pauses between the two of you—keep it going back and forth, as you can imagine it must have been between these two mortal enemies. You will *never* be friends; your intention is to *kill* each other.

David, make it obvious that you are talking to God by looking up. You know that God is listening to you and promising victory for his people, Israel. Remember your *attitude* will say as much or more than the words you speak.

- When you are not speaking, maintain your facial expression.

- Goliath *never* looks up to God since he doesn't recognize that there *is* a live god.
- David uses *every* opportunity to look toward heaven as he claims God's presence with him in this battle.

It's Tough Being a Servant Girl

Voices of Miriam and the Apostle Peter

Staging: Miriam and Peter stand far apart from each other. They never speak to or look at each other. They appear to be in different places.

Miriam: This place was a madhouse that night. The later it became, the crazier it seemed to get. The confusion just kept building and building until I thought I just might go crazy myself. People were running around, yelling at each other, ordering me around, and standing in corners of the rooms in small groups whispering to each other. From the looks on their faces, I was sure they were conspiring to do something evil. The whole day was the kind of day that would make a person want to change jobs.

After all, I was just a servant girl from Galilee working in the house of Annas, the high priest, and another high priest, his son-in-law, Caiaphas. Everyone knew these two men were appointees of the Roman officials. Oh, and by the way, those two had been in the high priest function longer than any other family had been. In those positions anyone who had those kinds of connections with the Romans, and had been in fact appointed by the Romans, so they received much of the disdain and hatred that we had for their bosses, the Roman authorities.

One of my issues with them had to do with my name. Sometimes the priests and their political appointees called me by my name, Miriam, but usually it was, "Hey, you." If I didn't respond immediately to whatever name they called me, they just yelled, "Hey you," more loudly. However, they made sure to let me know in many ways that I was in fact not a person, but just a no name nobody.

Peter: We were with Jesus in the upper room having an unusual meal: it was the Feast of Unleavened Bread, often called Passover. Jesus extended it with something different. He took some bread and wine and said he was instituting something he wouldn't be doing until we sat with him in his Father's kingdom. I figured I would ask Jesus what that meant when we left our meal. Sometime during the meal, I noticed that Judas was leaving the room with a face that looked contorted with anxiety. I asked the guy sitting next to me, "What gives with Judas? Why do you suppose he's leaving?" The only answer I got was a shrug of his shoulders. I did see, however, that he didn't take his moneybag with him, so I guessed he wasn't going to get something else for our meal.

Miriam: It was Passover time, and during the preparations for the Seder meal, a strange man came to the door demanding to see Caiaphas. I didn't know whether to let him enter or not. He seemed more than just a little strange, as if he didn't quite know what he was doing or why he was even there. I thought he looked dangerous. Against my better judgment, I let him in, and he and the priests talked for just a little while and then he left. In one way, he seemed to be quite happy, but in another way, he seemed like he was being torn apart inside. I could only see one difference in him when he left: he was carrying a small bag that jingled. Interesting, he didn't have that bag when he came to the house. To me, it sounded like money. Money never seemed to be in short supply around here, especially for one of the pet projects of the priests. Never in short supply, that is, until I needed some of it for shopping. Over time, I had learned about their money sources. They had locked up the rights to run the sales booths in the temple. They had the approval of the Roman officials for the franchises used for changing money into the appropriate currency with the usual interest rates, and for selling doves for the sacrifices. These franchises brought in a lot of "pocket change" for them.

Peter: When we left the upper room, I looked for Judas, but he hadn't come back from wherever he went. Strange! This wasn't like him. He was usually quite prompt in what he did and where he went. I guess that's why he was appointed as the "money guy" for our group.

Miriam: However, later that night that same strange man was back again, but this time he seemed more crazed than he had been earlier in the day. After more secretive conversations, he and a large group of men left together. It was late—actually, it had been dark for several hours. It was obvious to me that something suspicious was going on. I was sure the strange man who'd been here earlier seemed even more upset then he had been on his first visit. He was so upset that the priest had to speak harshly to him to get him moving. I was glad to see them leave so I could breathe again, but I was uneasy because I was sure they were not up to any good tonight! I couldn't help it—something was wrong about whatever they were planning. On the other hand, I was often uneasy about much that this group did.

Finally, there was some peace and quiet around here since I expected them to be gone for several hours. I was just hoping that whatever they had been planning was over, and that life around here could return to normal, whatever normal was in the home of this high priest.

Peter: There Judas was! But in a garden? Gethsemane Garden no less. With a mob? Jesus had brought James, John, and me up here with him and asked us to be on the lookout while he went farther up the hill to pray. Lookout? For what? Oh, good, Judas stepped away from the mob and walked up to Jesus. *What?* Why is he kissing Jesus? Is one of them leaving? This is getting too weird for me. Suddenly a man stepped up and grabbed Jesus to take him away. That's when I took charge, dashed up to the man, raised my short sword, and cut off his ear. Jesus took the ear and put it back on the shocked man just as if I had never cut it off! Then my buddies and I took off. We were afraid we'd be next. As we ran, I guess I must have remembered what I had promised Jesus about never leaving him, so I followed the mob to see where they were taking Jesus, and discovered that they ended up at the high priest's home.

Miriam: When they returned, some of them came into the house, laughing and saying, "Well, that's done. We got him, and now it's up to Pilate." I didn't know what they meant by "that's done," but I was certain by this time that I knew who the "him" was. That man was in danger, and I hoped that he would get away from them. My grandmother used to talk about feeling things in her bones. That night, in my bones I could feel the evil in this house. These religious people seemed to be often filled with hate, and more concerned about their unbearable rules that demanded much of others but demanded very little of themselves. Their hypocrisy was obvious every day to anyone who had to deal with them. They talked about their sacred rituals and proper ceremonies, but they didn't practice what they preached. These priests seemed to have no mercy, no grace, and showed very little forgiveness for anyone. Their concerns were more often than not focused on punishing those who had broken their endless laws rather than finding ways to forgive and help people.

When Annas, a high priest, came into the house with the group, he seemed to be in a positive mood, but when I heard what he said, I couldn't believe my ears. This was *unbelievable*! It was the worst thing that could possibly happen. This proved to me just how evil someone could be to even think and plan such a thing. Now I was totally convinced that people have the capacity to be worse than evil. I saw them drag Jesus into the house as though he were a common criminal. As I listened to them talk, I picked up on what had happened while they were gone. Judas, the crazed visitor, had led them to the Mount of Olives up to the Garden of Gethsemane, where he identified Jesus, his leader, to the high priests and the soldiers that were with them. Judas had told them that they would know which one was Jesus because Jesus would be the man he kissed.

Peter: I finally realized that this was bigger than anyone could possibly have imagined. What is this all about? I followed some of the men into the courtyard, where they were standing by the fire keeping warm. They were joshing about the night's task and how easy it had been to arrest Jesus. I wanted to say something, but I, the brave one, couldn't open my mouth.

Miriam: By the time the priests and the soldiers had gotten back to the house, the Sanhedrin made up of seventy men who served as a court, were ready to interrogate Jesus. It was almost daybreak when the priest called the court into session. These men were often called together to pass judgment on the rest of us for our failures to keep all the laws they had added to God's laws for our people. When they weren't finding fault with some of us, they did a lot of fighting among themselves. However, on that particular night there was no fighting among themselves. Jesus was the focus of all their anger, which they seemed to delight in directing at him. Our history has had many men just like these Jewish authorities—men of whom we are ashamed. They asked Jesus many questions about who he thought he was, and by whose power he did his miracles.

By this time, the house was full of people since the word had quickly spread around that something big was going on. In spite of the large crowd, when the priest asked witnesses to come forward and testify against Jesus, the crowd was silent. At least, I didn't see anyone step forward. No one said a word. *No one!* Finally, two men came forward and testified that Jesus had said, "I am able to destroy the temple of God and rebuild it in three days." I thought the court would have apoplexy. It was no longer quiet. The noise became unbearable. For the second time that day, people were yelling and screaming at each other but this time at Jesus too.

However, I remember Jesus saying something like that earlier in the week at the temple when I had gone to market to shop for the Passover food. On the way back from market that day, I had stopped by the temple; Jesus was there, so I hung around for a few minutes. I didn't dare stay very long even though I wanted to stay and listen some more. Jesus seemed so sincere and caring. He wasn't bragging when he said that about destroying the temple and rebuilding it in three days, but it seemed like he wanted us to know that he lived in the power of God. I knew that if I stayed very long, a priest would be asking me, "Where have you been?" I'd be in big trouble. You see, I had been listening in on some of their conversations about Jesus as I served their meals, and I had the impression that there was trouble between Jesus and these temple authorities. I can tell you this: if I hadn't needed this job, I would immediately have joined the group that followed Jesus.

On that day in the temple, I saw a loving spirit unlike anything that I had ever experienced around here in a house full of religious people. These priests and their cohorts were hung up on their own words and their laws, but they just laughed at the loving and caring actions of the rest of us. They seemed to know all the right religious words, but their behaviors were anything but religious. I couldn't help wondering if something happens to people when they get power over other people, or think they have that power. What happens to their humanity?

That day when I was coming back from the market, I heard Jesus talking about Dorcas and her two small pennies. I must've looked surprised, and even though I didn't say anything, I had the feeling that Jesus knew what I was thinking. He turned toward me and smiled. He even held out his hand to me and touched my shoulder. I knew then that he was a very special person, a person who knew God in a way that I didn't know God. That's when I saw Peter for the first time. Right away, I knew that Peter was devoted to his leader, Jesus. I took one look at Peter and thought that if any man would be my hero, it would be a man like Peter. He was handsome, rugged, and I thought he was probably one of the leaders of the group of people around Jesus. "That's the kind of man I want for a husband," I fantasized.

I'm sorry. Talking about Peter must have distracted me. Back to that night and the mock trial of Jesus. I didn't like the way they were treating this good person who seemed as if he could see right through all of us, and that he understood where all of this was going. Then my hero entered the house. I was positive that Peter would say something in defense of Jesus. Peter seemed like a forceful man who didn't take much nonsense from anyone. I asked him if he were one of the disciples, hoping that my question would make it easier for him to say, yes.

Now, I had heard about Peter from some of my family up in Galilee. People up there knew Peter as a good businessman, with a prosperous fishing business, but who gave up much of his fishing business to be with Jesus and the other followers of this popular rabbi. If anyone would speak up for Jesus, I was positive that Peter would. However, he said, "I am not one of his disciples." In fact, at least three times during that night he denied ever having known Jesus. How could he say that? I have so often been disappointed in men, but I thought Peter would be different. But he wasn't. I decided right then, that even if he were not married and he asked me to marry him, I would never marry such a coward.

This was starting to take on some heavy overtones. What was going on? What could be so critical about this sort of trial? That's when it hit me; they were planning somehow to stop Jesus from teaching about the spiritual kingdom of God. They wanted him out of their hair and out of their sight. I think they were afraid that he might uncover their money-grubbing activities and their political alliances with Rome. We common people might revolt against them if we found out all about Annas the high priest and Caiaphas, his son-in-law, and their cohorts, the Sanhedrin. From what I had heard, Jesus had already had a ruckus during the week with the moneychangers in the temple. He had tipped over their tables and opened the cages to release all the sacrificial doves. I guess they could see their dirty profits flying away with the doves.

Peter: What have I done? I said I would never leave him nor deny him. In fact, I told him that I would die with him. What's that? ... A rooster just crowed three times. Oh, Lord, what have I done? I feel so alone and so very lost!

Miriam: I was right there, so I could see and hear everything that was going on, and it was so easy to see the differences between Jesus and the Sanhedrin. These men playing at being a court that night seemed intent on pinning something on Jesus so they could charge him with criminal activities to make sure he would suffer, maybe even die. Their hatred of him was as obvious as the nose on my face. That hatred was certainly in sharp contrast to his quiet, peaceful responses to their questions, and he was anything but defensive. I had the feeling, in fact, that he had the whole wide world in his hands. After all, I had felt his hand on my shoulder, and it had soothed my spirit. I'm sure that anyone who was troubled, heavily burdened, and weighed down with care would find rest and peace if they came to know him.

In synagogue, I had learned just a little bit about the coming Messiah. As I remember, it was Isaiah who wrote about someone who would appear in the future and would be badly treated, but would not open his mouth in his own defense. Isaiah had written, "He would be like a lamb being led to the slaughter, but he would not open his mouth." Could this Jesus be that person? He certainly caused an uproar in this house that night. The chief priest had asked Jesus, "Are you the Messiah, the Son of the Blessed?" That's when everything hit the wall. Jesus said, "Yes, I am, and you'll see it yourself: the Son of Man seated at the right hand of the Mighty One, arriving on the clouds of heaven." That's when Annas went crazy. He tore at his clothes, and the trouble really began. The worst thing they could say about anyone was that the person had blasphemed God. In our system, blasphemy was judged to be the same as the death penalty. I didn't think that what Jesus had said was blasphemy, I felt sure that he really was the Messiah. But would anyone listen to me? No! They would not, and they did not. After all, I was just a servant—a woman.

They slapped him, laughed at him, spit on him, beat him on the head, condemned him to death, and finally decided to send him to Pilate for the legal charges. They planned to ask Pilate to crucify him. You see, they themselves could not carry out a death sentence. I hoped that Pilate would have more sense than these crooked men had. Talk about justice! In the future, I hope someone writes about these events to help people see just how unjust, immoral, and probably illegal this court and trial had been.

Peter: Where do I go? What do I do now? To whom can I talk? No one, especially my buddies, who won't want to see me ever again. It's too late to tell Jesus that I'm sorry. Even if I could, would he believe me, let alone accept my apology? I wish I were dead! I just betrayed the best friend I'll ever have.

Miriam: I decided on the spot that I had to get away from Jerusalem, from this house, and from these people. I had had it up to my eyeballs when what I needed was for someone to tell me more about Jesus, and his love for people like me. I was sure that there must be some followers of Jesus who would take me in and help me know more about Jesus. I planned to go home to Galilee and find someone there who would fill me in on the whole story of Jesus. My parents had once told me about a boy who lived in Bethsaida. One day he had carried his lunch to a large outdoor meeting that Jesus had held.[17] My father had told me that the boy, Zach, was telling other boys what he had learned about Jesus. But I don't know how to ask a boy for information. That just isn't done among our people. Maybe *you* could tell me. *Will you?*

Biblical reference: This story is an adaptation of the account in Mark about a young servant who was sure she had previously seen Peter with Jesus and is now telling her story.

Scripture: Mark 14:53–72

Discussion possibilities:

1. Who is in your life or was in your life that is like the servant girl, hungry for God, but didn't know anyone who could help her find a way to God? You know that God is seeking her, and you may be the one to bring them together.

2. What would you need to do to help that person satisfy her hunger for God?

3. If that makes you nervous, what can you do about your nervousness?

The Prodigal's Disappointed Dad

Voices of the Prodigal's Father and His Two Sons

Father: How can parents have two sons who seem to be exact opposites of each other? I'm not talking about the color of their hair and eyes, or their height and weight. I'm talking about the way they seem to think, the way they express themselves, and the way they relate to other people. *Totally* different!

Their mother saw them one way, and I see them differently. It seems to me that their mother always favored Aaron, the younger son, and she was usually the first to find fault with Jacob, the older son. Some of my male friends have noticed similar differences between their children and in the way their mothers treat them. Of course, we fathers are unbiased in the way we treat *our* sons and would never even think of favoring one over the other. Am I right or not? Oh, oh, here comes his mother's favorite now, probably to complain *again* about Jacob, his brother.

Prodigal Son: "Hey, Dad, 's up? Gotta minute? I'm not sure how much longer I can put up with the way Jacob treats me. This is the stuff I had to put up with just this morning. I counted the fights we had—exactly five of them. First, it was about the jobs you gave me and the ones you gave him—I got the toughest ones.

271

Second, who is responsible for taking care of the sheep this week? Third, who is responsible for cleaning up the shearing lot? Fourth, which field do the sheep go into after the branding? Fifth, why can't *I* go with my friends tonight? Jacob is going with *his* friends after dinner, and he doesn't even have a curfew time. None of my friends have to put up with this kind of stuff. Jake never listens to me or to my ideas. Just because he's older, he thinks he can run my life. I don't think I can put up with him much longer."

[Prodigal Son backs away from center stage]
[Father speaks to the audience in this next statement.]

Father: See what I mean? I try to be reasonable and talk some sense into both of them, but it never stops. I'll bet you never hear those kinds of complaints from your sons, do you?

Our situation came to a head one day when Aaron found me alone and asked if I had time to talk about an important issue. My first thought was, *Now what? More of the same, more griping about Jacob's this or Jacob's that? Come on now—Aaron is eighteen or nineteen years old. Shouldn't he be getting past this stage of his life?* I just wanted to say even before I listened to him, "Aaron, just suck it up and get on with your life." But of course, I didn't.

[Father speaks to Aaron.]

"Of course I have the time. What is it *this* time, Son?"

Prodigal: "Well, Dad, I've been thinking about my future."

Father: "That's great, Son. I hope you and this farm will share that future together. I've always had a dream that you and Jacob would share this place when I pass on. I have it all worked out."

Prodigal: "Dad ... *Dad*, just *listen* for a minute, okay? That isn't exactly what I've been thinking. I think I need to be more independent—a chance to try life out on my own, to experience life in another culture, meet new people, and try my hand at some other occupations. Know what I mean?"

Father: "No, Aaron, I'm not sure I do know what you mean. This comes as quite a shock. I thought you were happy here other than having a few disagreements with your brother. Does this mean you don't want to be a part of the inheritance of the farm, the flocks, and all our buildings here?"

Son: "Not ... exactly, Dad. Yes, I do want to share in my inheritance, but I want to have my share now to finance my own future—where I want to go and what I want to do. The inheritance will be mine someday anyway, so why not now? I don't think it will put a strain on your budget. Of course, I don't know that for sure since you never share any information about finances with us. You seem to have a lot of money available for just about anything we need around here. But I really want to get out on my own, experience life as a young man, and try out my skills in other situations."

Father: "Have you discussed this with your brother Jacob?"

Prodigal Son: "Naw, he wouldn't understand. He's satisfied with being right here for the rest of his life—doing the same old thing day after day, and probably year after year. Dad, I really think you are stuck with him forever.

"So, Dad, what'da think? I'm kinda in a hurry to get going. I know you have to get my share of the inheritance ready, but maybe you could pull some strings and get something going ... soon ... like now?"

Father: "Aaron, how can you be so sure that this is what you want? You're still young, and there is so much for you to learn right here. I'd be glad to spend more time with you so you can learn the business end of the farm, the market possibilities, and some of your ideas for growing our business even bigger. We could become a father-and-sons' business and also develop this place into a showplace for the neighbors to come and learn.

"Why not wait six months before you definitely decide what you want to do while you, Jacob, and I start planning for bigger things for our farm, our animal production, and our crops? In the meantime, you can start your planning, if you still care to, on where you can go and find suitable work, your transportation needs, and what and who you will take along with you."

Prodigal Son: "No, Dad, I've done all the thinking I need to do. I'm ready now. I'll just plan my trip as I go along. I'll be just fine. I don't need anyone else to go with me, and I don't need anything but basic supplies. I can get what I need along the way. I want to go now! I can't wait six long months!"

Father: "Okay, okay! I'm very disappointed, but I'll check and see what the banker has to say. I think I will be able to get it all wrapped up soon. I hope that fits into your schedule."

[The son exits and leave the father standing alone.]

Father: *[To audience]* Only a parent can understand how I felt. The bottom of my life seemed to drop out. First, it was my wife's death, and now Aaron, my little boy, the baby of the family, wants to leave me. I feel so alone with no one to talk with, no one to share my desolation with. Even Jehovah seems far away. I know He would understand, but I can't bring myself to share my heartbreak even with Him.

The banker put the money together although he was in shock about Aaron leaving. He didn't approve of dividing the inheritance now, saying that there would be more for each of the boys later as my account accrued interest over time. I tried to explain this to Aaron, but he either couldn't or wouldn't try to understand. He obviously had only one thought in mind and that was to get away from here and from us. I asked Jacob about his thoughts on his brother's leaving, but he seemed to think that his brother was just a headstrong kid who was bored with the quiet life around here. I thought I'd been lenient enough with Aaron, and that he was just a boy who couldn't live under my rules any longer. Jacob thought I hadn't been hard enough on his young brother, and that I had always let him get away with too much. Apparently, he could quite easily overlook the times when he fell short of my expectations for him. Maybe Jacob's right. I just don't know.

Where did I go wrong? Since sleep is avoiding me, I have had the dark hours to think about possible answers to my question. And after too many sleepless nights, I may have come to some answers. I realize now that all my attention has been on the farm, the crops, the animals, and the production numbers. My attention *has not* been on the most valuable but *non*-renewable resource that Jehovah has given me: my two sons. Somehow, I began seeing them as a *given* not as a *gift*. I stopped appreciating what they did and saw only what they did not do. It's so easy to make assumptions about what others need without ever asking them.

[Older brother reenters and speaks to audience, not facing father.]
Older Son: Dad and I really didn't talk to each other very much. But when we did … well, what I remember most is him pointing out the mistakes I'd made, the things I'd forgotten to do. He was always on me about keeping accurate books! Maybe he encouraged

me now and then, and I probably knew he cared. Though it would have been nice to hear it once in a while.

[Father is seen now lighted or as older son steps back.]

Father: I just assumed that most of the time they knew I cared. After all, I was their dad, and don't all dads care? Well, don't we?

I have come to a conclusion about why Aaron may have run away. He left because of me, not because of the workload or because of his brother. As he thought about the way things had developed, he could probably see no possible changes in me, or in the way I treated him.

I wonder how many parents have realized too late what went wrong between them and their headstrong son or daughter. Now I have those sleepless nights, wishing I could go back and correct those things I mistakenly thought were the important factors in running my business. I don't think that Jacob will take the same way out of his difficulty with me, but I'm sure that he is also bothered by some of the same issues that bothered Aaron.

Older Brother: *[from off stage]* Dad seems to be making an effort, and literately it really seems to be an effort, to be more encouraging, more interested in my concerns by listening to me, really listening, and in general just being more pleasant. I have been hearing words of appreciation and encouragement more than I ever heard before. But I can't let him know I have noticed, though, just in case it is only a short-term adjustment in his style. Whatever, little Aarie is gone, and I can relax a bit more.

Father: And he *is* gone! All I could think of this past week was:

- Will I ever see him again?

- If I only knew where he is going, I could go and bring him home.
- What if he gets in trouble and wants to come home?
- Will he waste his money or be robbed and left destitute?

Even after all the sleepless nights when I think I have figured out the reasons why my boy left, there are still those nights when I can't get to sleep worrying about him. As soon as darkness gives way to the sunlight, I keep looking down the road, thinking that maybe he will be returning to us, but I live in constant disappointment. That road is becoming accustomed to my footsteps and my tears.

Older Brother: *(off stage)* I keep telling Dad, "Don't worry, Dad, he's a grown man now. Let him find out for himself what life is like. Eventually, he'll come to his senses and he'll be back."

Father: *[back on stage]* But I'm not so sure. I wonder if other parents have been through similar situations. Oh, how I wish I could talk with someone who could help me deal with it, but I'm too embarrassed to let anyone else know that I'm having these concerns about my son, my Aaron, my little boy.

I guess eventually my heart and mind became accustomed to the idea that this was going to be my life—without Aaron. Sleep comes a little easier, the work is getting done, and Jacob seems more pleasant now that his brother has gone. I have even become more accustomed to Jacob's compulsions, and out of sheer exhaustion, I have let him have his way on some of his ideas. I find I am always reminding myself of my need to be more appreciative, to listen more, criticize less, and show how much I care. However, it is difficult after so many years to change my way of handling things.

[Prodigal son slowly begins walking down the center aisle toward his father]

Father: One day as I stared down the road, I saw a man walking slowly toward our farm. He looked like a very old man. He was alone, no camel or horse, and not carrying anything that even resembled a traveling bag. Could this be my son? No way! I put that possibility out of my mind, assuming that my mind was again playing its tricks on me. I've seen this apparition too many times before—for it to be true today. But I couldn't stop looking. There was something about his walk that took me back to my memories of my little boy. He had that odd little step that was unique to him. One foot was just a little slower to move than the other foot, so his walk looked something as though he was skipping. I remembered now how that had happened. He was racing some of his little friends when he tripped and badly hurt himself and then haltingly came into my arms for comfort.

By the time I had watched the old man's feet for a while, he was closer, and I could see that the man's face looked familiar although dirty, unshaven, and scarred. His clothes were *beyond* dirty and torn. He looked more like an old man than anyone I recognized. Even so, hesitantly … softly … I said his name, "Aaron?" I said it a second time but just a little louder, *"Aaron?"*

It *was* Aaron! My *son*! My *boy*! He's come home. Faster than I thought I could, I ran to meet him, threw my arms around him, hugged him close to myself, and kissed him as only a father could kiss his wayward but home-again son.

Prodigal Son: "Oh, Father, I have sinned against God, I've sinned before you, and I don't deserve to be called your son ever again."

Father: It sounded like a prepared speech to me, so I interrupted him and called for a couple of servants. "Quick, dress him in some clean and good clothes, get the family crest ring, and some sturdy sandals for his feet." To another servant I told to get the fattened calf we had been saving for a neighborhood barbeque, and get it ready for a celebration tonight. The servant looked at me as though I had lost my mind. I could see the question in his eyes. *"Why?"*

"Why? My son, my *son* was given up for dead and is now alive. Given up for lost, and is now found!"

So, in just a few hours the party began. The music was loud. (Not my kind of music, but the young people liked it.) In fact, it was so loud that Jacob, who was working in the field, could hear it. He asked one of the servants what was happening and was filled in on the whole story.

[Older brother steps out to front of stage looking extremely angry.]

Older Son: What? *He's* back? *This ... cannot ... be*! I was so furious that I had to confront Dad outside behind the house and asked the same question, *"Why?* This good-for-nothing son of yours shows his face after gobbling up your estate on undesirable women and treating half the world to wild parties, and you treat the whole neighborhood to a welcome home party." It's now my turn to ask why? Dad told me the same thing he had apparently told the servant: 'My son was dead, but is now alive!'"

Father: I feel certain that Jacob had no way of understanding my joy over Aaron's return just as he could not understand my sorrow over his decision to leave us. I hope Jacob never has to live through something as heartbreaking as a son announcing that he is leaving home. I learned through this situation that all the tears come from a parent's eyes.

Jehovah taught me that love is not conditioned on a child's behavior. I don't love my sons because they are good or dislike them when they misbehave. I love them because they are my children! Jehovah loves me and has been so good to me because I am his child. Our prophets called it "grace"—just because I *am* his child.

Scripture: Luke 15:11–32 and 1 Corinthians 13:4–8a
Biblical reference: This story is an adaptation of the account in Luke 15 about the lost boy, the lost sheep, and the lost coin. It's all about the joy in heaven when the lost is found.
Discussion possibilities:

1. How does the story relate to lives of families in the twenty-first century?
2. Describe in contemporary terms the areas of conflict in this family.
3. What did Dad do to deal with the conflict between the two brothers?

Suggested closing hymn: "Amazing Grace"

Hand Signals

(Triad for Cleopas, his companion, and Jesus)

The two companions are leaving Jerusalem after the events of Passover and the crucifixion of Jesus, as well as his resurrection. As they walk down the aisle of the church, hall, or auditorium, they will be joined by Jesus. He will be sitting in a chair or pew next to the aisle, and he will join them immediately as the two come to the row in which he is sitting. They will be surprised when he joins the conversation.

Companion: Well, Cleopas, here we are *finally* on our way home to Emmaus. I hope these seven miles won't seem as long as they usually do. They probably won't because it's downhill most of the way. Cleopas, I don't know if I have ever had such gut-wrenching experiences as we had this past weekend. My stomach just won't settle down.

Cleopas: Tell me about it. I feel pretty much the same way, except my head is in as bad a shape as my stomach. I can't stop thinking about what it all means, but I get nowhere—it all just keeps circling around in my head like a small windstorm down in the desert.

Companion: I realize that we weren't together all the time, so we probably have different pictures in our heads of what really happened. I only know that those pictures in my head are so excruciating that I wish I could somehow get rid of them.

Cleopas: You are so right! I feel the same way. I wish we had met Jesus earlier in his ministry. One year doesn't seem enough time to get to know another person very well. The last twelve months have flown by, and now he's gone like a bird that just flew away. Where were you on Friday during the crucifixion? I couldn't locate you in that huge crowd. Did you hear what Jesus and the thief next to him were talking about? All I heard was that Jesus promised the thief, "Today you will join me in Paradise" (Luke 23:43).

Companion: *Jesus said that?* You aren't kidding me, are you? I can't imagine what that meant, if you really heard him correctly. What was the thief's response to Jesus, and I wonder how they even got into that kind of conversation, what with all the distractions that were involved?

Jesus unobtrusively joins the two walkers, but keeping his hands in the folds of his robe.

Jesus: Hi, guys. You seem quite agitated. Are you both okay? You seemed so intent that I began to be concerned when I realized you didn't even notice that I had joined you. Where are you going? Up to Galilee, maybe? That's where I'm heading, and that's a long walk—long enough for you to share with me what has you so concerned.

Cleopas: No, sir, we're only going to our homes down in Emmaus. But I don't think we know you, do we? Where are you from?

Obviously not from around here or you would know why we are so agitated. By the way, you were in Jerusalem over Passover, weren't you? My friend and I were talking about all the things that happened during those three days. If you were there, I guess you know what has us so concerned.

Jesus: What things are you talking about? And, yes, I was there for Passover. Did something important happen to both of you? What happened? Come on now, you can tell me. I'm a good listener.

Companion: *What happened?* Are you sure you didn't sleep through the entire Passover? If you were there, there's no way you could sleep with all the noise the crowds were making. You were probably the only one who didn't know what was going on.

Jesus: Well, tell me what you remember that seemed so important to you. It *was* important to you, wasn't it?

Cleopas: *Important?* I'll tell you it was! To us it seemed like the end of the world—it was that important. Am I right, buddy?

Companion: Absolutely! *Very* right!

Stop in the aisle to talk together. There's more to tell before you get to Emmaus. These directions will tell you when to go up onto the chancel or stage.

Jesus: Keep going. Tell me what you remember.

Cleopas: It was all about Jesus of Nazareth, a small town up in Galilee. Nazareth is on the west side of the lake. Maybe you knew him. The Sanhedrin became furious about the teachings of Jesus about the kingdom of God: who would be there, and how we could be a part of it. They said that he didn't have the authority to teach and perform the miracles that healed people and so on. They nabbed him while he was praying up on Mount Olivet, took him off to the high priest's palace, put him through some kind of trial, and then gave him to Pilate to get the death penalty. We had hoped that he was the one who would free us from the scourge of the Roman rulers.

Companion: That's right. He was hung on a cross on Golgotha, and actually died on Friday, that same day. Simon of Arimathea had prepared a new tomb for himself, but he asked Pilate if he could take the body of Jesus to his tomb. We went into hiding with the other followers of Jesus—about eleven of us. We thought that maybe we were next on their death list because we had been with Jesus during those days.

Jesus: Then what happened? Apparently you were *not* on their death list.

Cleopas: You haven't heard any of this until now? Amazing! Well, there's more. The next morning some of the women in our group went to the tomb to embalm him with spices, and the tomb was empty when they got there. Angels were there, *angels* no less, and told the women that Jesus had gone up to Galilee and that he would see them there. The women, except for Mary, came back to the city to tell us the story and about the angels, too.

We had difficulty believing their story so Peter and a couple of the others, took off for the tomb. Well, some walked to the tomb, but Peter ran. Strong guy, that Peter. Quick to talk, and quick to run. The followers found out that the women were right ... again, as usual.

Companion: Right, as usual. But sometime after the others had left, Mary was weeping by the tomb, when a man walked up to her and asked her why she was crying. She thought he was a gardener, but learned that the guy who was talking with her was Jesus. She said she was overcome with joy and hurried back to tell the rest of us. And you didn't know about all of this? Wow! That's hard to believe.

Cleopas: *(to the audience)* About this time, the man began teaching us from our own scriptures what God had said about the Messiah—his life, his death, and that he would be raised from the dead. His understanding of our scriptures more than made up for his lack of information about the weekend. Suddenly, we were back home in Emmaus. Wow! Time flies when the conversation is exciting.

Companion: *(to Jesus)* How did you learn all that information about the Messiah who will be coming soon ... we hope? I wish he were here now to comfort us and our friends. By the way, it's time to eat, so why don't you stay here? At least have a meal with us. We have an extra mat so you could stay overnight if you'd like, but we hope you'll at least have supper with us.

(Go up onto the stage or platform and sit around a table with Jesus facing the audience.)

Companion: Sir, as our guest, will you ask God to bless our meal?

Jesus: Of course, thank you for praying with me.

(As Jesus stands to pray, he will take a loaf in his hands and break it in half, exposing red marks on his palms and the back of his hands. This is done as Cleopas is saying the following.)

Cleopas: *(to audience)* I think you know what happened. As the visitor took the load of bread, he took it in his two hands, held it up to heaven, and broke it. As he broke the loaf apart, we saw his hands—they were the wounded hands with pierce marks from the nails. We sat there in awe, realizing who our visitor was … he was Jesus. He left us at that moment with our mouths open but our minds at peace.

(To companion) Did you just see what I think I saw? No, don't answer that. Just tell me what you saw. Yes, we both know it—he is alive! Now what! We must tell the others what we have just experienced.

Companion: I've got it! Let's both go back to Jerusalem and tell them … tonight, now! It's uphill all the way. Is that okay with you? The walk will do us good. We can both stand to lose a little more weight. When we arrived and met them in the upper room, they had trouble believing us, just as all of us had trouble believing the women this morning. While we were telling them our remarkable story, we heard, "Peace be with you!" We were all in shock as Jesus showed us his hands and feet. He asked for some food, a piece of baked fish was all that was left. He ate the fish, and we could see that he was real and not a ghost.

Cleopas: Every time we eat the bread and drink the cup, you can believe that the two of us will see Jesus sitting at *our* table, praying, breaking the bread, and revealing his scarred and wounded hands. That table became *his* table that night. We both trust that you will experience the same excitement every time you sit at *His* table that we felt on that busy day in Emmaus.

Notes:

1. Have a loaf of whole bread that can be broken at the table.
2. Use the material at the end of the "Hand Signals" *monologue* on page 219 for references, scripture to read, and the possible points for discussion.)

How to Use These Stories

These stories may be read as just that—stories. They may also be used as dramatic presentations in many different venues. They could be helpful in Bible studies, at campfire devotions, at student meetings, or as sermons. Feel free to use them in any way that assists others to find their way to God, as was the experience of many of the characters in these stories.

Each story is a statement describing the viewpoint of the person who is experiencing God in everyday circumstances. Sometimes the words will spill out of the person's mouth in a rush of emotion, and at other times, the words he or she uses may slowly and carefully express the thoughts of that person and may be uncomfortable for that person to face and then to express.

If the story is being used as a performance, you will find performance suggestions as you would in a play script. If you are using it as a performance, it would be helpful to prepare yourself to express the emotions and concerns of the biblical person you are representing. This usually involves:

1. Getting into the feelings and the mind of the character you are portraying.
2. Reading the story carefully (probably more than once or twice).
3. Reading it to another person as practice.

4. Discussing the listener's suggestions after the practice reading.

The last four stories require the participation of three people. For these, there are some dramatic suggestions to assist in the presentation. You may want to rehearse these presentations multiple times to increase the comfort of the performers.

Bibliography

Archaeological Study Bible, New International Version. Grand Rapids, MI: Zondervan, 2005.

Bruce, A. B., *The Training of the Twelve.* New York: Harper Bros, 1901.

Common English Bible. Nashville, TN: Common English Bible, 2011.

Geike, D. D., Cunningham, *Hours with the Bible,* 3 Vols. London: James Pott & Co., 1889.

Hastings D. D., James, ed., *Dictionary of the Bible,* 4 Vols. Edinburg: T & T Clark, 1908.

———, ed., *Dictionary of Christ and the Gospels,* 2 Vols. Edinburg: T & T Clark, 1906.

———, ed. *Dictionary of the Apostolic Church,* Edinburg: T & T Clark, 1918.

———, ed., *The Greater Men and Women of the Bible,* 6 Vols. Edinburg: T & T Clark, 1915.

Lockyer, Herbert, *All the Men and Women of the Bible.* Grand Rapids, MI: Zondervan, 1958.

Orr, D. D., James Orr, ed., *International Standard Bible Encyclopedia,* 5 Vols. Grand Rapids, MI: Eerdmans, 1946.

Peterson, Eugene H. *The Message, The Bible in Contemporary Language.* Colorado Springs, CO: NavPress, 2002.

The Living Bible, Paraphrased, Tyndale House Publishers, Wheaton, Illinois, 1971.

Whyte D. D., Alexander, *Bible Characters.* New York: Fleming Revell Co., 1901.

Notes

1. Genesis 18–20.
2. Genesis 22:1–19
3. 1 Samuel 11:1–8
4. Psalm 23
5. Pikes—sharp spears at the end of long poles that foot soldiers carried as weapons.
6. 1 Samuel 19
7. 2 Samuel 16:1–4 and 19:24–30
8. The "Great Sea" is what we currently refer to as the Mediterranean Sea.
9. Jeramiah 31:15
10. Isaiah 61:1–3
11. Isaiah 1:18
12. Deuteronomy 21:17
13. Exodus 28:6–12
14. Numbers 9:14
15. 1 Peter 5:13–14
16. 2 Timothy 4:8–13
17. John 6:1–15

Printed in the United States
By Bookmasters